What is Religion?

We all know what religion is – or do we? Confronted with religious pluralism and cultural diversity, it manifests itself in many forms. *What is Religion?* serves not only as an introduction to the different belief systems flourishing throughout the modern world, but asks us to consider how the very boundaries of faith might be drawn now and in the future. How might religion interact with political ends, or permeate culture, society and everyday life? Is the postmodernist world in thrall to 'religions' of its own kind – materialism, humanism, medicine, science? And what logic separates 'common sense' or academic knowledge from the immutable but unstable boundaries of faith? Which is the more certain? What does it *mean* to believe?

Combining clear accounts of contemporary global religious practice with an incisive philosophical interrogation of the dynamics and aims of belief, *What is Religion?* offers a fresh and wide-ranging introduction to the perennial human questions of ritual, faith, ethics and salvation.

Robert Crawford is a professor currently working with the Open University. He has taught in England, Ireland, the USA, Nigeria and South Africa and has recently published *Can We Ever Kill?* and *The God/Man/World Triangle* (nominated for a John Templeton Award for Theology and the Natural Sciences). He has also written accounts of South African Apartheid and Ulster Protestantism.

Also by Robert Crawford

Can We Ever Kill? (Second Enlarged Edition)
Journey into Apartheid
Making Sense of the Study of Religion
A Portrait of the Ulster Protestants
The Saga of God Incarnate (Second Enlarged Edition)
*The God/Man/World Triangle: A dialogue between science
    and religion* (Second Paperback Edition)

What is Religion?

Robert Crawford

London and New York

First published 2002
by Routledge
11 New Fetter Lane, London EC4P 4EE

Simultaneously published in the USA and Canada
by Routledge
29 West 35th Street, New York, NY 10001

Routledge is an imprint of the Taylor & Francis Group

Typeset in Sabon by Wearset Ltd, Boldon, Tyne and Wear
Printed and bound in Great Britain by TJ International Ltd, Padstow,
Cornwall

British Library Cataloguing in Publication Data
A catalogue record for this book is available from the British Library

Library of Congress Cataloging in Publication Data
Crawford, Robert G. (Robert George), 1927–
   What is religion? : introducing the study of religion / Robert Crawford.
      p. cm.
   Includes bibliographical references and index.
   1. Religion. I. Title.

BL48 .C722 2002
200–dc21
                                                     2001048101

ISBN 0–415–22670–8 (hbk)
ISBN 0–415–22671–6 (pbk)

To all the Open University students whom I have taught over the years whose hard work and interest has encouraged me to write this book.

Contents

Introduction   ix

1 Can religion be defined?   1

2 How is religion studied?   9

3 Rituals   22

4 Scriptures   37

5 Behaviour   48

6 Women   64

7 Liberation   75

8 Divisions within religions   89

9 Why can religions not unite?   112

10 Confessing a murder   123

11 Is the world designed?   134

12 What are we?   142

13 Mind and brain   151

14 Other belief systems   159

15 The existence of God   174

16 A definition of religion   192

17 The future of religion   203

    Notes   216
    Index   227

Introduction

We live in a pluralist, inter-racialist and multi-faith society and the need to understand one another is greater than ever before. Much misunderstanding arises from racialism and nationalism and could be avoided if people knew more about the beliefs and practices of one another. It is hoped that this book will make a contribution to a better understanding and sympathy with those who differ from us in race and creed.

Another aim is to try to dispel the idea that religion and science are in conflict with one another. Some scientists do hold that religion is grounded in superstition and belongs to a 'primitive' stage of mankind whereas science advances and provides remedies for modern problems. But others recognize that religion is asking different questions than science and is still needed for living the good life and giving meaning and purpose to existence. In order to clarify some of the issues there are a number of chapters devoted to science and its relation to religion. But many people are concerned with social problems, deprivation, injustice and imbalance of wealth throughout the world and subscribe to belief systems intended to bring about change in the human conditions. Hence there is attention to two of the most influential: Marxism and Humanism.

Some scholars have insisted that such movements which are normally designated as secular are religious because they understand religion in a broad way. Usually they operate with a functional definition: religion does something in and for a society. But it can be argued that while this is true, it is a somewhat limited idea of religion. Alternatively, some scholars have sought to distil the essence of religion from the study of religions but it has not proved to be possible. The way chosen here is to examine six religions and note characteristics or aspects of religion which appear in them in order to try and advance beyond the functional to something more substantial. The six religions are Judaism, Christianity, Islam, usually known as the Semitic, and those that developed in an Indian context, Hinduism, Buddhism and Sikhism.

With regard to the method of studying religions, writers follow a pattern of discussing religions separately rather than a thematic approach. The latter option is followed throughout the book for a number of reasons. First, we want to compare and contrast the various themes and make it easier for the reader to detect similarities and differences. Second, the approach may help students and the general reader to remember more easily what is being taught on major themes. Students of world religions say that while a course which deals with each religion individually is helpful, it often happens that when they have reached the sixth one they have forgotten what they had learned about the first! Third, since examination questions often refer to a particular theme and require it to be considered in relation to two or even three religions, a thematic study should be helpful in at least giving direction. Ideally, if the thematic and the detailed study of each religion separately can be combined, it should enable the reader to get a good grasp of essentials.

It would also help to counter the objection that the thematic neglects the fact that religions emerge in an historical context. For, in this book the historical has been taken into account to show how religions have developed and the divisions which have ensued. In describing the religions the attempt is made to move from the concrete – what is visible and happening in an everyday context – to the abstract – the reasons why people believe. It begins with rituals, use of scripture, moral behaviour, and the activity of women in religion, before moving on to the beliefs. Visits to places of worship can be helpful, because in considering the architecture of the buildings, furniture and decoration, and listening and participating in the services, questions soon arise as to why people behave in this way.

We continually encounter on the streets of our large cities, Sikhs, Muslims, Hindus, Jews, Christians and Buddhists. In describing and analysing what they believe and do we will not try to establish what is of more value in one religion than another or to judge from a particular standpoint. But comments will be made on what seems inconsistent with modern knowledge or lacking in relevance. Religions do change as they develop in their context and the question will be raised of whether the changes which have taken place accord with their origins.

Because of the extent of the areas considered, these matters could only be dealt with in a limited way, but it is hoped that the attempt will stimulate discussion. God does not have a gender, but it is impossible to write about the concept without using gender-specific terminology. I have used the masculine pronoun with reference to the deity except when writing about the Hindu Brahman which is normally referred to as neuter. I have also tried to alternate between 'he' and 'she' but it may be noted that 'man' includes male and female.

I would like to record my appreciation of the dialogue with students in various parts of the world and show gratitude for the questions that they have raised. I also owe a debt not only to the authors of the books mentioned in the footnotes to each chapter but also to the writers of Open University materials. The educational outreach of the University not only in the UK but elsewhere has been a great success and there are thousands of people throughout the world who acknowledge their debt.

I have tried to acknowledge any quotations or ideas derived from others but wide reading may mean that I have missed an acknowledgement and if this is so I would apologize in advance. I would also like to thank the Editor and staff of Routledge for their interest in and the publication of the book and those colleagues who read the manuscript and made suggestions.

Robert Crawford

1 Can religion be defined?

When someone is asked 'What is religion?', they usually point to a mosque or church or Hindu temple or Sikh gurdwara and say that people who go there have 'got' religion! But this is drawing attention to the places of worship and members of the various religions, it is not telling us what religion is. Can it be distilled from a study of these religions? Some scholars have tried to do it but an essence of religion fails to appear so most seek to understand its effect on society. We will begin with stating some definitions and then go on to comment briefly on them:

> The cosmos is a gigantic flywheel making 10,000 revolutions a minute. Man is a sick fly taking a dizzy ride on it. Religion is the theory that the wheel was designed and set spinning to give man the ride.
>
> (H. L. Mencken)

> Religion masks the face of God.
>
> (Martin Buber)

> A system of beliefs and practices by means of which a group of people struggle with the ultimate problems of human life.
>
> (J. M. Yinger)

> A belief in spiritual beings.
>
> (E. B. Tylor)

Religion is what the individual does with his solitariness
. . . institutions, churches, rituals, bibles, codes of behaviour, are the trappings of religion, its passing forms.

(Alfred North Whitehead)

Any beliefs which involve the acceptance of a sacred, transempirical realm and any behaviour designed to affect a
person's relationship with that realm.

(Peter Connolly)

It is the presence in the world of something spiritually
greater than man himself . . . man's goal is to seek communion with the presence behind the phenomena.

(Arnold Toynbee)

It is an emotion or morality touched by emotion.

(Matthew Arnold)

Ancestor worship is the root of every religion.

(Herbert Spencer)

Religion is an illusion.

(Sigmund Freud)

Religion is not born out of speculation or reflection, still
less out of illusion or misapprehension, but rather out of
the real tragedies of human life, out of the conflict between
human plans and realities.

(Bronislaw Malinowski)

It is the sigh of the oppressed creature, the feeling of a
heartless world, the soul in a place without a soul; it is the
opium of the people.

(Karl Marx)

Religion is a virus.

(Richard Dawkins)

A religion is a unified system of beliefs and practices relative to sacred things, that is to say, things set apart and for-

bidden, beliefs and practices which unite into one single community called a church, all those who adhere to them.

(Émile Durkheim)

It is a way of life.

(Most religions)

A religion is a seven-dimensional organism, ritual, doctrinal, mythical or narrative, experimental or emotional, ethical or legal, organisational or social, material or artistic.

(Ninian Smart)

Religion is a revolutionary urge, a psycho-social impulse to generate a new humanity.

(Aloysius Pieris)

Religion is a sense of the numinous, the 'wholly other', the *mysterium tremendum et fascinans*.

(Rudolf Otto)

These definitions reflect the perspective of anthropologists, sociologists, philosophers, psychologists, biologists, theologians, historians, scriptures, and show that there is no universally accepted definition of religion. The experts differ even with regard to definition! So much so that a feeling of despair is created. John Hick writes:

Religion is one thing to the anthropologist, another to the sociologist, another to the psychologist (and again another to the next psychologist!), another to the Marxist, another to the mystic, another to the Zen Buddhist and yet another to the Jew or Christian. As a result there is a great variety of religious theories of the nature of religion. There is, consequently, no universally accepted definition of religion, and quite possibly there never will be.[1]

The anti-religious strain is clear when defined by Freud and Karl Marx and more recently by the biologist, Richard Dawkins, who compares religion to a computer virus passed from one brain to another. Dawkins reacts to any 'wheel of design' in the cosmos: we are here because of a random process. The definitions also raise questions: How can religion simply be a private affair since it develops in communities and has an impact on social and political life? If it is a way of life how can we keep it private? But how can it be demonstrated that it has contact with the sacred or supernatural or something greater than ourselves, as Toynbee said? And what is it that religion is pointing to, since the presence of God has different forms in the religions? Perhaps it would be easier to think of religion as emotion and morality with Matthew Arnold, but would that not make it so subjective that validation would be difficult? If it is a way of life there must be some beliefs connected with it.

The definition which relates religion to ancestor worship impressed itself upon me when teaching large numbers of students in Africa. They told me how they venerated their ancestors, had a special place in the home where they went to consult them before an important decision, and generally showed that respect for them was akin to worship. So was Spencer right when he saw the origin of religion in ancestor worship? It is largely discounted today as applicable only to certain tribes and we cannot simply define something by its origins and fail to notice its development. The African students were mainly Christian yet held on to this belief. Perhaps some of their respect for the dead and the living would be helpful in Western society today.

Some of the definitions are functional, stating what religion does, but others are substantive, stating what religion is. If we say that religion unites or separates people or comforts those who suffer and so on, then we are thinking of it in a functional way. Functionalism is a theoretical perspective in sociology but function refers more to the role of an institution in society. A substantial definition seeks to highlight key features of a religion such as belief in God. Durkheim appears to supply both a functional and substantive definition but his beliefs do not include what those who want a substantive definition consider crucial, the supernatural dimension. Religion concerns only the human: a creation of society. His view has been followed by many modern scholars.

We will look at the sociological approach to religion in the next chapter but note here that the functional approach can lead to disagreement. Some conclude that religion has declined as religious symbols are less important, supernatural causes are not acceptable, and religion has little to say about society. A demystification of the world has taken place with a fall in attendance at places of worship. The sacred and magical have little place in civilized societies and religious values are being steadily eroded. Religion in any vital form, it is argued, survives only in the cults.

But other sociologists disagree, contending that it is based on the assumption that past communities were more religious than today. A consideration of history does not support the assumption since even the domination of Christianity in the Middle Ages did not prevent paganism and mass superstition. Today global religion is flourishing. For example, in the United States the majority of Americans believe in God and there is a resurgence of religious fundamentalism. It believes in a return to tradition, certainty, community, sanctification of politics and commitment, and opposes the modernity characterized by relativism, individualism and bureaucracy. Religion has not kept out of politics but has supported freedom movements to abolish injustice and exercises a world-wide influence.

If we estimate the world's population at about 5400 million, there are 4333 million in the various religions – approximately 80 per cent.[2] And there is a mass of people who are not members of religious communities but say that they are religious. All sociologists recognize the growth of religious cults, with the British media in 1998 reporting that science's popularity was waning and that there was a boom in New Age mysticism and spiritual belief. Books on chemistry and physics showed a drop in sales of more than a quarter but New Age titles and books on Eastern and minority faiths published in Britain shot up by 75 per cent.

Whitehead's definition stresses individualism which figures in religions, but usually there is a community to which one belongs and receives help. John Wesley said that there was no such thing as a solitary Christian and organized his movement on a communal basis. Whitehead understands that the trappings of religion, churches, rituals, institutions, bibles and ethics are the passing forms, but would the religion not disappear without these? Of course, if they are being used as a substitute for a change of heart then he would have the support of Wesley, the Hebrew prophets and some of the founders of the religions. It is true that visions of God often occur in 'solitary' quiet places away from not only secular affairs but also the performance of religion.

Marx's definition means that religion is the compensator, justifier and concealer of exploitation. It endorses the status quo by enabling the poor to accept their inequality and teaches that the capitalists' power was God given. But Marx also saw it as a protest and would surely have endorsed the stand of Gandhi, Martin Luther King's civil rights movement and Liberation theology in Christianity. Christians and Marxists joined together in Latin America with the common goal of defeating injustice. Protest ceased to be passive and became active resistance. Neither Marx nor Freud studied religions other than Christianity but Max Weber did, and he argued that religion could spearhead change in society.

It may be that the definitions are complementary rather than contradictory and that elements from each might be combined to form a satisfactory definition. If broad, it would allow secular belief systems, such as Marxism and Humanism and new developments like Transcendental Meditation, to be termed religious. In the latter, members claim that there is a field of consciousness which can be tapped into in order to exploit our inner energy and reach maximum intelligence. A deep relaxation is induced to reach subtle levels of the mind and eventually transcend it altogether. It is believed that we can then contact the source of thought. What this is, however, remains somewhat vague and there is little indication if it is natural or supernatural.

Definitions can be too broad, including what dominates or appears of ultimate concern: work, home, children, entertainment. Some of these have rituals which are similar to those of religion. Football has its assemblies with crowds displaying ecstasy and wonder at their team's performance. There is the hallowed turf, the flags and banners, the hymn singing, and so on. Nationalism also extols the flag of the nation, and some lands are so sacred that they must be defended at all costs. But all of these consist of visible objects whereas religion, while having outward signs, refers to the invisible.

If the definition can be too broad, it can also be narrow and miss something which is essential. In an effort to distinguish between sacred and secular it may be defined by reference to sacred persons or places or rituals or relics. But, while these can be a focus, the religions insist that God is everywhere and cannot be confined to one place. He pervades the world and hence the secular and sacred cannot be kept apart. But if 'God' is essential in any definition then what about Buddhism which in its early beginnings moved away from the Hindu gods? This question has often been raised about Buddhism and we will attend to it in later chapters.

Ninian Smart opts for a broad understanding of religion by reflecting on the characteristics of religions in his seven dimensions. But why only seven? He does not mention the political which was very prominent in the last century, with religion protesting about apartheid in South Africa, poverty in Latin America, and injustice in the United States. What is it that makes Smart's dimensions religious? It would seem that he is operating with some definition of religion, a broad one, so as to include Marxism, Humanism and Nationalism. Smart thinks that the search for an essence ends in vagueness, for we have to go on and define the supernatural or the ultimate or the transcendent Being. There is pluralism within traditions and he looks for patterns by considering the dimensions. If a movement has these seven dimensions he thinks there is a religion so there is no need to define it.[3] But some religions in their beginnings did not have the material dimension of buildings, and he admits that non-literate societies are weak on the doctrinal dimension and the narrative one is absent among Buddhist modernists.

Perhaps it might be helpful to consider where the term religion originated. *Religio* is a Latin word originally meaning a kind of superstitious awe. It developed into scruples or conscientiousness implying religious feeling and worship of the gods. The awe-inspiring nature of deity has been captured by Otto who pointed to the experience in all religions of the phenomena. His view has been very influential but is opposed by those who see religion as an illusion and man-made. Whatever the source of religion it soon developed a cult of sacred things and persons forming a religious system. Thus the definitions that emerge try to embrace these elements or concentrate on one of them.

Religion can also mean to bind a worshipper to the deity by the observance of cultic ceremonies and acts of devotion. Perhaps if we consider the particular expressions of religion as found in six religions it may be possible to arrive at a definition. In so doing we will be taking Max Weber's advice that trying to define religion at the start is a mistake.[4] Indeed it is rare for a contemporary sociologist of religion to do so at the beginning of the investigation.

One of the difficulties is that religion is so mixed up with other things that it is not a distinctive category and it varies in different places and at different times. Hence some, like D. F. Pocock, prefer to talk about beliefs rather than religion.[5] William James remarked that there were so many definitions of religion and so different from one another that the word cannot stand for any single principle or essence but is a collective name. However, we will see that each religion has its own particular distinctiveness; and it is possible to see signs of it in other belief systems that purport to give some meaning and purpose to life and supply some answers to the ultimate question of death. Are they religions or surrogates for religion?

Some of the proposed definitions will receive more attention in the next chapter as we seek to understand the different approaches to the study of religion.

2 How is religion studied?

There are various methods of study and we begin with the evolutionary approach which developed in conjunction with anthropology. Societies evolved from the lower to the higher. 'Primitive' man saw his world in terms of magic and impersonal forces (animatism) and then came to think of spirits dwelling in trees, mountains and rocks (animism). Animals were worshipped as the symbol or emblem of a tribe (totemism) and the spirit of an eminent chief would be venerated with sacrifices. His grave became a shrine (ancestor worship). A sense of awe in the presence of nature led to the worship of nature gods and this polytheism became the religion of ancient Greece and the Romans, and is still a feature of Hinduism.

Scholars in the nineteenth century believed in a progression from animism, totemism, polytheism to monotheism, a belief in one supreme God. Auguste Comte (1798–1857), the father of sociology, detected three stages: theological, metaphysical and scientific. In the first, things were explained by a supernatural cause, in the second reason took over, and in the third by a scientific understanding of natural causes. Despite his scheme, Comte saw the need for religion and founded the Religion of Humanity which was shortlived. Soon exceptions to the evolutionary development were noted, for progress is not so simple and straightforward. The scenario was too tidy and neat and did not allow for deviations and complexities. Tribes were discovered worshipping one God when they should have been committed to many. Andrew Lang (1844–1912) referred to it as the 'High God among Low Races'. Many of the investigators were 'armchair anthropologists' who had not ventured into the field and wanted to see everything as part of a grand evolutionary plan.

The nineteenth-century idea that we were morally and spiritually better than previous generations, moving upwards and 'letting the ape and tiger die', received a devastating blow in the two world wars of the twentieth century. So-called civilized nations behaved in a savage way and released weapons of inconceivable destructive power. Science and technology can be misused and there is no guarantee that an advance here will be accompanied by ethical progress. While it is not denied that religion does develop in its understanding of God, humanity and the world, the so-called 'primitive tribes' can surprise with subtle ideas about spirituality. Societies must be studied in their own terms, not placed in a higher or lower level, or placed in frameworks that we erect. Eric Sharpe points out that some anthropologists refused to go and look at the Palaeolithic cave paintings in France because such artistic expression did not fit into their views of 'primitive' culture! Such prejudice is not acceptable in any area of study.[1]

Historical

The history of religion approach relates what has happened and tries to interpret it. It examines primary sources such as literary and archaeological material (inscriptions, monuments, artefacts, etc.) connected with a religion and compares its development with other religions without any thought of one religion being superior to another. Secondary sources are considered but not treated with the same respect as the primary. The question of truth is usually left to the philosopher, though judgements of value often occur. The methods used are scientific and objective and the sacred books of the faiths are treated like any other book. Thus an historian writes concerning Sikhism that little can be known about its founder, Guru Nanak. Sikhs join Jews and Christians in deploring the radicalism of some scholars in their approach to the scriptures.

But one of the difficulties is that the sources are the response of believers and are considered subjective. There is little attempt to relate events to the contemporary culture or the forces that moulded the religion, so the conclusion is that they are theological rather than historical. We shall return to the problem when discussing the scriptures of the various faiths but comment here that the writings, though often related to history, particularly in the Semitic traditions (Judaism, Christianity, Islam), do not stress it. They are doctrinal, philosophical, impressionistic and imaginative. Such narrative does convey truth and therefore the historical must be wedded to other approaches to understand the significance of the writing. The theologian may fasten upon the patterns which the historian discovers in history and speak of the purpose and revelation of God, but the historian is likely to think of it as showing a progressive understanding by humanity.[2]

The history of religions developed in the nineteenth century with the desire to compare different religions. But it was based on the evolutionary idea from the false to the true instead of a concern with religions per se. And it was the policy to compare other religions with Christianity to show their limitations, but such a procedure is not acceptable today.[3]

Theological

There are many theologies in the various religions based on the sacred writings and traditions. Doctrines may be explicit in the scripture or implicit. Thus, it is contended that the Christian doctrine of the Trinity, while not in the Bible, can be deduced from various statements of the relation of Father, Son and Holy Spirit. Unitarians and Muslims believe that such a deduction is not valid and it becomes a point of issue in inter-faith dialogue. Theology is derived from *theos*, meaning God, and it tries to explain and validate His existence and revelation. Doctrines are established which form the basis of the ministry, sacraments, authority and organization of a religion. They can cause divisions within the community and discord with other religions.

Theology produces creeds and confessions of faith. To take Christianity as an example, there is the Nicene (325 CE), which is concerned with the status of Jesus Christ, and Chalcedon (451 CE), dealing with his human and divine natures. Confessions of faith are the Thirty-Nine Articles (1574) and the

Westminster (1643), which clergy of the Anglican and Presbyterian Church subscribe to but today are signed with mental reservations. In each faith there is a theology which is theoretical and practical, with the latter trying to understand the devotional and mystical writings. Other faiths such as Judaism and Hinduism pay little attention to creeds and see religion as a way of life.

The theological approach traditionally rested on a given faith position, but during the last two centuries has adopted a more liberal stance with a freer interpretation of scripture and a much greater interest in religions other than Christianity. But revelation in its various forms – free inquiry, truth claims – continues to be a subject of debate. An impact on theological methodology has been made by the rise of Religious Studies which considers religion in general and each religion in particular and uses the various approaches that we are describing in this chapter. Religion is seen as part of the history of ideas.

Philosophical

Philosophy can consider the methods employed in the study of religion, evaluate the evidence and arrive at the truth or otherwise of belief statements. In the past, philosophy asked ultimate questions about the purpose in the world, the existence of God, evil, morality, immortality, and so on. These questions went beyond science and were called metaphysics. In reaction, modern philosophy emphasized observation, experiment and induction (moving from particular experiments to formulating a general law), so religious statements were often treated as meaningless. The logical positivist philosopher said: 'I do not understand what you theologians are saying, it is non-sense because we cannot verify or confirm it by the senses'. In such a method there were difficulties too for morality and aesthetics. If I say, 'You stole that money', I am referring to a fact that can be verified by witnesses, but if I say, 'You ought not to have stolen it', I am merely expressing an emotion or moral disapproval. Moral approbation or censure statements were treated as 'Hurrah' or 'Boo' utterances.[4]

But within philosophy itself there has always been a scepticism about the ability of the senses and Immanuel Kant (1724–1804) was driven to declare that there was a reality behind things (things-in-themselves) which we could not grasp. He distinguished between the world of appearance which we could observe and the world of reality which we could not. The question becomes: 'Am I really seeing the world as it actually is or is it just an image or representation in my mind?' The problem will surface again when we consider the Indian religions. But in reply it could be asserted that we could check one sense against another: it may look like cheese but taste will show that it is butter. With science, observations are checked by experiments.

But what of mathematics, which is not based on sense observation? The Greeks who did so much in this area (we all remember the horrors of Euclid at school!) spoke of an unseen dimension and an invisible world of ideas and forms. The reply of the school of Logical Positivism was that both mathematical statement and statements of logic were valid because of the acceptance of the meaning of numbers and concepts. Thus, 'All husbands are married men' is true given the definition of the terms. They are analytic statements, validated by analysing the words used. But the philosophy failed to do justice to the fullness of human experience, though it had drawn attention to the importance of language and meaning.

The enquiry into religious language came to prominence in the work of Ludwig Wittgenstein (1889–1951). Language is compared to a bag of carpenter's tools, each with its particular function and technique of use or with a range of games each with its own rules and equipment and criteria of success or failure. We have to understand these if we are to know the game. Language is social, it cannot be uprooted from the life of the community in which it originated. A stranger in a foreign country needs not only to master the rules of the language but also to study the culture, customs and traditions if he wants to fully understand the people. The language of religion is intelligible within a mosque, temple, church or gurdwara, and is subject to internal rules. It is personal and cannot be reduced to what is connected with objects.

This means that we cannot define religion as a private affair as it takes place in a community and has rules for the interpretation of sacred texts and for the regulation of the behaviour of its members. The social dimension of religion must be recognized. Also, as Wittgenstein pointed out, while games have their own rules they need to be brought into relation with other games and similarities in language and rules observed. A religion needs to consider its relation to other religions and areas of knowledge for there are family 'resemblances' as well as family 'differences'.

Empiricism is not ruled out by many of the religions for they make the empirical claim that the sacred books are based on the evidence of eyewitnesses who kept company with the founder. It was the experience of the founder of the religion which led them to believe in God and pass on to others what they had experienced. The historian needs to sift out the kernel of experience from the later additions and the theological viewpoint of the writers of the Gospels or the Adi Granth or the Qur'an and so forth. While the development of religions shows change, we cannot imagine Christianity without Christ or Islam without Muhammad or Sikhism without Guru Nanak. Otherwise we make the followers greater than the founder himself! But all of this means that the philosopher has to turn to the historian to see what the critical interpretation of the texts is and he will find that they vary from the conservative through to the radical.

The language of religion has a great variety of expression: metaphor, simile, analogy, symbol, allegory. In speaking of God we are limited, for we are using human language to describe what is beyond the human. But this does not mean that such figures of speech do not impart information, for at times they can be more effective than literal statements, just as a poem can startle and arouse in a way that a factual statement cannot. We can sum up the problem of empiricism and verification by a simple example used by John Wilson. If I say, 'Mary is sweet', I am not going to confirm it by trying to taste her! But if I say 'Sugar is sweet', I can taste to verify. The two statements are different though having points of contact by the use of the same word. How I verify a religious assertion has some contact with empiricism, but there are other ways of verification.

Psychological

The emotional aspects of religion cannot be ignored so psychologists examined religious experience. Many psychologists treat religious experience like any other human experience and religious writers have followed the procedure by arguing that it is normal experience in depth. But some people contend that they have had extraordinary trances, ecstasy and visions. Ninian Smart thinks that a religious experience involves a perception of the invisible world or of some person or thing which reveals that world. Psychologists tend to be sceptical about this and explain such states as psychological conditions of the mind. The scepticism appears in the religions: Catholicism, for example, is distrustful of individual claims of conversion and direct communication with God and relies more on the sacraments of the Church and other mediating channels extended to the faithful. But much study is now devoted to mystical experience which appears in all the religions.

Many have written on religious experience. One of the most notable was William James (1842–1910) who thought it was better to believe in God since it often produced good results. This stemmed from his pragmatism which did not concern itself with the truth of a belief but its effect on our lives. Religion, he thought, is the belief that the world is part of a more spiritual universe and has the goal of achieving harmony with it. The result is a zest for life and a sense of inner peace. He distinguished between the religion of the sick soul which seeks salvation from sin and is reborn by conversion and the religion of healthy-mindedness which is less pessimistic about its spiritual condition and feels no need of conversion. There are the 'once born' and the 'twice born'.

Rudolf Otto (1869–1937) argued that the numinous or uncanny could be experienced, and that religious experience was beyond normal experience. It was a unique experience based on the awesome (*tremendum*) but attractive (*et fascinans*). It was the essence of religion and he had observed it in Hinduism and Islam as well as in Christianity. The awareness of the numinous results in a feeling of unworthiness, as Isaiah experienced in the Temple (Isa. 6), but it is difficult to describe in rational terms since it is super-rational. Otto does not attempt to prove the existence of such a Subject or Supreme Creator since this is the rational way and does not make contact with the numinous. It was enough for him to conclude that the experience of the numinous conveys its existence.[5] Such an experience could be envoked through nature, music, ritual, architecture, art, the use of a language which is mysterious and sacred, and chanting. Fear, majesty, energy, mystery, are all elements in the experience of the 'Wholly Other'. It would seem to imply a negative approach to God, since He is so unlike us we are only able to say what He is not, but Otto introduces the fascination or attraction of God and thereby agrees with Thomas Aquinas: 'We are only able to say what God is not if we also know in some sense what he is.' It can be experienced in nature as Wordsworth said: 'a presence that disturbs me with the joy of elevated thoughts'. But it can also be awakened by the Spirit of God in Judaism and Christianity and the suppression of the rational in Zen Buddhism to reach satori.[6] It is done by enigma and riddles; for example, what is the sound of one hand clapping? There are questions which have no answer and the rational mind collapses in trying to solve them.

Sigmund Freud (1856–1939) was not convinced and thought that such experiences can be explained psychologically. He wrote of God as an illusion or a projection of the father image whom the son respects but hates because he is jealous of his love for the mother. Repression of such ideas gives way to exalting the father into a divine figure. The theory may reflect more Freud's own experience, for it is difficult to establish it on a general basis. It could hardly apply to Muhammad since his father died a few days before his birth and his mother died when he was only six years old! Carl Gustav Jung (1875–1961) differed from Freud, seeing religion as having great practical value for it gave people hope and a happier outlook on life. Thus he would have agreed with William James. It was not an illusion but a natural function which affects humanity just as much as the will to power (Adler) or sexuality (Freud). He propounded 'the collective unconscious', images or archetypes which we experience in dreams and religion and the God image was one of them. He insisted that a religious outlook on life was essential.

In more recent times the question has been raised of whether drugs can induce a religious experience, but psychologists differ on this and produce many conflicting theories about religion. With regard to defining religion, most psychological attempts are rather negative, implying that it is based on fear or an attempt to escape from the demands of life or wish projection of a better time. Guilt is regarded as a neurosis which can be dealt with by realizing that we are the product of heredity and environment, so why blame ourselves? Problems of free will are often not attended to, nor are reasons given for the continuance of the fear of death.

The whole question of religious experience is important, and psychology is a useful and relevant tool. It can examine what has been called the religious instinct, the charisma of the religious leader, and the effect of suggestion in mass evangelism. But it is argued that the psychologist cannot settle the difficult question of whether or not there is a God or a transcendental dimension to which many think religion refers. But it must ally itself to sociology since religion is social as well as individual.

Sociological

The approach tries to avoid personal commitments and prejudices and formulates hypotheses which can be tested empirically. It stresses that the understanding of another society requires knowledge of the culture which influences behaviour. Questions are raised: How does religion function in a society? Does it bind together or cause division? Will it last? Augustus Comte believed religion would disappear but his sympathy with it is shown by his tribute to theologians whom he thought were aware of what human nature was like. He commented that but for them, 'human society would have remained in a condition much like that of a company of superior monkeys'.[7]

Émile Durkheim's work based on the Australian aborigines showed that the totem, a sacred object, points to an impersonal force in objects and of the tribe itself. In his *Elementary Forms of Religious Life* (1912), he argued that religion is society itself and by its rituals cements social unity. It pertains to the sacred aspects which can be distinguished from the profane. Durkheim's definition of religion is both functional and substantive: beliefs provide the substance and the practices are their functional aspects. But beliefs can divide as well as unify, and was he right in thinking that the sacred and profane are so distinct? The view is challenged in the religions, but even in such ceremonies as the coronation of a monarch or the swearing in of the President of the USA, nationalism and religion are blended. Durkheim was right in seeing religion as social but it can also be individualistic.

Max Weber opposed Durkheim, arguing that it was religion that produced social groupings. Capitalism owed much to Christian Calvinism which insisted on hard work and thrift as a sign of faith in God and His election. Ambition, saving and hard work were pleasing to God and since money was not wasted on dress or adornment or entertainment, the Calvinist invested it, leading to more capital. Sociologists are often limited in their findings because they concentrate only on the Christian religion, but Weber studied world religions and showed the nature of ethical and exemplary prophecy. The former encouraged social change while the latter held on to tradition. The traditional forms of religion supported the status quo whereas the sect could upset it. His work ranged over the area of bureaucracy and types of authority and charismatic leadership. While some of his arguments are regarded with scepticism by sociologists of religion, it is clear that his influence has permeated their writings today.[8]

Karl Marx followed Durkheim's view that religion was a human construction, though he went on to an interpretation which was quite different. It will be developed in a later chapter. More recent work such as that of Peter Berger refers to the sacred canopy: beliefs in the sacred providing an overall explanation of existence and supplying meaning in a confusing world. In his book, *A Rumour of Angels* (1971), he reacted to the general idea that religion is human in origin by pointing to signals of transcendence found in humour, hope, justice and play, and our sense of order in the world.

Sociologists are interested in how institutions react to changing circumstances: a religion founded by a charismatic figure can develop into an institution which seeks the power to consolidate and spread the faith. There are a number of examples. One is the peaceful religion of Sikhism, founded by Guru

Nanak, which developed a military style of organization called the Khalsa. Another was the development of papal power in Christianity, which sent the crusaders to take the Holy Land from the Muslims. A third is the military power of Islam, which developed from Muhammad's defence of his revelation to worldwide conquest. Even in normal times, religious organizational structure can exchange spiritual power for temporal with a diminishing of spontaneity and enthusiasm as arguments continue about ritual or beliefs or leadership. The worst scenario occurs when the faith fails to adapt to society and retreats into a religious ghetto with little social outreach. Conversely, the religion may so conform to the values of the society that the original message virtually disappears. Every religion is faced with conserving the best of its past with accommodation to the present. How it balances these factors is not easy.

Many Sikhs when they migrated to Britain abandoned their turban. The Punjabi word for turban is *sikhna*, meaning to hear, hence the Sikhs listen to the word of the Guru and are continual learners. When their wives and families arrived in Britain religious ties were renewed, and the turban reappeared. The first gurdwara (Sikh temple) was built in 1958 in Yorkshire and regular attendance observed. Where there was no temple a religious service (*diwan*) was held in the home. It was a social event as well as religious and helped to strengthen the Sikh ethnic identity. But with them and other religious groups such as the Muslims, there is often a tension between the values inculcated in the schools and their religion. The stress on individualism and choice comes into conflict with the family loyalties and the tradition of arranged marriages in accordance with parental control and religious belief. Racial discrimination is evident still in Britain and elsewhere, and a secular society makes little attempt to understand religious values. In connection with Sikhism, the transport authorities tried to force Sikhs to wear the regulation cap and it was a long time before Parliament agreed to Sikhs wearing their turbans instead of crash helmets when riding motorcycles. The wearing of the turban also reasserts the ethnic pride of the Sikhs in the face of white rejection of their colour and treating second and third generations of them as foreigners.

While religions have to accommodate to survive it is obvious that a society needs to know something about the culture and customs of migrant people if racial discrimination is to be eliminated. One factor that would help is more religious education in schools so that children will know something about and learn to appreciate the customs and beliefs of everyone living in their society.

The sociologist is aware that only by participation in a religion and its culture, language, customs and values can it be understood. Many go to live with communities to gain their trust instead of standing away from them as objects to be examined. The discipline tries to be scientific, using statistical methods and surveys. Secularization is a main theme with some saying that it has occurred and others disagreeing. Much work has been done in connection with sects by J. M. Yinger, David Martin and Bryan Wilson. But there does not seem to be any single model created by sociologists to fully explain the role of religion in society.[9]

Phenomenological

The method is descriptive, looking at similarities and dissimilarities, and tries to be free from value judgements and to show empathy with the culture and beliefs. It endeavours to 'walk in the moccasins of the faithful', looking at the phenomena from the viewpoint of the people themselves, and tries to discern patterns in the religions.[10] Limitations are imposed on the investigation in that it is the observed data which are interpreted and no attempt is made to deal with the truth or otherwise of the faiths. But it cautions about seeing what we want to see or expect to see and calls for imagination to enter into the lifestyle and mind-set of those who differ from us. It draws on all the other approaches but favours participation or 'field work' studies. The approach is a good one for it is difficult to understand the conflict in Northern Ireland or Israel or other parts of the world without living among the people there. Yet while the phenomenologist does not project her own views but maintains a neutral viewpoint, it is difficult to escape one's own background and presuppositions and not exercise some judgement on what is observed.

Feministic

We shall be thinking in detail about this approach in a later chapter but comment here that it opposes masculine assumptions about the inferiority of women in leadership roles. It contends that the scriptures of the religions are male orientated and neglect the proper place of women. The continual use of the masculine gender in referring to the deity is to be deplored and in some cases feminists have campaigned for a new edition of scriptures and prayer books which will deal with the problem.

In conclusion we note that the different approaches blend in various ways so in any study of religion all must be taken into account. No one approach gives a total view of religion and its characteristics. We will attempt to use all of them as we proceed. In the next chapter we begin our study of six religions by considering the importance of rituals.

3 Rituals

In this and the following chapters a theme in each religion will be examined, beginning in each case with the Semitic (Judaism, Christianity, Islam) and then the Indian (Hinduism, Buddhism, Sikhism).

The Jews have no temple because the first, built by Solomon in about 950 BCE, was destroyed in 586 BCE, and the second, built in 516 BCE and replanned by Herod in 19 BCE, was destroyed by the Romans in 70 CE. The Jews pray constantly at the Wailing Wall of the old Temple in Jerusalem for its restoration and the return of former glory. But the destruction meant that the synagogue, which probably dated back to the time of Ezra, became the focus of worship. The home too is a place of prayer with the family table replacing the temple altar and the father imitating the duty of the High Priest during the Passover ritual.

The synagogue is the meeting place on the Sabbath or *Shabbat* (Saturday) since the creator rested after his work and it is also a weekly remembrance of Israel's deliverance from slavery in Egypt (Exod. 20:11, Deut. 5:15). It houses the scrolls of the Law, the Torah, the first five books of Moses, has a pulpit-reading desk (*bimah*) and the stained-glass windows are adorned with Jewish symbols. Images are strictly forbidden. During a service it is impressive to watch the opening of the cabinet where the scrolls are kept and the carrying of them in procession to the reading desk. The chest containing the tablets of the Law stood in the innermost sanctum of the old Temple, the Holy of Holies (Exod. 37), and now each synagogue has scrolls. Fastened to the right doorpost of each house is the *mezuzah*, a small metal container holding pieces of parchment inscribed with biblical texts, but neither the home nor the synagogue are consecrated as holy places. In both, psalms are sung and prayers recited and in the synagogue there is usually a sermon. The service may be in Hebrew or English.

In the orthodox branch of Judaism men wear a skull cap and women sit apart in the gallery, but in more progressive Jewry they worship together. The holy place of the Faith is the ruins of the Temple in Jerusalem. Worshippers in an orthodox synagogue can touch the Torah with their shawls as it is carried in procession, but women are not allowed to. At the time of religious maturity a thirteen-year-old boy attends the Bar Mitzvah ceremony and is called to read the Law and receive a set of *tephillin*, two small boxes containing biblical texts, and a *tallith*, a white shawl with fringes in which there is a blue thread. These are worn at morning prayers.

Rabbis learned in the Law lead the worship and offer counsel and guidance. Historically it was the rabbis (masters of the Torah) who brought about changes in Judaism after the fall of the Temple. They stem from the Pharisaic tradition which received a 'bad press' in the New Testament for its attention to detail and the many laws. Traditionally they believed that both a written and oral Torah was given to Moses on Mount Sinai but the Sadducees trusted only in the written law and performed the priestly function in the Temple. The office (*kohen*) was instituted through the family of Aaron, the brother of Moses, and was hereditary, but both priests and sacrifices disappeared with the Fall of the Temple in 70 CE. Hence it was left to the Pharisees to lay the foundation for Rabbinic Judaism and through the centuries nourish the faith in the synagogues. Usually the rabbis had other ways of earning a living, but in the nineteenth century they were salaried and today officiate at rites of passage. They are authorized teachers, having had a training and examination in Jewish law. In progressive synagogues a greater role is given to them than in the orthodox.[1]

In Judaism there was the idea of 'outside in', meaning that purity was associated with the inner parts of the Temple and any extension outwards of the building became increasingly impure. Thus there were courts of the Gentiles considered most impure and courts of the Jews with degrees of purity until the innermost sanctuary was reached. Only the High Priest could enter this sanctum once a year on the Day of Atonement. The courts point to both a religious and a social separation.

The Muslims built a mosque, the Dome on the Rock, on the ruins of the Jewish Temple, and Jews have to remain at the Wailing Wall of the old Temple and are not allowed near it. This is a focal point of tension. But there are places other than the remains of the Temple which are special because of connections with outstanding teachers and the patriarchs. Also it can be argued that since God is always present with Israel the community itself could be considered sacred.[2] How then, if God is everywhere, as most religions believe, can there be sacred places? The Rabbis explained it by pointing out that God in the Temple was like the sea in a cave. The cave can be full without reducing the amount of water in the sea. Theologically it means that God is transcendent, far beyond us, but also immanent, within us. The *Shabbat* itself signifies the replacing of sacred space by time, and may be understood as a foretaste of the world to come, a replacement of the Temple as the focus of messianic hope.

Festivals and feasts are joyous times for most religions. The Jews have three main Festivals: Passover (*Pesach*), Pentecost and Tabernacles (*sukkoth*). The first (Exod. 12:21–4) recalls the escape from Egyptian bondage. The ritual (*seder*) follows the *haggadah* or prayer book of the Jews and at the meal there is roast lamb, a reminder of its blood smeared on the doorposts of the house so that death would be avoided, the unleavened bread (*matzah*) since their ancestors had no time to allow the bread to rise, and the bitter herbs eaten in remembrance of the suffering. Pentecost celebrates the giving of the Torah to Moses on Mount Sinai and the Feast of Tabernacles recalls the time when the Israelites of the Exodus lived in small shelters or tabernacles *en route* to the promised land.

Other important days are New Year (Rosh Hashanah), remembering God's act of creation when a ram's horn (*shofar*) is blown in the synagogue and is sounded again on the Day of Atonement (Yom Kippur), recalling Abraham's sacrifice of the ram in place of his son, Isaac. In Judaism male children are circumcised at the age of eight and in progressive synagogues there is now a Bar Mitzvah for girls. In the synagogues there is the impressive *menorah* which is a candelabrum and reminds them of the eight-branched candelabrum which stood in the ancient Temple. During the Feast of Chanukkah, the Festival of Lights, the candelabrum is lit and the victory of Judas Maccabaeus over Antiochus V Epiphanes is celebrated.

The place of worship in Christianity has a style and decoration depending on the divisions of the Faith. Some have altars, stained-glass windows, elaborate choirs and music, images and icons, while others may not have even a cross on display. The Reformed churches often retain their central pulpit, emphasizing the preaching of the Bible, but the altar for the celebration of the mass has the prominent position in the Catholic, Anglo-Catholic and Orthodox traditions. It is celebrated frequently, contrasting with the Protestant denominations who may only hold the service once a month. A plain table replaces the altar for Holy Communion. Christians celebrate the birth, death and resurrection of Jesus and the pouring out of the Spirit at Whitsun. Some churches also celebrate events in the life of the Virgin Mary and the saints and martyrs. Others believe in adult baptism by total immersion, but some sprinkle water to remove the guilt of original sin. It is the equivalent of circumcision in the Hebrew scriptures. The belief is that God advances with grace towards the child which is later confirmed by an act of faith.

The Mass, or Eucharist or Holy Communion, is based on the final meal that Jesus had with his disciples, but different views are presented of its significance. Some see the bread and wine as symbols while others believe that when the elements are consecrated they become the body and blood. The Eastern and Western churches differ in their ritual. Both prepare the elements before the service but in Eastern orthodoxy there is the symbolic action of slaying Christ by piercing the bread with a miniature lance. At the offertory the dead Christ is intended to undergo resurrection through the Spirit. The Mass was to become a bone of contention during the Protestant reformation in the sixteenth century.

There is a variety of worship in Christianity but some elements are generally common: preaching, congregational singing, use of organ, sacraments and leadership by priest or minister. There are differences regarding images or icons (paintings or mosaics of Jesus Christ or one of the saints) and in the Quaker denomination there is no music or preaching but waiting silently for the coming of the Spirit. Many Protestant churches have expanded their ritual, departing from what is called the non-conformist sandwich: hymn, prayer, bible reading, hymn, and so on. But ritual is elaborate and a sacred place marked out for it in Catholicism, Anglo-Catholicism and Eastern Orthodoxy. The space around the altar is usually regarded as holy. In Greek orthodoxy a screen or iconostasis divides the area from the rest of the church. Sacramentalists are inclined to view the building and its contents as sacred, but the Early Church had no buildings and the church was identified with the people. Where the church community gathered was a sacred place and today some argue that it is the ritual which makes a place sacred. Others think that a building is sacred because of its connection with persons and objects. They point out that particular places have always been regarded as sacred because they were connected with Christ, the saints and martyrs of the Church.[3]

The twelfth century has been called the century of relics and it was laid down that altars in churches should have a martyr's relic. Graveyards became consecrated ground and sacredness was linked with the dead. Today the performing of ritual at a crematorium has developed to the extent that many regard it as a sacred place. Pilgrimage to shrines acquire merit or healing, e.g. Lourdes, but it is opposed by Protestantism. However, their leaders do organize visits to the Holy Land and other sites. The Reformation destroyed many valuable works of arts, icons and images, but mental images are formed in the mind when hymns like 'There is a green hill far away' are sung.[4]

The leaders of worship and organization were defined by Ignatius Bishop of Antioch (100 CE) – bishop, presbyter and deacon – and these were endorsed by Catholics and Anglicans, but other denominations insist that bishop (*episkopos*) is equivalent to presbyter (*presbuteros*) or elder and exclude bishops. The word priest is derived from presbyter and was connected with sacrifice in Judaism. The Reformers replaced it with minister or servant. Women have been ordained for some time in the Reformed Churches and more recently the Anglicans have followed the example. Christianity has had monks since the third century and these exercised quite an influence in theological debates; there were also some monasteries for women. In Ireland monasteries existed before churches and they did much to preserve and foster learning.[5]

The Islamic mosque is not consecrated and there are no priests. The mosque is usually in the form of a square with an open courtyard and from the tower (minaret) the muezzin calls the faithful five times a day to prayer (*adhan*). The mosque contains a watertank for ablutions. The Muslim washes his hands, forearms and legs below the knees before worship and he also rinses the face, mouth and nose. There is an area for prayers, a pulpit and recess or niche in the wall (*qiblah*) indicating the direction of Mecca, the holy city. The Muslims originally prayed towards Jerusalem but soon the focus centred on the sacred shrine (Ka'bah) in Mecca. The worshippers, having removed their shoes and the women covered their heads, pray using certain words and postures of the body. Hands are raised on both sides of the face crying '*Allahu Akbar*' (Allah is most Great) and the right hand is placed on the left one and they recite the opening chapter of the Qur'an acknowledging that Allah alone is worshipped.

Eleven different postures follow which include bowing from the hips and full-length prostration and sitting cross-legged on the floor. The words uttered include the Al-Tashahud (Testimony) which bears witness to Muhammad as the servant and apostle of Allah. Islam acknowledges Abraham as the founder of the Faith, so it is incorrect to say that it began with Muhammad. But it contains a denial of the Christian belief that God had a son, Jesus Christ: 'Allah is One: He begets not nor is He begotten. And there is none comparable unto Him.' The Imam who leads the prayers is in the recess (*mihrab*) which marks the direction of Mecca (*qiblah*). Calligraphy is used in the mosques with decorated texts of the Qur'an, but like the Jews no image or visible symbol of God is permitted. The mathematical design of the mosques represents the order and design of the universe. There is no music and the women pray separately from men. Purity of intention (*niyyah*) is necessary for all ritual acts.

The Muslims have a number of feasts and festivals and it is only possible to mention a few of them. There is the Feast of Sacrifice associated with the annual pilgrimage to Mecca. It resembles the Jewish Yom Kippur and the Muslims believe that it was Ishmael that Abraham intended to sacrifice, not Isaac. Ishmael is considered to be the father of the Arabs, and according to the Qur'an he helped Abraham to build the Ka'bah and place the Black Stone, brought down to Abraham from heaven by the archangel Gabriel, in the east corner of the shrine. Ramadan occurs in the ninth month of the Muslim calendar and calls for a complete abstinence from food and drink during the daytime. The end of the Fast is celebrated with much entertainment and there is a distribution of food to the poor. Gifts are exchanged and the mosques are full of worshippers. The New Year Festival is celebrated in different ways by the various divisions of Islam according to historical experience or religious beliefs. Other feasts are connected with Muhammad. The first commemorates his birthday and is marked by special prayers and reading of the Qur'an and processions and the second remembers his nocturnal journey to Paradise which is usually interpreted in a spiritual sense.

Everything is sacred in Islam but sacred places act as a focus. *Haram* means prohibited and usually refers to the women's quarters, but by extension it can mean sacred when applied to places. Mosques are sacred by use and the Muslim is called upon to pray five times in the day. Mecca (Makkah) is the archetypal sacred place and the Ka'bah signifies where human life began. Pilgrimage to it assures the Muslim that Allah has forgiven sin. Medina (Madinah) gets its sacredness from Mecca, for it was the place to which Muhammad migrated in 622 CE. It is his burial place and when the Muslim worships there he expects that the Prophet will intercede on his behalf. The archetypal shrine is Jerusalem's Dome on the Rock and some argue that such a building symbolizes the superceding of Judaism and Christianity by Islam. The majority of Muslims are Sunni and revere these sites but a minority, the Shi'ah, have the sacred place at Karbala, ninety-six kilometres southwest of Baghdad. They remember that it was there that their leader Husain and his followers were massacred in 680 CE by the Sunni. The event is commemorated annually in the Passion of Husain. Pilgrimage (*hajj*) is one of the five pillars of Islam and it is expected that Muslims will travel at least once to Mecca, the birthplace of Muhammad and the spiritual centre of Islam.[6]

The ancient Hindus engaged in nature worship (*puja*) and as there were no temples it took place in the open air. The use of images was introduced by the devotees of the gods Shiva, Vishnu and Shakti. The temple is the residence of the deity and when the image is housed in it there are rituals intended to breathe divine life into it. The image is bathed, decorated and wakened in the morning with songs of praise, and when the worshippers bring their offerings a bell is rung to warn the god and a ritual is performed by the Brahmin priest. He receives the offerings and prays in the classical language of Sanskrit. Music is played and hymns sung. The gift includes food offerings which are then distributed to the worshippers as *prasad*. Prayer is individual rather than corporate, with the lighting of a lamp or candle as a token of devotion. The *prasad*, being dedicated to God and yet consumed by the worshippers, means that they have shared in the life of the divine.

The home has a shrine to the god, usually in the kitchen, which must be kept scrupulously clean. The mother, having washed, brings offerings to it. Here the family gathers for worship in the morning and evening with the women taking responsibility for it. Local deities are more prominent in the villages since it is believed they are interested in the daily needs of the people. The ceremonies are conducted by the village priest (*bhopa*). But many Hindus argue that religion is to be equated with the human spirit, hence external places such as shrines, temples and places of pilgrimage are not that important. True pilgrimage is within the body, which is regarded as a sacred place. Secular art is prevalent in the temples, with scenes of erotic love, because it is believed that sexual desires are to be conquered and nothing in human life must be excluded from religion. There are also wayside shrines which resemble those dedicated to the Virgin Mary and other saints in Catholicism.[7]

Natural phenomena such as mountains, rivers, lakes, caves

and woodlands are awe inspiring and invoke prayer. The soaring towers of Hindu temples are modelled on the mountains and have a bathing tank and rivers. Mother Ganges conveys blessings on those who bathe in her. Hinduism, like Islam, resists the distinction between the religious and the secular, but the deity resides in the sanctuary of the Temple (*garbhagriha*) so there is a sacred area. This 'holy of holies' resembles the inner sanctum in the Jewish temple and the iconostasis which acts as a division in Greek orthodoxy. Pilgrimage includes fasting, ascetic practices and celibacy, and involves going to a temple or a special place such as Allahabad, Badrinath, Dvaraka, Ramesvaram and Puri. There are also seven sacred rivers and bathing in the Ganges conveys the forgiveness of sins. If Hindus die at Benaras they are guaranteed liberation from the cycle of rebirth, but all pilgrimage to obtain merit and the cure of disease and so on must be undertaken with purity of mind.[8]

There are life-cycle rites (*samskaras*) which are observed at birth, initiation, marriage and death. A prayer of blessing is said for the infant and a youth is invested with a sacred thread (*janeu*). Traditionally the ceremonies were for the initiation of the higher classes, the twice-born. Nowadays in most families the various stages of life are recognized and one of the most important is marriage. It is arranged by the parents with the consulting of horoscopes to ensure that the couple are suitable for one another. At death the body is cremated and the ashes committed to a holy river, but holy men (*sadhus*) and small children are often buried. The mourners take ritual baths to avoid pollution, and food for the ghost of the departed is laid out by the son. Only he can perform the duty (*shraddha*) so every family wants a son. In Hinduism the god of death is Yama and the soul according to its deeds is sent to a place of ghosts or to one of the twenty hells for purification before rebirth. Animals are respected, especially the cow, which is sacred, producing much that is necessary for life: milk, curds and butter. Killing it is one of the worst crimes.

Both gods and goddesses are worshiped with Krishna, the incarnation of Vishnu, and female deities such as Durga, Kali and Radha, being very popular. There are many festivals in their honour. One of the most colourful is Divali, the Festival of Lights, held at the end of the Hindu year and the beginning of the new. Lamps are ceremonially lit and presents exchanged. The Kumbh Mela Festival is held every twelve years in India, and it is estimated that in 2001 seventy million Hindus attended, making it the largest gathering ever assembled. Worship is connected in Hinduism with *bhakti*, loving devotion to the god Vishnu, based on the *Bhagavad gita*. But yoga (*yoke*), which is a method of self-control and meditation, can be linked to one of the six schools of Hindu philosophy and need not involve the gods.[9]

In Buddhism there are celebrations of the Buddha's birth, enlightenment, first sermon and death. In Theravada Buddhism a full-moon festival (*Vesak*) is held to commemorate these important events. It is the Buddhist New Year when food and alms are distributed. The initiation of the novice into the Faith is a joyous occasion and he arrives wearing his best clothes with a cotton cord placed around the top of the head and the community engages in the chanting of the teachings of the Buddha. There are refreshments and entertainment. On the second day there is continued chanting of the scriptures and on the third his head is shaved. He sleeps in a cell, dresses in an orange/yellow robe, carries a begging bowl and a string of beads to help him to meditate. A filter is also required to strain drinking water in order not to harm any insect that might have fallen into it. With these few possessions he spends his life in the monastery or, having learned a lot about self-control, he returns to the outside world.

Worship developed in Buddhism even though the Buddha reacted against the gods of Hinduism and showed little interest in them. Faith and devotion can be observed in Theravada Buddhism with the main focus being the Buddha whose statue is in the home and the temple. Monks chant or recite passages from the scriptures and there is devotion to the Buddha's relics. The chanting can shade off into meditation which involves control of the breath and the calming of the mind. The purpose is to develop an attitude of loving kindness to all beings. We will look in more detail at this practice later.

The Buddha did not advocate pilgrimage, stressing that it was the dhamma or teaching which was important because of its sacred quality. However, the devotional current developed and Mahayana Buddhism elevated the Buddha to the status of a god. Thus there are temples where worship is offered to the transcendent Buddha of Infinite Light (*Amitabha*). Worshippers bring gifts of food, money, flowers and candles and carry a prayer mat, bowl, betel-nut box, spittoon and a teapot. Like Hinduism, there is a stress on the individual rather than the communal, with music, the waving of incense sticks and much bowing before the image of the Buddha or Buddhas. There is coming and going, some standing before images intoning prayers while others listen to a monk reading scripture. Mantras are used, which in Buddhism, Hinduism and Sikhism are sacred formulas or chants invested with mysterious qualities and efficacy.[10]

Stupas or funeral monuments have been built containing relics of the Buddha or images of him or parts of scripture. The architectural design reflects the movement away from Hinduism in that there is no particular space which secludes the deity and excludes the worshippers. Such a 'central cell' would not have been able to accommodate the members of the monastic community (*sangha*) which are the fraternity of monks founded by the Buddha. A daily recitation of the monks is, 'I take refuge in the sangha.' The stupas have a base, dome and spire, representing the world of desire, the world of form and the world of formlessness which are the three spiritual states. Pilgrimage to them acquires merit. But the Buddha was not keen on pilgrimages and did not want his relics preserved. He said: 'He who sees the dhamma sees me', meaning that it was the teaching that was important and his body was only a temporary vehicle for its transmission.[11]

The dhamma, being sacred, is not a quality of time or place, teacher or ritual. Nevertheless, there are sacred places associated with the Buddha and his followers with the qualification that everywhere and everything is sacred. And in the development of the religion, persons did come to be regarded as sacred, for example, the Dalai Lama of Tibet. Again, despite the Buddha's rejection of externals, hairs and teeth belonging to him were found in Rangoon and Sri Lanka and many other places. In India, Tantric Buddhism (*Vajrayana*) had more than twenty-four places of pilgrimage and in Tibet, where the land was considered to be the body of an ogress, stupas and temples were erected in order to pin her down! It is contended that these sacred places meet the needs of the laity, not the ordained sangha, whose minds are concentrated on higher things.

The founder of Sikhism carried the protest about the external trappings of religion much further and called for their abolition. The earliest Sikh meeting places (*dharamshalas*) were not places of worship but served as accommodation for pilgrims. Eventually they became gurdwaras and housed the scripture (Guru Granth or Adi Granth). But they have no images or altars and cannot be called temples in the Hindu sense. Guru Nanak taught the practice of repeating the name of God in worship and service to the community. There are no priests, any member can read the scripture and conduct the worship (*diwan*), but usually it is done by the committee of the gurdwara. They organize the services and sometimes there is a *granthi*, who acts as a religious teacher and custodian of the building.

The Sikhs remove their shoes and the women cover their heads and approach the scripture which has been placed on a raised platform with a canopy over the top. A fly-whisk made of yak's hair, a sign of royalty, is waved continuously over it and as each worshipper passes the book, he bows and places an offering in front of it. Prayers are said, passages of scripture repeated and devotional songs (*kirtan*) sung. The hymns of Nanak are very popular. The service is very lively, using a variety of musical instruments and the hymns are read first and then explained before singing. A sermon is preached to inspire conduct and at the end of the service there is the distribution of food (*kadah prasad*) held in the *langar* or kitchen, sometimes referred to as '*Guru ka Gangar*' (the Guru's kitchen). It is a mixture of ground wheat, sugar and butter in equal parts. The seated congregation receive it in their right hand. *Karah* is the Punjabi name which means a gift or present. The purpose is to show that they are one united family of equals: caste distinctions are rejected. But it is not a sacrament.

The Golden Temple at Amritsar is linked with previous gurus and Hindu gods and houses the Guru Granth Sahib. It is a sacred place and attracts pilgrims. Other gurdwaras have been built where gurus have died but pictures of them are not in the same place as the scripture but hung in other rooms.

While there is a concentration on the presence of God where the Guru Granth is, the Sikh sees Him everywhere, so again the sacred and the secular combine. The sacred primarily resides in the human heart. Nanak opposed pilgrimages to sacred places but the division of Punjab between India and Pakistan meant that Sikhs needed to travel to Pakistan where Nanak had been born. There is also at Amritsar the Akal Takht (the eternal throne), once the residence of the historical gurus and now the most important of the five seats of authority. It means the unity of spiritual and temporal power. The impressive Golden Temple is a model for all gurdwaras.[12]

In Sikhism, on the birth of a child a ritual can be organized or *ardas* (formal prayer) is offered as a thanksgiving, but it is not strictly an initiation. A name must be chosen before the child is forty days old and is done by consulting the Adi Granth. Sugared water (*amrit*) applied to the lips of the infant is part of the ceremony. But the main initiation into Sikhism is the *Khande di pahul*, which was introduced by the Guru Gobind Singh in 1699 when he created the Sikh brotherhood or Khalsa. It is an elaborate ceremony using amrit and the call for commitment to the essentials of the Sikh faith. They must promise to pray daily, pay tithes, and always wear the five Ks: *Kes*, unshorn hair and beard; *Kangha*, a comb to keep hair tidy; *Kaccha*, knee-length breeches; *Kara*, a steel bracelet on the right wrist; and *Kirpan*, a sabre or steel knife. These are the symbols of the faith. The founding of the Khalsa is celebrated by a Festival (*Baisakhi*) in January when it is recalled that the Guru baptized five followers, giving them the name of Singh and the five symbolic emblems.[13]

There are arranged marriages but no dowry is demanded and it is not a sacrament but an act of spiritual union. It must take place in the presence of the Guru Granth Sahib, commencing with prayer (*ardas*), obeisance to the scripture, recital of a scriptural page taken at random, and four marriage vows. Hymns are sung, advice given, and the conditions of marriage outlined. At the conclusion the *kadah prasad* is distributed, the couple garlanded, and greetings exchanged by all. The death ritual requires the bathing of the body, dressing and placing in a container and then cremation. There is singing, prayers and *kadah prasad* distributed. It is not necessary to sprinkle the ashes at any particular place but they may be immersed locally in flowing water or the ocean. There is no wailing since death is inevitable and normal. After the funeral, verses of the Guru Granth Sahib are read over a period of ten days. Nanak said that death had no finality but was a 'half-existence' before rebirth.[14]

Many Hindu festivals are kept by the Sikhs since their founder was a Hindu, but in addition they celebrate his birthday and that of Guru Gobind Singh. They are joyous times accompanied by fairs, animal races, wrestling contests and other sporting events. Divali, the Hindu festival, is remembered as it coincided with the return from prison to Amritsar of the sixth Guru, Hargobind. The birthdays of other gurus are celebrated, especially those who were martyred.

In conclusion, we note that ritual is important in religions but some stress it more than others. Hinduism, for example, believes that a Brahmin must engage in ritual, and nonperformance for one year entails loss of caste. Rituals are essential in devotional Hinduism and Tantric since it is thought to be the way of joining the spiritual world. The rituals pertaining to initiation and marriage must be done properly. It is particularly the case with death, otherwise the soul will be unable to find peace. But the founders of other religions, while calling their followers to prayer and fasting, insisted that purity of heart and intention is more important than any ritual. Without it pilgrimage is useless. The Hebrew prophets condemned ritual divorced from justice and mercy, and it is said that Nanak called for the abolition of religion, i.e. its trappings. No doubt these protests would have pleased Whitehead!

There is also an individualism in Hinduism and Buddhism and in the Protestant protest of the sixteenth century where again ritual was a focus of criticism. But it is difficult to do without some form of ritual and even Nanak instituted a basic ritual with *nam simran*, remembering God, and *nam japan*, meditation and repeating the name. Ritual re-enacts past events which are crucial to the Faith and with care and attention can foster the inner spirituality of the worshipper. Christians, for example, remember Christ in the celebration of the

Eucharist and imaginatively enter into the experience of the disciples on the night when the sacrament was instituted.

Icons and images have been a source of controversy and conflict in some religions, but there are also aids to worship called prayer beads. The Buddhist uses one hundred and eight in two parts, each part representing the fifty-four stages of becoming a *Bodhisattva* (one who has attained enlightenment); Muslims have ninety-nine, one for each of the names of God; Roman Catholics have about 160 plus a crucifix, usually termed a rosary.

Most religions have sacred places and spaces in their places of worship, but the presence of God is everywhere and in their way of life they do not separate the sacred and secular which challenges Durkheim's definition. Islam is inclined to focus more sharply on its sacred places than Hinduism, which believes that God permeates all places. In pilgrimage to the sacred shrines the faithful are identifying themselves with the total Faith past, present and future, e.g. hajj in Islam. The observation of what people do in these rituals and the architectural design of the buildings is a way of entering into the doctrinal and mystical dimensions of the Faith. What is common in worship is the acknowledgement of some reality or dimension that is beyond this world and yet can be experienced.

Hence it would appear that any definition of religion must take into account the ritual dimension and what is being worshipped. What we have also noted is that scriptures play a role in the rituals and in the next chapter we consider what they are and how they are to be regarded today.

4   Scriptures

The rituals are based on custom, tradition and scripture teaching. All religions have a special book or books which contain the revelation of God or teaching about Him and in worship the book is prominent. The Jews and Christians read from it while the Muslims recite, the Buddhists chant and the Sikhs consult. It is generally believed that the books contain history, myths, stories and legends. Some of the events described can be verified historically but there are various meanings attached to them. For example, that Christ died on the cross, though denied by the Muslims, can be verified historically, but the theological meaning held by Christians cannot. Scholars often use the word 'myth' when dealing with scriptures, not meaning to imply a judgement of value as to what is true or false but a narrative about the meaning and purpose of life and the world. Perhaps 'story' would be a better word to use with interpretation clarifying the meaning.[1]

We look first at the Jewish experience. It is said that the Hebrews were nomads and that the name Jew originates with Judah, one of the sons of Jacob. Israel was the name given to Jacob after he had wrestled, according to the story, with God (Gen. 32:28). Though the name persists it was originally given to the northern kingdom which vanished into Assyria in the eighth century BCE. Abraham, one of the patriarchs, is regarded as the father of the faith and he is also claimed by Islam. The scripture records the Hebrews in Egypt in the second millennium BCE, their escape from slavery, the revelation to Moses in the desert, and the settlement in Canaan. The land is now known as Israel or Palestine.[2]

The record indicates that the Jews are an elect people with whom God has made covenants: Abraham, Isaac and Jacob, and then with all the people at Mount Sinai (Exod. 6:2–8). The covenant (*berit*) is a unique conception and, like the Exodus, of major importance. By agreeing to the Sinai covenant they had a responsibility to live holy lives and were a 'treasured possession', but would be punished if they failed to keep to it. In their scripture there is a developing idea of God from the particular to the universal, for He becomes not only their God but that of all nations (Amos 9:7), and they must be witness to his justice, love and mercy. He is not confined to Sinai or the Ark of the covenant or Temple but is everywhere. But He can be concentrated in one place to meet the needs of the people. After the Fall of the Temple in 70 CE the priest disappeared and the rabbi or master who was learned in Jewish law offered counsel and guidance.

The orthodox Jews believed that God gave Moses both a written Torah (first five books of the Bible) and an oral Torah (interpretation) at Mount Sinai (Exod. 19). They hold, like Islam, that the scripture is verbally inspired. While the oral Torah was given to Moses it was only gradually made public in the light of changing conditions, which opens up the possibility for the Rabbis to modify and accommodate the scripture to modernity. Literal interpretation of an 'an eye for an eye' and 'a tooth for a tooth' can be modified to the payment of compensation. A hierarchy can be detected in observance of the commandments so that keeping the Sabbath may give way to saving a life. *Mitzvah* (commandment) can also mean duty or obligation and may be considered equivalent to dharma in Hinduism. Also the Rabbi can depart from the literal and discern levels of meaning which are metaphorical and allegorical.

The codification of the oral law was completed in the second century CE and is known as the Mishnah. From it arose the Talmud which classifies the material into *halakhah* and *aggadah*. The distinction is significant for the *halakhah* refers to the keeping of external practices but the *aggadah* means the inner condition of the heart. It is not only what you do but how you do it. Mechanical obedience without good intentions is not acceptable to God, nor is the practice of ritual without mercy and compassion in daily life. Hence true religion is connected with the inner person as the prophets were to preach. The Talmud is the major source of Jewish law and exists in two recensions, the Palestinian and the Babylonian, and is the lens through which the Torah is viewed.

The Torah must be taught to the children so that their 'eyes will shine with it' and it will be a privilege for them, when older, to study it. The orthodox Jew pays the same deference to the Torah, which can also have the general sense of teaching as Islam does to the Qur'an. The Torah is the word of God, a kind of mystic tool by which He made the world. It has a parallel with the word or logos in Christianity (John 1:2). To obey the Torah is a sacramental activity. The reform group, however, while regarding it as a holy or priestly law, do not obey it blindly, place stress on conscience, and have modified many of the commandments which flow from the oral law. It is estimated that at one time there were 613 commandments, but the orthodox assert that now there are only 100.

During the nineteenth century both Jewish and Christian scriptures were subjected to historical criticism and treated like any other book. A number of authors were detected not only in the Pentateuch (first five books) but in other parts of the Hebrew Bible, which showed changes in the name of God, simplistic views of man, and primitive ideas about the cosmos. In particular, the Genesis account of the creation of the world was in conflict with science. The orthodox refuse to accept such criticism but the progressives do and the conservatives try to mediate between them saying that divine authority rests on tradition. It is loyalty to it which is important, not the origins of scripture. But the answer is unsatisfactory since tradition as well as scripture can be questioned. Allegorical interpretation of scripture has proved helpful and the rabbis over the years have reached a high level in it and benefited from their contact with Greek thought. But some Jewish philosophers took it too far, resulting in a view of God removed from human affairs.

Christians recognized the Jewish scriptures, incorporating them in their Bible. In many churches at the start of worship the Bible is carried in and placed reverently on the reading desk or on the communion table. Historical and literary criticism of the New Testament cast doubt on the authorship, content and dates of the various Gospels and Epistles. One of the problems is that there is a difference between the Synoptic Gospels (Mark, Matthew, Luke) and the Fourth Gospel (John) with the latter from the start declaring that Jesus is in a very special relation with God, and dates and events do not synchronize. But if they were all alike it could mean that they had copied and perhaps 'dissimilarity indicates authenticity'. It is usually thought that Matthew's gospel reflects a Jew writing for Jews while Luke is more interested in the Gentiles and so they differ in events and details. The Fourth Gospel is much more theological than the others, ascribing a very high status to Jesus but, it is argued, even in the synoptics his words and actions produce awe and astonishment. High titles are ascribed to him, such as Son of God, which shows a close affinity with God: he called God Father (Abba) instead of the more formal address of 'Our Father, Our King'. From these and other titles scholars go on to assert that Jesus claimed a unique filial relationship with God as is shown, for example, in the parable of wicked tenants (Mark 12:1–9).

Some Christians insist on the inerrancy of scripture but others say that it witnesses to Jesus Christ and should be interpreted in a mythical or poetical way. While this is correct for the interpretation of many passages it runs into difficulty when applied to events like the resurrection of Christ which the scripture itself regards as a unique event. The New Testament narratives centre around the person of Jesus and much space is devoted to his passion. It is asserted that he was recognized by many as the promised Messiah with his miracles being signs of the inauguration of his kingdom. Such a spiritual kingdom involved suffering and he saw himself as the suffering servant of Isaiah. He spoke with authority, interpreted his death as removing the barrier of sin which existed between God and humanity, and taught that he would return eventually to bring about the ultimate defeat of evil. If this is correct there is no real contradiction between the preaching of the Early Church and what is taught in the Gospels.[3]

But there are three new features in the apostolic preaching: they are dependent upon Jesus as exalted Lord, the Spirit has been poured forth, and there is the hope of an immediate return of their Master. Perhaps the apostles read too much into what Jesus said about it for he did not specify any date; they may have been influenced by apocalyptic literature and Old Testament prophecy, and longed for a quick vindication of their faith.

There has been much debate about what the title Son of God means. It cannot be understood in the physical way because God is a Spirit. Some see it as a perfect relationship with God which demonstrates the love of God and is the medium of atonement for sin. Others go further and think of God becoming man in Jesus Christ, having both a divine and a human mind, though the latter does not have complete access to the former. But the divine mind has full access to the human so that both are united in the one person as the Council of Chalcedon (451 CE) stated. A third view stresses the human nature of Christ but the divine means that he was uniquely filled with the Spirit of God.[4] It is not unlike the view that the Buddha had the spiritual force of the dhamma. What is essential in Christology is to preserve the humanity, for he 'was bone of our bone and flesh of our flesh', but how the divine functions in such a person has never been fully resolved.[4]

Muhammad was born in Mecca about the year 570 CE and may have been influenced by Judaism and Christianity. Mecca was ready for a more stable pattern of society than tribalism and many gods. The Qur'an is the speech of God and therefore it has a place equivalent to that of Christ in Christianity. It compares with the position of the Adi Granth in Sikhism. But it is also admired as a great prophetic and literary book. There are 114 chapters or *surahs* and tradition holds that it was revealed to Muhammad by Allah. It deals with wisdom, doctrine, knowledge, worship, history and law, but its main theme is the relation between God and His creation. The Muslims believe that it provides a basis for a just society and for a system of economic relationships which avoids both capitalism and socialism.

Most translations of the book do not convey the beauty of the Arabic original, and since it contains the words of Allah given to Muhammad, it is verbally inspired. It is pre-existent in heaven (*surah* 85:22) and sent down (*tanzil*) to the Prophet who passively received it. In 656 CE a definitive canon of these revelations was announced. In addition there is Hadith, containing information about the Prophet which helps us to understand what he said and how he acted. But the Qur'an itself mentions metaphorical verses and points to allegorical interpretation, i.e. 'the face of God', which cannot be taken literally.[5] It accuses the Jews of corrupting the scripture and the Christians of worshipping Christ as the son of God. In so doing they have gone astray and must be brought back to the religion of Abraham which was obedience to the will of Allah.[6]

The question arises: Is the Qur'an created or uncreated? Muhammad was in a trance-like state when he received the revelations and differs from the Hadith which contains his normal speech. The official text was adopted under 'Uthman (644–66). The traditionalists argued that if created, the book would be devalued as God's speech but the rationalists, the Mu'tazila, denied this saying it was created. The dispute has never really been resolved despite attempts at compromise.

The Hindus have many scriptures and the dating of them is approximate. There is the Rig Veda (1500–1000 BCE) which is a collection of ten books consisting mainly of hymns; the Brahmanas (800 BCE), instructions about sacrifices and rituals intended for the priests or Brahmins; the Upanishads (800–400 BCE), which teach that there is one supreme God called Brahman; the Laws of Manu (250 BCE) concerned with ethical behaviour; and the *Bhagavad gita* (fourth or third century BCE), which shows what kind of religion Hinduism is and what true worship involves. This latter scripture ('The Song of the Lord') is probably the best loved of all and forms part of the great Mahabharata (200 BCE) epic. But it is not regarded as revelation.

The Vedas are revelation received by Hindu seers and are sacred books (*shruti* – 'that which was heard'). The Upanishads, third part of the Vedas, probably composed between 800 and 400 BCE, reflect philosophical speculation and are regarded as higher knowledge of Brahman. The way to obtain it is through yoga. But there are schools of philosophy which do not accept the Vedas as revelation (Nastika). The laws of Manu (progenitor of humanity) are 'that which is remembered' (*smriti*) and essential for understanding the duties attached to caste and the stages of life. They are based on tradition. They are found in the *Sutras* which also contain texts about dharma, yoga and Vedanta. All of these texts come from the upper class and some think that they do not reflect the practices of the masses. The epics which include the *Ramayana* (200 BCE) have had a much greater popular appeal and have been filmed for television. There are also the Tantras (eighth to ninth century) which feature the goddess Shiva and encourage practices opposed to the teaching of the Brahmins. Such Tantras also emerged in Buddhism, texts said to be revealed to the Buddha and thought by Tibetan Buddhists to have magical power. The *Paranas* are mythological texts (300 to 900 CE) and tell the stories of gods and goddesses.

Hinduism has no founder or canon of scriptures and the sacred writings are of limited importance in understanding what people believe, so the sociologist and anthropologist are involved in understanding customs, practices and beliefs. But scriptures are important for the scholars and it is recognized that the Upanishads supply a more formal doctrine than the Gita which is used for devotional purposes. Hinduism does not have the same problems about history as the Semitic religions and weaves together fact and fiction without much distinction.[7]

Siddhartha Gautama, the Buddha, was born between 500 and 485 BCE and experienced enlightenment through meditation after he had given up wealth and family and wandered in the company of Hindu monks for many years through India. He had been jolted out of a complacent lifestyle by the sight of suffering and death and felt that he must find an answer to the impermanence of life and the problem of how one could escape from rebirth (karma). Unlike the materialists he accepted the idea of rebirth and karma and became convinced that happiness comes through the effort of controlling the mind. His experience of enlightenment was both intellectual and mystic, and the way to obtain it was followed by a group of monks called the sangha, or order. The sangha have a code of rules called the Vinaya which according to tradition were handed down from the Buddha. The sangha were responsible for the writing of the scriptures in the everyday language some four hundred years after his death.

The first basket, the Vinaya Pitaka, contains narratives concerning the establishment of the sangha and instructions about the monastic life. The second is the Sutta Pitaka, containing the five collections of the Buddha's teachings (dhamma) and to a lesser extent that of some of his disciples. The third is the Abhidhamma Pitaka which analyses and classifies the doctrine and is abstract and impersonal. The intention was to reveal the right way for all aspects of life, providing a model or an ideal, and leading to nirvana. It became the Pali canon of scripture for the early Theravada Buddhists and these texts were written in about 80 BCE. Divisions soon developed between the two forms of Buddhism, Theravada and Mahayana, over what texts were authoritative. The latter rely more on sutras, short sentences which reflect the tradition of what the Buddha said. Thus from 100 BCE onwards literature was written by monks on the basis of communication from heavenly Buddhas and these new sutras were mystical, poetical and rich in imagery, e.g. the Lotus Sutra. There are the *Saddharma-pundarika* (White Lotus of the True dharma), the *Vimalakirti-nirdesa* (Exposition of Vimalakirti) and *Prajnaparamita* (Perfection of Wisdom). They became the basis of disputes and divisions. It was held by some that the Bodhisattva, one who has attained enlightenment but renounces entry into the full nirvana in order to help others, actually eclipses the earthly Buddha.[8]

In addition there were treatises (*shastras*) written to interpret the texts and tantras. Some see their language as sexual but others dispute this. The sutras are used as guides to meditation and are integral to religious practice. The writing of the texts helped the development of Mahayana for it enabled them to introduce new material. Sutras were written based on the belief that the Buddha can have access to human beings other than by human contact. In Japan a school of Buddhism, headed by Nichiren, ranked texts in a hierarchy and showed a particular devotion to the Lotus Sutra. This followed the Mahayana who taught that certain texts were more important than others, but Nichiren went to the extreme of contending that the Lotus Sutra was the final revelation of the Buddha. A mantra was chanted in order to invoke the power of the scripture and gain enlightenment. Nichiren was sure that he was right and dismissed other Buddhist practices to such an extent that he had to spend much of his life in exile.[9]

Guru Nanak (1469–1539 CE) was influenced by a leading

exponent of bhakti, Kabir (1440–1518 CE), and some of his hymns are included in the Adi Granth, the holy book of the Sikhs. Nanak was born at Talwandi, near Lahore, and became a government official but was distressed by the suffering endured by the people of Punjab under Muslim rule. His life story is told in the *janam sakhi* or stories, which recount that he questioned Hindus and Muslims from an early age and had a spiritual experience at the age of thirty. Afterwards he travelled widely and made disciples (*sikhs*) who were impressed with his teaching and miracles. He died at Kartarpur in 1539, but before his death chose one of his disciples as successor: Angad (1504–1552 CE). In so doing he showed preference for spiritual leadership rather than hereditary claims.

Despite Nanak's insistence that scriptures should be regarded as part of the paraphernalia of religion, his words were to become holy writ for the Sikhs. The scripture assumes the place of a living Guru occupying a central place in worship. One of the Gurus, Arjan (1581–1606 CE), made a compilation of the founder's hymns and other material from Hindu and Muslim writings and produced the Sikh scripture. It is the Word of God; hence its prime place in the faith. Since Indian and Muslim writings are included it not only commends Sikhism to both religions but also shows that the message of the faith is universal. It also assumes importance because of its use in the naming of children, at marriage, the initiation to the Khalsa brotherhood and the comfort and guidance it gives to the members.

The Sikhs believe that it is necessary to cleanse themselves with water before handling such an important book. They have been accused of being book worshippers, since this living Guru is put to bed in the evening and in the morning throned on a dais above the congregation. When it is opened the first paragraph gives guidance to the faithful. The treatment is similar to the Hindus installing images in the temples. Is it not idolatry to venerate a material object like the Adi Granth? The Sikhs reply to this criticism by saying that in every religion a material object can symbolize a spiritual power, e.g. bread and wine in Christianity.[10]

The *janam sakhis* are a collection of narratives about the life of Nanak and according to historians consist of historical events and legends reflecting a later period. Nanak believed in salvation by the grace of God, but some of the stories in this literature teach that it is the result of human merit. There is also a claim to his performing miracles, but Nanak did not accept them. The Sikhs do seem to recognize these problems, hence the *janam sakhis*, or the Dasam Granth, which has the hymns of Guru Gobind Singh, do not have the same authority as the A*di Granth* (first book) which contains the teaching of Nanak. It is written in Punjabi, has 1430 pages and contains 5894 hymns. Some Sikhs do not accept its authority as a guru, and dissension and division occurred after the death of guru, Gobind Singh.

In conclusion, it would appear that scriptures play a more prominent part in some religions than others, but what is their influence today? A lot will depend on the literacy of the population and in the case of Hindu villagers custom and tradition probably have a more determining effect. They are dependent on the priest to interpret the scriptures for them, but even in religions such as Christianity the view of the expert is required. The Catholic Church, for example, reacted against the Protestant view of laypersons reading the Bible for themselves since the interpretations would be so varied that a crop of denominations would result.

The historian has problems with trying to find not only the original texts which usually have perished but also the time gap between when they were written and today. With changing circumstances and a more scientific and technological view of the world and human nature, what can these ancient scriptures say to us? Modern historians seek a sympathetic rapport with the past, but they are aware of cultural difference, change and development. What has been called the hermeneutical problem is posed by the 'gap', the need to fuse 'two horizons'. In brief, there is a great difference between the ancient and modern way of thinking.

The point about the scientific view will be taken up in later chapters, but there is a danger in making the present the critique of the past. It is also possible to argue that if the records have any validity then they appear to know more about God than we do. It is common nowadays to say that everything is relative but those who write authoritative books on this basis seem to forget that what they write is also relative! If the founders of religions were really in touch with the divine, then what they say can hardly have the same degree of relativity as our thinking about Him. Some will counter this argument by saying that we do not know what they really thought or said since the sources were written by believers. But the argument depends on a radical approach to the scriptures and we will seek to steer a middle course between it and the verbal inspiration position. The historian will take into account records written from within the faith, but also keep in mind that it is difficult to find objective sources for any event.

The criticism also judges one culture by another, but how can we do it in an age of relativity? The student of religion cannot approach Indian religions with the view that her culture is better than theirs. How then can we say that our culture is better than the ancient one? What criterion do we use? We can use a scientific criterion, but what about a moral one? Before the awful destruction of two world wars and man's inhumanity to man it might have been argued that we were better morally than the first century, but what do we think about it now? There will be various answers to the question but perhaps the best way forward is to try to maintain a balance between past and present and recognize both continuity and discontinuity.

In connection with our concern about what religion is, we recall that it is not only the following of rules or commandments but the inner condition of the heart that matters. The prophets of Israel were conscious that the people had not kept the commandments and had drawn near to God with their lips while their hearts were far from Him, so they insisted that God would make a new covenant with them: the Torah would be written inwardly not externally (Isa. 29:13; Jer. 31:31ff). True religion requires not only right action but purity of motive and intention.

We also noted that mitzvah in Judaism could mean the same as dharma in Hinduism when thought of as duty or obligation, hence it is the moral quality of the law which will be attended to in the next chapter. Most people think that good morality should be the result of religious teaching and some even define religion as ethics or a certain way of life. It is a test of religion, but can it be confined only to this dimension?

5 Behaviour

In modern societies there is a lack of objectivity in morals due to the belief that morality is relative and varies from one place to another. There is not the traditional framework of values supplied by religions but a stress on individual autonomy. In a context of a wide range of conflicting opinions there is a need for moral maturity on the part of the individual in order to avoid anarchy. Thinking on morality has been influenced by philosophers: the rationalism of Descartes, the empiricism of Hume, the utilitarianism of Bentham and Mill, the principles of Kant and the personal choice of the existentialist as seen in Sartre.[1]

But most religions have a moral framework that flows from scripture and tradition. Morality can be observed and people often test a religion by how its members behave. In the Hebrew Bible religion pervades all things so that the people are called upon to be holy as God is (Lev. 19:2) and show love to Him and one's neighbour. The religious law called *Halakhah* prescribes in detail how people should behave: caring and love for parents, hospitality and charity to strangers, visiting the sick, attending the dead to the grave, making peace between one another and studying the Torah. In the orthodox form much attention is paid to dietary laws (*kosher*): an animal must be slaughtered in the proper manner; pork is forbidden and only fish which has both scales and fins is acceptable. Milk products should not be eaten after meat.[2]

Morality is good behaviour in Judaism but belief is important. It is argued that natural law corresponds with the Torah, but the groups will differ about this. Progressive groups of

Jews hold that the Torah has a human input and has been edited by scholars over the years. They also consult rabbinic commentaries and philosophers when making decisions. Overall there is a basic principle: life is given by God and is sacred, so questions asked about any action are: Does it benefit humanity? Does it preserve life? But it can happen that there is a tension between conscience and law with some saying that the former cannot overrule the latter.[3]

Halakhah and civil law are not always in agreement. Zionists in Israel object to being subject to a religious law which is adjudicated by the rabbinical courts and applicable to most aspects of life. An example is divorce. Traditionally, the husband initiated it for such trival reasons as spoiling his food or finding a better-looking woman, but such reasons are ludicrous today. There is also inequality; a woman has to get her husband's permission for a divorce. He often will not allow it or will demand a large sum of money which she cannot pay. The civil law may grant the divorce but religious law will not and insists that if she marries again it is adultery and any children will be illegitimate. The basic principle operating in orthodoxy is that there can be no divorce without mutual consent. Many women want to remain in orthodoxy and be allowed to continue to attend the synagogue, but have mounted public protests demanding change in the religious laws. Sometimes the rabbis and the synagogue have helped them by withdrawing the synagogue privileges of the husband. With regard to converts, the orthodox are cautious and do not recognize those who have been admitted to other groups because they have not been circumcised and immersed in a ritual bath. They insist that a Jew is one born of a Jewish mother and are concerned about members who marry a non-Jew because they fear a diminishing of their nation.[4]

Good behaviour is more important than ritual and the latter must not be a substitute for the former: cease to do evil and learn to do good is commanded (Isa. 1:1–20; Psalm 15). Suicide is expressly forbidden, monasticism is frowned upon, and Jews must serve their community. It is recognized that everyone has the inclination to do good, *yetzer tov*, and the inclination to do evil, *yetzer hara*. Jews refuse to accept original sin, the causal connection between the sin of Adam and the subsequent sin of humanity (Ps. 51:5; Rom. 5:12), but see the disobedience of Adam as a prototype, not a burden of guilt transferred to his descendants. Everyman is 'the Adam of his own soul'. When one of the rabbis was asked to summarize the Torah he said: 'That which is hurtful to you do not do to your neighbour, everything else is commentary.' Hillel balanced this with: 'If I am only for myself what good am I but if I am not for myself who will be for me?'[5] Turning the other cheek is not acceptable for it is agreeing to an injustice, but an exception is the prevention of an innocent third party being injured.

The law forbids Jews to wear clothes of the opposite sex but women's slacks with the zipper on the side are permitted. The orthodox have detailed rules about not working on the Sabbath, so that they do not switch on an electric light but rely on someone to do it for them or set a timer. Jews are kind to animals, so hunting is a cruel sport but it is permissible to kill animals for food or for research that will aid humanity. Confining animals is not acceptable.

Good company and willpower are defences against sin. Jewish mystics did believe in reincarnation but there is little evidence of the belief today. faith-healing is still practised among the Hasidic and other orthodox Jews, but transplants are accepted to save lives and even a pig's heart can be used, though food from the pig cannot be eaten. Euthanasia is allowed when the illness is terminal and pain-killing drugs can be given to relieve suffering resulting in an earlier death, but it is not the intention. Life support should be cut off if there is no further hope.

When a woman suffers too much in childbirth contraceptives are permitted. Abortion is permitted to save the life of the mother or if the birth might lead to her insanity or a deformed child, or was the result of rape. Traditionally, the foetus had no status until birth: babies of thirty days who died were not given a funeral. Abortion is not murder but is very serious, so economic circumstances or the desire not to have children are ruled out. Artificial insemination is permitted if the donor is the husband, but if the semen comes from a stranger it is adultery. Homosexuality is not permitted in orthodoxy since the scripture teaches that Sodom was destroyed because of it. But reform and progressive Jews accept homosexuals despite the fact that the Talmud does not even allow two males to be alone together. Nudism is opposed for the wearing of clothes distinguishes us from the animals. Polygamy is sanctioned by scripture but not practised today and pornography is not permitted.[6]

With respect to capital punishment Israel has carried out executions, especially of Nazis who had committed war crimes. War should be for self-defence and scripture states that enemies must be warned before engaging in battle (Deut. 20:9–12), but Israel has engaged in pre-emptive strikes against the Arabs and achieved such success in the Six-Day War of 1967 and the Yom Kippur War of 1973 that many have seen the hand of God in it. Israel occupied Jerusalem, the West Bank, Judaea and Samaria. Zionism was delighted with these successes but the ultra-orthodox (*haredim*) were not pleased since they believe that the coming of the Messiah should set up the state of Israel. Only protracted negotiations resulted in the return of land to the Palestinians and currently there is little sign of tensions being resolved. The difficulty of judging when a defensive war becomes a war of aggression is posed and some Jews question if it is morally right to wage wars of conquest to strengthen their defence. Some say nuclear arms are a good deterrent but others contend that no weapon has been invented which has not been used.

Christianity accepts the Jewish Ten Commandments and adds the Sermon on the Mount and the teaching of St Paul the Apostle. But Christians must go beyond the law (*nomos*) in their concern for others. They are called upon to receive the Spirit of God from which flows the ethical virtues of love (*agape*), joy, peace, long-suffering and self-control. In the history of the Church moral decisions were based on scripture, natural law, tradition, reason and conscience. Today in various groups there can be a conflict regarding these guides and their relation to the values of society. How, for example, does the apostle Paul's instructions to masters, servants, husbands and wives and advocation of celibacy fit into a modern scene? Commentators find a solution by insisting that he was giving the instructions because he considered that the end of the world was at hand. But they were related to the world of his day as seen by the fact that he does not condemn slavery but insists that slaves obey their masters. To what extent then are the other moral teachings related to his time and not ours? Debate still continues about the issue.

The monastic life soon appeared in the Church resulting in communities of monks and nuns. The principle of the sanctity of life is held by all the Churches, hence suicide was outlawed, but gradually Christians moved to seeing some suicides as not blameworthy because they were due to torture, rape or mental derangement. A distinction was made between taking life and giving it, so that when persons were involved in a suicidal act which benefited others they were not condemned. But active euthanasia as the intentional termination of life is not permitted since it could lead to the slippery slope of removing those who had become a burden on society. The Catholic Church modifies this by the doctrine of double-effect which means that death is the side-effect of an action intended to relieve pain. The easing of suffering outweighs the possibility that death may eventually ensue as drugs increase.

Abortion continues to cause debate especially in the Catholic Church which only permits abortion when the life of the mother is threatened. Anglicans accept it for a variety of reasons: if there is a risk of a deformed child or it is the result of rape and if the social conditions would prevent the parents from rearing it properly. But in America church members have joined groups incensed with abortion on demand and lobbied politicians, held protest meetings, and even threatened the lives of doctors at clinics. Capital punishment continues in some American states despite the opposition of many churches. Yet it is in the Jewish scriptures, which are part of the Christian Bible, and the apostle Paul insisted that the state has the power to take 'retribution on the offender' but without saying what punishment there should be for murder (Rom. 13:2–5). In the tradition of the Church there have always been those for and against capital punishment.

With respect to war, Christianity was pacifist but that did not mean passivity. Jesus in the Gospels is portrayed not as the victim of circumstances but as the one who deliberately chose to go to Jerusalem, the place of danger, and his activity in the Temple seems revolutionary. He resisted the ecclesiastical system of his day in word and deed but called for love and understanding of the enemy. While the faith remained a minority religion the issue of military service was not important, but after the conversion of Constantine, the Roman Emperor, Christianity became the religion of the State and there was the need to establish the Christian attitude to war. One way of resolving the dilemma was the concept of the Just War, put forward by Augustine (354–430 CE), to secure justice and peace. A list of criteria was drawn up for such a war including that it must be a last resort and the innocent should not suffer. Wars in the twentieth century conducted by Christian nations infringed most of the criteria, subsequently leading to a variety of Christian and Humanist peace movements. In the context of a possible nuclear war pacifism has come into its own, for who could win such a conflict?

Liberation theology opposed injustice and it emerged in Latin America and South Africa in the last century. The ethical question was: Can violence against dictators ever be justified? The answer was that violence could be used as a last resort to overcome tyranny. But what was the attitude of Jesus towards an unjust state? Attempts have been made by modern theologians to see him as a political activist, but it is more apparent that he was not violent and the cleansing of the Temple was an exception. He respected the rule of the state and Paul too called for obedience to the 'powers that be'. But Liberation theology backed various revolutions. Ironically, John Paul II, elected pope in 1978, challenged communism in the Polish state but urged no political action in Latin America. Certain churches actually sided with an oppressive state: the Dutch Reformed Church in South Africa supported apartheid and had to apologize when the regime collapsed. Liberation theologians charged the mainstream churches that unlike their founder, they had not identified themselves with the poor. A desperate situation required extreme measures. Religion is not a private affair. It cannot stand aside from unjust politics and decide whether the resistance is to be non-violent or violent. Religion involves a community which calls for justice, mercy and opportunity for all. We will refer again to Liberation theology in a later chapter.

Protestant theology has also been involved in politics in the

USA. The Moral Majority movement initiated civil disobedience in its opposition to abortion and even resorted to violence. Some of their leaders put themselves forward for President of the USA while others, named the Promise Keepers, earned the wrath of feminists and homosexuals. The New Christian Right is Republican and disliked the former president, Bill Clinton, a Democrat, for his liberal views and conduct.[7]

In Islam religious and social morality are interpreted by the various Law schools which can provide different judgements. Muslims have five pillars which govern their conduct. The first is the confession: 'There is no god but God, and Muhammad is his Messenger (the *shahadah*).' The second is prayer (*salat*), and the third fasting (*saum*), so that the Muslim may share the suffering of the less fortunate. The fourth pillar is charity or *zakat* and the last is pilgrimage (hajj) which entails going to the holy city of Mecca. There was also a sixth pillar (*jihad*) or holy war which the Qur'an imposes on Muslims to fight against polytheists (Q. 8:39) or Christians and Jews (Q. 9:29) but it is generally interpreted now in the spiritual sense: war against sin in oneself. Muslims are also forbidden to drink alcohol, eat pork or gamble, and basically subscribe to the Jewish Ten Commandments. Islam is a religion of submission and obedience and is often couched in legal terms and obligations. The Muslim must not kill and it is only justified if wrongful killing has taken place. The ideal is to follow the example of Muhammad.[8]

Just as the Torah is important for Judaism, the Shari'ah, which is the Canon Law of Islam, applies to all human activities. It is sacred and embraces the social, economic, civil and criminal, personal and communal. Using the Qur'an, Hadith, tradition, analogy, consensus of the community (*ijma*), and the interpretation of scholars (*ijtihad*), the Shari'ah developed to meet new situations. We shall be looking in detail later at the various groups within the religions but would note here that in Islam, the Sunni, who are the majority, make their decisions on the communal basis but the Shi'ah accept the ruling of their imam. The impact of modernity with its individuality has had an impact on the youth and some of them regard particular laws of the Shari'ah as valid only in their context and it may even apply to specific rulings in the Qur'an itself.

Militancy erupted in fundamentalist Islam with the killing of Anwar Sadat in 1981, and Hamas, the Arabic Islamic Resistance Movement, demanded a jihad against Israel. It opposed the Palestinian Liberation Organization led by Yasser Arafat because it was not strictly Muslim. In Afghanistan the success of the Afghan Muslim (Mujhadin) in 1992 created the fear that such militancy would spread to other countries and it was confirmed by the repression which followed under the Taliban. The militancy of Islam also has its roots in the protest against the Western system of taking interest on money loaned. Capitalism, it is asserted, means that the rich get richer and the poor poorer. The Shah of Iran, accused of destroying the Islamic state, was deposed in 1979 and was replaced by Khomeini, who bluntly embraced the jihad proclaiming that people could only be made obedient by the sword. But Iranians are Shi'ite, a minority, whereas the mainstream Sunni rejects such violence. They would not accept the elevation of an imam such as Khomeini and a state ruled by religious jurists.[9] Islam suffered in Turkey in the early twentieth century when their religious laws were set aside and the secular attained prominence. But it would seem that Muslims emerged stronger than ever from the conflict.[10]

With respect to everyday conduct the religion calls for hard work, the pursuit of knowledge, care of parents, and the avoiding of alcohol, eating pork or gambling. It places stress on intention contending that an action is good only when it has a pious intent (*niyyah*). The role of free will is a problem since there is a strong doctrine of predestination. There are severe penalties for murder, theft and adultery, but in the case of the latter there must be four witnesses and a confession. It is stressed that Allah is compassionate and forgiving, but the Qur'an has many warnings about the judgement of evildoers. In Islam suicide and euthanasia are forbidden (Q. 4:29).

In dealing with abortion it is believed that the foetus has the right to life from conception, but not if the mother's life is in danger. Abortion on demand is unacceptable but there may be cases where a mother cannot cope with a child. After 120 days abortion is murder and accidentally induced miscarriage is considered to be manslaughter. The foetus can inherit property. Premarital sex is forbidden and rape is murder, but contraception in marriage is permitted. There is the curious idea of the sleeping foetus (*ar-raqid*) which is a legal fiction (*hilah*), meaning that a pregnancy might be potentially dormant for years. It operates to shield a woman guilty of sexual sin. Today Muslims are generally opposed to such an excuse.[11]

When Muslims live in an Islamic state the law forbids the lending of money at interest. In the West, negotiations with established banking houses has resulted in the setting-up of special arrangements for Muslims to use these facilities without offending their laws, and when a mortgage is required then it is permissible to borrow money for the purchase of a home.

Understanding the ethics of Hinduism is more difficult than any other religion for a number of reasons. First, there is the great variety of belief and ritual and the different ways of liberation from evil propounded by the schools of philosophy and theology. Second, there is the class and caste system. From early times Indian society was divided into four classes: the *brahmin* who performed the religious ceremonies, the nobleman or *kshatriya* who was a warrior and statesman, the merchant or peasant or *vaisya*, and the *s'udra*, consisting of menials and labourers. Class forms the framework for caste and good conduct is related to both. The priest must maintain purity and his duty (*dharma*) is to study scripture and conduct the rituals. A person of lower class would be committing a sin if he tried to do it, but he could drink alcohol which would be a sin for the brahmin.

Modern Hinduism owes much to Mahatma Gandhi (1869–1948) who opposed the caste system and encouraged passive resistance and non-violence (*ahimmsa*) which he saw as *satyagraha* or holding to truth. From 1915 he organized mass civil disobedience rallies and fasted, but was unable to prevent the partition of his country. It was thought that he was supporting the Muslims and was shot by an extreme Hindu on 30 January 1948. Gandhi was very conscious of the plight of the untouchables (*harijans*) and protested about the inequality of women.

Dharma, which can mean law, duty, justice and virtuousness, comes closest to what religion means. Santana dharma is eternal law but *sadharana dharma* is general morality incumbent upon all Hindus. It aims at firmness, forgiveness, charity, purity, not stealing, sense control, prudence, wisdom, truthfulness and freedom from anger. dharma refers to behaviour (*praxis*), so it is conduct rather than creed which is stressed. Religion or dharma permeates all of life with no division between sacred and secular. Occupation plays a role in caste status, for if work is ritually unclean it has low status.

Money is important but it does not guarantee a high caste ranking, so brahmins can be poor and yet have a high status. Behaviour is related to the four stages of life: the student, householder, dweller in the forest, and the *sannyasin*, who is a hermit or member of a monastry. Legal texts were developed to define behaviour so that everyone would know what their dharma was, but in practice it applied only to the upper castes. The *Bhagavad gita* spells out the duty of the warrior Arjuna and the paths that lead to the disciplined life: knowledge (*jnana-yoga*), action (*karma yoga*), and devotion to Vishnu/Krishna. Liberation will be discussed later but it is by offering actions to God, not simply religious ritual, that one experiences His grace. The legal texts are called Manu, the progenitor of the human race or the primal man, and were completed in about the second century CE. They deal with marriage and the place of women who are called upon to be obedient to fathers and husbands.[12]

Hindus are not allowed to gamble, engage in illicit sex or get drunk. Many of them embrace *bhakt*, which is love or devotion to Vishnu whose major incarnation, Krishna, appears in the Gita. There is common ground between Hinduism and Roman Catholicism in that merit is rewarded by God. Hinduism teaches that a good life will follow if actions in a previous one have not been bad (karma). But a radical trend is Tantrism which relativizes the usually accepted values. It is claimed that 'what is injurious becomes spiritually useful and what is unethical becomes ethics'.[13] The trend originated in asceticism which rejected the normative Hindu dharma and went on to indulge in caste-free sexual intercourse. Substances such as meat, fish and alcohol were freely consumed and sex was seen as a way to unity with the goddess Shiva. Women are portrayed as channels of power and knowledge and engage in what orthodoxy would see as immoral practices. But it is said that such sexual licence is exceptional and depends on how radical the group is.

Euthanasia as a quiet waiting for death is favoured by many Hindus, but it does not meet the problems raised by medical technology which can keep a person who is terminal alive for years. Abortion was legalized in India in 1971 but many Hindus oppose it because of the sanctity of life and the function of marriage as childbearing. It is asserted that the killing of newborn girls has taken place. Gandhi opposed suicide since it was not an escape from life's problems: karmic forces continue into the next life. But some see *sati* or *suttee*, a wife burning herself at the death of her husband, as acceptable suicide. It would be a case of giving a life rather than taking it, but the practice was banned in the British states of India in 1829 CE.

For Gandhi celibacy would appear to be better than marriage because love can be extended to all instead of being confined to the marital state. He opposed untouchability as a cruel boycott of human beings. But despite his stress on nonviolence, he was assassinated in 1948 which sparked off a rise in nationalism, a stress on Hindu identity, and conflict with Islam. Right-wing movements like the Bharatiya Janata Party supported campaigns against the Muslims and disputed the building of mosques. The mosque at Babri was destroyed and thousands were injured in riots. In 1991 Prime Minister Rajiv Gandhi was assassinated, resentment against Muslims was high and the humanitarian work of Mother Teresa was criticized because it was a foreign input. The use of force is contrary to the tolerance of Hinduism and has induced fear in the hearts of Indian minorities.[14]

Buddhism has strict rules for the monks who are forbidden intoxicating liquors and not allowed food after noon. They must be temperate in eating, not engage in or witness singing, dancing or the acting of plays. Garlands, perfumes and ornaments are not to be used and they must not rest on high or luxurious beds or accept gifts of gold. The early Theravada Buddhists believed that the right action was to withdraw from the world, showing that desire for the objects of sense had ceased. In this form of Buddhism the monk is very important and the only hope for the laity was a better rebirth that would lead to becoming one. The Buddha taught the four noble truths: all life is suffering or unsatisfactory, it is due to desire and of ignorance of what really mattered, desire must be eliminated, and the way to do it is to follow an eightfold path.

A favourite symbol is the wheel of life with nirvana at its centre. Spokes in the wheel begin with right viewpoint and right intention. When objects are looked at in the light of the four noble truths they are seen as fleeting and impermanent, thus desire will not be aroused. The ego is illusory and must be replaced by love and kindness for others. Then there is right speech, not swearing, avoiding gossip, lying, slander and engaging in right action which abstains from stealing and wrong in general. Right living follows, not killing or harming other people by selling them drink or trafficking in women and slaves. Right effort is required. The last two spokes are right mindfulness and right concentration. These are the most difficult to master.

The sangha or group of monks has a code with upwards of 227 offences and confession must be made even in connection with diet. Some offences result in permanent exclusion: killing a person, sexual intercourse, theft, and falsely claiming higher knowledge. The Buddha showed the way to liberation (nirvana) but each person must find his or her own enlightenment. No matter how depressed one may be, suicide is not the way out of the problems, for the operation of the law of karma will mean a poorer existence in the next life. Only if the act has no intention of getting a new body can it be blameless. The Buddhists can point to monks like Channa and Vakkalie and Godhika who committed suicide and were not condemned, for they had no longing for a new life.[15]

In Mahayana Buddhism the lay person has the opportunity of seeking nirvana and help ethically is provided by the Bodhisattvas who delay their ultimate nirvana in order to help others. The tradition is more flexible regarding the keeping of precepts: not telling the truth is possible in a difficult situation (skilful means). Vajrayana Buddhism goes further and encourages practices that violate the usual precepts. Killing is possible to prevent someone committing actions that would send him or her to hell, stealing to stop another stealing, and so on.

Buddhism believes that all life is sacred but situations must be taken into account. Life-sustaining processes that merely prolong life are pointless, people should die naturally in a peaceful atmosphere. Living wills are good, indicating wishes in advance of death. Passive euthanasia or letting die is acceptable with the understanding that it is not a wish to end life but to prevent suffering. Buddhists oppose active euthanasia and would advocate the care of the hospice. Concerning abortion, the foetus will be reborn and take on a new existence. Those who feel remorse for having an abortion can seek forgiveness through various rituals and by helping others. Abortion is permitted if the life of the mother is in danger and in most Buddhist countries a woman in the early stages of pregnancy has the right to have an abortion. Buddhists accept contraception but under Chinese rule in Tibet they were forced to abort whether they wanted to or not.

Generally the Buddhist is tolerant, but there are militant groups and there has been conflict in Tibet with forceful resistance by monks against the Chinese. It is argued that it prevented greater suffering and was based on the principle of compassion. But leaders have not been unanimous about militancy, with the fourteenth Dalai Lama opposing it and the thirteenth contending that it must be in self-defence. In other parts of the world monks have immolated themselves and been involved in ethnic violence, e.g. Sri Lanka in the 1960s. The most religious group is the Janata Vimukti or the National Liberation Front, which mounted an insurrection in 1971 and was not put down until 1990. The opponent was the Tamil Tigers and Buddhists continue to refuse to make any concessions to them.

Sikhs would also oppose stealing, murder and adultery and only resort to force in the face of evil. Love, hard work, dietary restrictions, service and tithing characterize their lives and they regard marriage and the family life with respect. The five deadly sins are lust, anger, greed, worldly love and pride. Celibacy or the single life is not the norm for them. Brotherhood is stressed with the Khalsa but some Sikhs are not members of it. There is a strict prescription against drugs, alcohol, tobacco and gambling, reflecting the influence of Islam upon the faith. But the Muslim stress on pilgrimage is unacceptable as their founder, Guru Nanak, opposed it, yet as we noted, Sikhs do visit places associated with their founder and other Gurus and especially Amritsar where their Golden Temple stands. But pilgrimage as such is not of any great significance.

A Sikh must believe in one God and have faith in the teachings of the ten Gurus and not hold with idols, caste divisions and untouchability. The hair must not be cut and voluntary social service should be undertaken: helping in the *gurdwara*, cooking meals in the *langar*, cleaning footwear of members and assisting in schools, hospitals and orphanages. Adultery is forbidden. Sikhism, like Islam, does not have priests or any religious hierarchy. Any man or woman knowing the order of worship can read the scripture and conduct a religious ceremony. Beards must not be dyed or dowry accepted in marriage. The turban is worn to make sure that the hair is ritually clean at all times and it identifies the Sikh. Monasticism is not acceptable for this is a householder's religion. The Rahit Maryada is the authoritative manual of Sikh conduct and defines a Sikh as a person who believes in one God, the ten Gurus, the teachings of the Guru Granth Sahib, recognizes the initiation ceremony (*amrit*) of the tenth Guru and professes no other religion.

In the twentieth century there was conflict between Sikhs and Hindus. Sant Jarnail Singh Bhindranwale, who believed that many Sikhs were not living according to their traditions, occupied the Golden Temple in 1984, and the Indian army launched an assault on the sacred place. He and his followers and many worshippers were killed. In turn the Sikhs assassinated Prime Minister Indira Gandhi and violence continued with Sikh killing Sikh and Hindus taking revenge on them. The demands of the Sikhs are political, economic and religious. Most live in the Punjab which cuts them off from other Sikhs who dwell in Pakistan. Thus they are exposed to oppression from both Hindu and Muslim and feel insecure. They demand a homeland (Khalistan) and many are prepared for martyrdom in order to achieve it. But some see Khalistan as a state of harmonious relationships between people rather than a particular place or political homeland. In 1995 the Chief Minister of Punjab, Beant Singh, was killed by Sikhs because they believed he had betrayed them. The world Sikh Sammelan convened in 1995 and tried to achieve a consensus but it did not enter into debate about Khalistan and some of the militant parties stayed away. Doubts remain if the militant tendency will ever disappear, for the Jats, who are a large group, believe that war or the threat of it will attain their objectives.[16]

The Sikhs accept the 'just war' concept, tracing it back to Guru Gobind Singh who said: 'When all efforts to restore peace prove useless and no words avail, lawful is the flash of steel, it is right to draw the sword.'[17] But there should be no enmity or desire for revenge, land should not be taken or property captured. Soldiers must not drink or molest women and a minimum of force must be used. The death penalty can be imposed for grave offences. Marriage is a sacred not a civil contract, but divorce is allowed. There does not seem to be much opposition to contraception and abortion is permissible for the usual reasons but termination must be done in the early stages. There is a debate among commentators on Sikhism regarding the discovery of the gender of the foetus. Some point out that Sikhs follow Hindus who outlaw the practice of scans and amniocentesis, the pre-natal birth test. But others disagree, saying that the preference for boys has increased the use of ultrasound by Sikhs and Hindus and in consequence abortions have increased.

Suicide is not permissible since life is a gift from God and euthanasia should only be thought of when relatives realize that they can do no more for their loved one. Sikhs would not believe in keeping a person alive when there is no hope of any ultimate improvement.

In conclusion we recall that a common belief in these religions is that life is God-given and therefore sacred. Intention in the moral issues is important. Some show a more liberal attitude to them than others, but all oppose abortion on demand. Suicide as the giving of life rather than taking it appeals, but some exert heavier penalties for crimes than others, e.g. capital punishment. War in most religions begins with self-defence which easily slips into aggression. How these attitudes will be affected by the context of the 'global village' remains to be seen.

Morality exists in communities and while the individual has

rights and freedom, he or she must conform to what the group believes. But even in modern secular societies there are laws sometimes based on traditional religious ethics that limit what the individual can do. Within a religion, however, there are different views of what can and cannot be done. Some religions allow more latitude here than others: Tibetan Buddhism allows a morality which the mainstream Buddhism would not permit; for example, it is accepted that there is nothing immoral in a sexual relationship between a man and his stepmother.[18]

What can we learn from this ethical discussion regarding a definition of religion? There are two terms appearing in the religions. The first is dharma which in Hinduism has a variety of meanings, but taking it in the ethical sense it points to religion as concerned with conduct. The Buddha's teaching (dhamma) is also basically ethical and in Sikhism it stands for duty. Hence we might be tempted to equate religion with ethics and go on in a later chapter to see affinities with Humanism.

But there is more to religion in these faiths than ethics and we can understand this in the context of Islam, for *din* means religion in general and religious duties in particular: it incorporates the five basic obligations of the Muslim. *Din* has a correlative, namely *iman*, which means faith or the activity of belief. The first pillar is of major importance: faith in Allah or belief in a sacred and spiritual dimension. Hence any definition of religion according to Islam and other religions must pay attention to it, but how we are to understand the divine will concern us later.

It has been said that the test of a religion is how it behaves towards its women members, so we turn to this theme in the next chapter.

6 Women

We note at the start the interesting fact that in most religions the status of women was higher in early times than in the later development and that theory and practice often differ.[1] We begin as usual with Judaism.

In ancient Judaism women participated in synagogue life and held positions in them and were members of religious councils. But in general the birth of a boy was greeted with more joy than that of a girl. He was circumcised with a specific ritual but only a record kept of the birth of a girl. One of the reasons was, as in other religions, that the son was required to work for and look after his parents when they became old. Marriage and motherhood were the acceptable roles for women and this continues in the orthodox tradition. Public activity is restricted to fund-raising and catering in the synagogue in orthodoxy, but the progressives allow women to become rabbis and cantors.

Feminists argue that the covenant at Sinai was made with both sexes and women were honoured as matriarchs: Sarah, Rebecca, Leah and Rachel. Changes do seem to be happening in the ultra-orthodox since they have to work to support husbands who are committed to the study of the Torah and Talmud. By engaging in such study men can claim exemption from military service, but they are dependent upon the earning power of the wife. It gives the women much more experience of the wider world and a freedom which will affect their thinking about religion.[2] Feminists want more freedom and an equality of status with men so that across the board they might be recognized as leaders of the Jewish community. They also ask why God cannot be addressed as mother. Language in the Jewish Bible and liturgy enforce male superiority. Change is needed and the instituting of ceremonies recognizing the important cycle of events in a woman's life.[3] But orthodoxy points to the rabbinic literature where the male has economic and sexual rights within marriage and the status of women is respected as a mother. A Jew must have a Jewish mother regardless of the faith or ethnicity of the father.

While Judaism recognizes disobedience on the part of Adam and Eve, the latter is not the catalyst of the Fall of humanity into sin. She was simply curious about knowledge, a curiosity which may have caused rabbis to discourage the education of women. But progressives contend that it is wrong to teach that a woman is ritually impure so that she is not permitted to touch the sacred scrolls in worship. Feminists argue that a change in attitude is necessary towards the menstrual period since the Jewish laws applied to worship in the Temple. But orthodox women reply that these laws of *niddah* prevented a man demanding sex at this time so the women had control. Feminists ask whether women really want to leave the religious life to men while they do the cooking! And as we mentioned, divorce laws need changing for at present the wife cannot get a divorce unless the husband agrees and that at a price. More stress needs to be put on regulations in Jewish law which provide for a woman's conjugal rights.[4]

While feminism is strong in Judaism, orthodox women react against it. Many in Britain are quite happy with a life related to laws over 5000 years old which rule that they cannot display their hair, touch their husbands for two weeks during a month or wear certain clothes. One is reported as saying that she dressed modestly and wore light make-up except on the Sabbath. She did not show cleavage or wear short dresses or trousers and accepted that only her husband was allowed to see her hair fully. She wears a wig when at work and does not do chores on the Sabbath. If a button falls off her blouse she cannot sew it back on until after the day of rest. She believes that Sabbath rest is essential and provides an opportunity to teach biblical values to the children. Many orthodox women in Western society and elsewhere work in the professions and offices but the job comes second to being a wife and mother. It is more important, otherwise society can undermine the family. They argue for Jewish rather than state schools and for socializing within the community. Physical relations between the sexes before marriage are frowned on and dietary laws must be observed. These wives accept a subservient role, recognizing that the husband is head of the household.

Hopeful signs are seen in reconstructionist Judaism which had equality for women since its foundation in 1968 and has worship in non-sexist terms. There is equality in the reform group and changes in liturgy, so that the prayer 'God of our fathers, Abraham, Isaac and Jacob' becomes 'God of our ancestors . . .' now includes the women Sarah, Rebekah, Rachel and Leah. Inclusive language is in the new Prayer Book (1995) of the liberal and progressives but the conservative group's decision to ordain women rabbis (1983) caused a split in their ranks. Orthodoxy has segregated seating and there is no intention of ordaining women, although their education has improved.

A prominent factor in the distrust of women in Christianity is Eve's responsibility for the Fall of humanity. The second creation account in Genesis teaches that Adam was created first and woman for him and from him. But it is balanced by the first account (Gen. 1:27), which insists that both male and female are in the image of God. Paul in the New Testament subordinated women, but this may be explained by the cultural context and his expectation of the immediate return of Christ. Jesus kept company with the harlots and sinners and protected women caught in adultery (Jo. 8:1–11). The disciples were amazed that he talked to the woman of Samaria (Jo. 4) for she was not only a woman but a Samaritan. However, as in other religions his attitude failed to prevent a subordination in the development of the faith. Some feminists assert that it is Jesus who makes Christianity bearable for them.[5]

There were extraordinary women such as the fourteenth-century Julian of Norwich.[6] But Augustine (354–436 CE) thought that women did not properly reflect the image of God and his view set the pattern. Luther (1483–1546) had a better understanding but thought that women suffered because of Eve's involvement in the Fall and should be restricted to Kinder (children), Kuche (kitchen) and Kirche (church). He did react against the Catholic Church's insistence on celibacy and prizing virginity. In 1139 it became illegal for a priest to marry in the West but only the bishops were celibate in the East. The cult of the Virgin Mary was developed by the Catholics with the doctrine of the immaculate conception of Mary (without original sin) and the continuance of her virginity throughout life. When questions were raised about the scripture references to the brothers of Jesus, it was said that they were his cousins! The culmination of the high status of Mary was the doctrine of the Assumption in 1950. Mary is an ideal as the Queen of Heaven, who, unlike Eve, obeyed God. Though it is difficult for the ordinary woman to follow her example, the mother image of devotion and love is an inspiration and feminism has used the Mary model in contending for the struggle against poverty and injustice.[7]

Monasticism was open to women and provided more freedom for them, but the thought of ritual impurity in women may be one of the reasons why some churches refuse to ordain women. Others do, arguing that the Church must not be seen as the last bastion of male privilege. In 1997 the first woman priest was ordained in St Paul's Cathedral, London, following the ruling by the Church of England in 1992 that women could fulfil the role. But it meant that some priests left the church to join Catholicism, arguing that it was against tradition and could affect ecumenical dialogue. Some feminists have left the Church of England but others remain to reform. They recognize that one of the obstacles is that many women continue to support the male dominance. But another reason is that the opponents of women's ordination contend that scripture teaches the subordination of women to men (1 Cor. 11:2–16, 14:33–6; 1 Tim. 2:11–14; Eph. 5:22). But these passages have to be set beside the equality of all: 'For you all are the children of God through faith in Christ Jesus, for as many of you have been baptized have been clothed in Christ. There is neither Jew nor Greek, there is neither slave nor free, there is neither male nor female' (Gal. 3:28). Racial divisions and slavery have been abolished, why not discrimination against women?

Some question whether or not we have what Paul wrote originally in the subordination texts, but assuming that we have, there are other passages that show women participating equally with men in worship (Acts 1:14), and Paul's letters mention women who were essential to him in his ministry: Phoebe, Prisca, Apphia, Euodia and Syntyche, etc. They and others were 'leading women' (Acts 17:4). There may have been anti-women tendencies to exclude women's place in the church and in any case Paul is giving instructions to local communities. Can they be made into universal laws? If men are so essential to the ministry and women cannot be ordained, how is that no male was required, according to the New Testament, when Christ was brought into the world?[8] Women have become saints in the history of the church but are not fit to become priests! Reformed churches who ordain women cannot agree with arguments against the ministry of women since they hold to the priesthood of all believers.

It is interesting to see the attitude of feminists when they engage in dialogue with other faiths. We mention what is occurring in Jewish/Christian dialogue. Jewish feminists accuse Christian feminists of being anti-Jewish. They say it shows in the Christian feminist writing which blames Judaism for patriarchy and making Jesus the liberator of women in contrast to the Judaism of his day. But when the Mishnah (*c.* 200 CE), the authoritative collection of Jewish oral law which forms the basis of the Talmud, is compared with the writings of the Christian Fathers, the treatment of women is better in the Jewish writings. Central to the argument is the assertion that Jesus never condemned patriarchy. More radical Christian feminists go further, however, with regard to the status of Jesus. Rosemary Ruether thinks a male saviour encourages male dominance since it stresses male suffering, not female. But the argument is questionable: What about the suffering of Mary? She goes on to call for a New Testament to be written concerned with the oppressive experience of women.[9]

It is argued that Muhammad improved the status of women with basic rights in marriage and opposing female infanticide and giving rights of inheritance to widows and orphans. He insisted that birth control to prevent the birth of daughters should not be exercised, but in the case of divorce, seven-year-old boys are to go with their fathers. The husband must provide for the mother and children, and the men are limited to four wives. But women are inferior legally because their inheritance is only half the portion of their brothers and they can be physically chastised by their husbands as a last resort. The Qur'an states that with a disobedient wife, a husband must admonish, then ask her to leave his bed, and if this fails he may beat her. It is contended that it does not mean assault and battery but only used when other measures have failed. But there are stories about Muhammad which indicate that he never beat a woman, and when his wife Umm Salama complained that the scripture spoke only about men his response was gender-inclusive language: 'believing men and believing women, obedient men and obedient women, truthful men and truthful women.'[10]

But in some countries women have been denied their inheritance and the lower-class woman has difficulties even when the marriage is viewed as a contract. The dowry is provided by the husband and the marriage is usually arranged by parents, but it is the husband who can divorce easily. If she divorces him she loses the dowry, but he can do so by simply saying that he does not want her! He need only support her for a limited period and if she gets his permission for a divorce, compensation must be paid to him.[11] She cannot refuse sex during the course of the marriage. The Twelver Shi'ah have a temporary marriage contract which can easily be dissolved. She is not permitted to marry someone of a different faith. The Qur'an allows men to marry Jewish or Christian women (*surah* 5:5), but if equality was genuine a woman should be able to do so. A woman could remain faithful to Islam in such a union. Christians and Jews are people of the scriptures and not treated like pagans in the Qur'an, so should *surah* 2:221, which forbids women marrying non-Muslims, not be modified? In countries such as Turkey, the United Kingdom and the United States they are legally able to do so.

In Islam women have been leaders: Aisha was one of the Prophet's wives. She was famous for leading Muslim armies and has become a model for the feminists, but we cannot cite such women as typical of how Islam regards and treats women in general. While in theory they are equal to men, they are called upon to wear the veil. Some women see it as an imposition but others think it is a good thing since it prevents harassment by men. It would seem that more Muslim women are now not wearing it, but Western dress is frowned upon as too revealing and immodest.

Feminists argue that there is a contradiction between the social justice that Islam insists on and the subjugation of women. But women are not blamed for the original disobedience, their motherhood is greatly honoured, and all the law schools insist that women can perform religious rites. While this is true, women can only conduct worship for other women. But they can become authorities in the law and have a choice regarding marriage. Some of the law schools teach this but others state that she must have the consent of her father. Feminists protest about all these matters but some argue that subordination is due to the culture not Islam.[12]

In Hinduism there were pre-Aryan feminine deities and women were regarded as equal to men in early Vedic times. They were teachers and composers engaged in the rituals but this ceased in the Brahmanas because they were impure and must be trained for the home. In the Upanishads knowledge is the way to liberation with asceticism and celibacy praised, but learned women are mentioned and they took part in the debates. However, by the first century women were not allowed to study the Vedas, their education was limited to the needs of the home and there was no need for them to renounce the world in the final stage of life. But unmarried women were allowed to enter monasteries. Hindus speak of Mother India and Mother Ganges, the most sacred of all rivers. Worship is centred on this feminine dimension especially among the masses.

In the epics we have Sita, Draupadi and Savitri, who are dutiful wives and mother models but challenge the gender-based ideology. Tantrism argued that menstruation is not a pollution and the Kama Sutra praises the breakdown of sexual rules and the use of sex to achieve spiritual fulfilment. But the Manu-Smrti in the sixth century teaches that a woman's place is in the home and that she must be supervised by a man. In childhood she should be obedient to her father, in marriage to her husband and in widowhood to her son. She is responsible for training the daughters in household tasks and for the family worship. Child marriage was possible but today the civil law prohibits it and the legal age for marriage is eighteen for girls and twenty-one for boys.[13]

Changes have taken place in modern Hinduism stemming from the Arya Samaj and Brahmo Samaj movements. Since goddesses were always in the faith, God can be female as well as male. Self-denial and inner strength are major virtues in women and were demonstrated in their membership of Gandhi's independence movement. The existence of the mother goddess in Hinduism points to great respect and honour for the position of woman in the reproductive cycle, but in the Semitic religions the goddesses were repudiated as worship of nature and patriarchal religion dominated. Today, women in India have been granted equal rights with men, but this is evident in urban cities rather than in the villages.

The 1956 Marriage Act placed men and women on an equal legal basis, with civil marriage recognized and divorce allowed at the request of the wife. Dowries were outlawed but in practice they continue and can bankrupt a father. Hence a son is desired rather than a daughter for he is not an economic burden, continues the family line, and performs the last rites at the death of his parents. Modernity has not prevented female infanticide and aborting female foetuses. There have been outstanding women such as Ramakrishna Paramahamsa's wife, who had the role of the 'holy mother' in the founding of the Ramakrishna mission, and Gandhi's wife, Kasturba, was invaluable to him. Women have founded organizations, monasteries and temples in the West. The bhaki movement of the sixth and seventh century CE improved the status of women religiously but not socially. It opposed the Brahminic teaching and challenged caste hierarchy and ritual and taught that the worshipper of Krishna should be female so that the man had to psychologically identify with her to satisfy the god. Bhakti raises the question: If women are more loving and devoted than men, does it not make them spiritually superior to men?[14]

Some contend that feminine deities are important in Buddhism and think that the Buddha was subject to a female force: the mother of the Buddhas who is the source of all goodness. But there are a variety of views about women, some positive and some negative. The Buddha, it is said, had to be persuaded to allow them to become nuns and their order was controlled by men. Nuns (*bhikkhuni*) were ordained but were subject to eight rules which compelled them to bow even to the most

junior of monks. The Buddha thought that admitting women
to the order would mean that the faith would be short lived.
But he did think they were capable of enlightenment. Scholars
today challenge this interpretation of the Buddha's teaching by
saying that the texts were added later or they have been mis-
understood. However, it is still a fact that women do not have
the advantages of men in most of the parts of the Buddhist
world except Taiwan and Korea. In contrast to the ordination
of women in early times, there are now no Theravada nuns
anywhere in the world, but many continue to live according to
the precepts that are relevant to them and try to learn the
texts.[15]

Pollution of women plays little role in the religion, nor is
celibacy or virginity prized. World renunciation in Theravada
Buddhism is essential if nirvana is to be reached, so attachment
to the family must be set aside. Monasticism is central.
But Mahayana upgraded the householder, holding out new
hope for the laity to achieve nirvana. Mahayana recognized
women's potential for spiritual development, but there is little
evidence that their roles were enhanced. Female birth is unfortunate and the scripture, Lotus of the Good Law, teaches that
for a woman to be a bodhisattva she must psychologically
become a man! In Tibet the word for woman means low-born
and female birth is unfortunate.[16]

But Vajrayana (Tibetan Buddhism) advanced the idea that
sexuality governed not by lust but by the wish for spiritual
attainment was permissible. It is not what you do but how and
why you do it! The body is not degraded but a vehicle that can
be used on the way to enlightenment. Today there is the hope
of reintroducing the ordination of women in Theravada countries as is the custom in Mahayana and Vajrayana Buddhism.[17]

Women enjoy equality in Sikhism and participate in
worship, but again in the early beginnings of the faith they
appear to have had more freedom than today. Amar Das, the
third Guru, had the practice of *sati* (widow burning) banned
and encouraged widow remarriage at a time when widows had
no social status and were often outcasts. He appointed four
women *manjidars* responsible for preaching Sikhism and the
collection of tithes in the areas that they governed. Infanticide
was forbidden under Guru Gobind Singh, the tenth Guru.

Mata Gujri, the wife of the ninth Guru, Tegh Bahadur, assumed leadership of the Sikh community after her husband was murdered, and her daughter-in-law Mata Sundri succeeded her. But Islam, Hinduism and the British in India ignored the equal status accorded to women by Sikhism.

Amrit (initiation) was given to men and women and both have equal rights and responsibilities in the *langar* referred to as the Guru's kitchen. Celibacy is not prized, although some groups do exist, and there are no taboos regarding women's impurity. Marriage is encouraged and monogamy for Sikhism is a householder's religion with monasticism considered as an escape from one's duties in the world. A woman is considered good and is not required to wear a veil or have a dowry when getting married. All Sikhs are expected to marry and the mother is highly honoured.[18]

This is the theory, but is it actually seen in practice today? Rajinda Sanghera married Tarbinder Singh at the Guru Gobind Temple in Bradford and her father provided the dowry. But the marriage broke down after she had been ill-treated and she divorced him and was legally compensated. Apparently it was the hierarchical structure of the home with the mother-in-law at the top and the new wife at the bottom that was to blame. Rajinda said in these circumstances she had been treated like a skivvy.[19] Despite the Sikh belief in the spirituality of the women and that they are not inherently evil, it has few leadership roles for women except that they can say prayers, recite scripture and lead worship. The tradition also persists that it is better to have sons than daughters.

In conclusion we remember that even Gandhi saw celibacy as the best state and marriage to be better for women as they were spiritually inferior. But the mother role is prized in all religions as having such a formative influence on the children. The first women's movements were religious,[20] but perhaps some religious feminists go too far when they contend that it was the culture not the faith that suppressed women. The argument is difficult to sustain on the basis of scripture teaching and tradition which endorses the view of impurity both in childbirth and menstruation. However, in all religions there are signs of the rise of women to positions of influence and feminism is steadily growing. In any case, subordination does not mean inferiority: a concert pianist is subordinate to the conductor but it does not mean that he/she is inferior.

Women have been idealized in the religions but there is the male suspicion of their sexuality and fear that they might get out of control! Patriarchy has ruled despite feminine protest. In general, feminists in Judaism do not worry about the male concept of God to the extent of Christian feminists, but it is agreed by them and women of other religions that they need more dialogue together about this controversial issue.

In the next chapter we examine the spiritual liberation of both men and women which is a major theme in religions.

7 Liberation

Every religion recognizes that there is something wrong with human nature and offers salvation. In general in the Semitic religions, humanity needs to be delivered from disobedience to God but in the Indian it is usually ignorance which is the problem. How the liberation is envisaged differs, with some religions stressing that God delivers but others believing that mankind must help itself. The goal of liberation is for betterment of life here and an ultimate paradise or nirvana elsewhere. We consider in detail the problem and the remedy in the various religions.

The Jew believes that there is in humanity a good and an evil impulse. Mankind comes from the dust of the ground (Gen. 2) but there is a gulf between animals and humans. We are made in the image of God, have aspirations, conscience, and can communicate abstract ideas about the universe and ourselves. We have cared for nature and exploited it, leading to pollution and destruction. The possession of a divine spirit makes us like the Creator, and we imitate Him in doing things with a purpose. Mankind is unique in knowing good and evil, but ambition, arrogance, vanity, hatred, lust and greed have led to disaster. The Greeks called it hubris: the loss of the sense of human limitations.[1]

The Jews saw the way out of the condition is by obedience to the Torah. They were conscious that God had revealed Himself, made a covenant with them, delivered them from Egypt and led them into the promised land. They responded with partial obedience and the offering of sacrifices for sin. Jews believe in free will, hence the individual can choose to obey the Torah, but salvation generally refers to the nation. If it obeys God a contribution is made to the redemption of the world. They must aim at it now but they also look forward to the perfect state when the Kingdom of God is established by the Messiah. The orthodox believe in a national and universal liberation and when the new age comes it will mean the judgement of the evildoers in the resurrection of the dead and the enjoyment of a closer communion with God by the obedient. But there are other views among the divisions of the faith which we will consider in the next chapter. Everyone has a soul, but it is not the Greek idea which disparages the body. Soul and body are joined in a psychosomatic unity so there will be a resurrection of the body as in Christian belief. But again there are differences among the Jews, with the reform group deleting reference to the resurrection of the body in their prayer book and inserting 'life eternal'.[2]

Christianity also believes in obeying God but Christ as saviour is central and without faith in Him we cannot achieve it. There is the problem too of how much free will we have since the religion holds the doctrine of original sin (Ps. 51:5; Rom. 5:12). Opinions differ about the extent of corruption. The doctrine means that there is a causal connection between the sin of Adam and the sin of all, but some theologians have disputed the doctrine and believe that human beings are born good and corrupted by society. Christianity relies on the redemption achieved by Christ whereby humanity was reconciled to God, but there are various meanings of atonement: expiation, moral example, sacrifice and victory over evil.

Saint Anselm of Canterbury in the twelfth century thought that the death of Christ made amends for the offence of humanity's sin which had affronted God's majesty. In reaction, Abelard believed in the moral theory of the atonement: Christ by his death set an example of sacrificial love that all should follow. But all the theories insist that evil was so grievous that only God could redeem, hence He became incarnate in Jesus Christ. By His Spirit he lives in the heart of believers, enabling them to live a good life. Jesus preached the kingdom of God as both present and to come. At the end there will be a reward for the faithful but judgement and punishment for the evildoer.

It was the dispute about salvation that divided the Western church in the sixteenth century as we will see in the next chapter.

The Muslims, like the Jews, do not accept the doctrine of original sin but recognize that we are imperfect. When Adam and Eve confessed their sin, according to the Qur'an they were forgiven. Muslims are responsible for their actions but there is a strong doctrine of predestination. Attempts to reconcile the latter with free will have been made by the philosophers without much success. In order to be saved the Muslim must follow the Five Pillars and be obedient to the various laws. Submission to God is a major feature of the faith and the religion is a way of life, making little distinction between the sacred and secular. It is asserted that the faith did not begin with Muhammad but was in the world from the beginning and is the only religion which has preserved the scripture in pure form. Muslims refer to the promise in Deuteronomy of the prophet who would come and believe it was fulfilled by Muhammad. He was unlettered as we mentioned but God put His words into his mouth. The faith envisages a Paradise, judgement and hell. There is a messianic element in the Shi'ah group who look forward to the revealing of the 'hidden Imam', but the Sunni emphasize a day of judgement.[3]

The life of the Hindu villages is dominated by what the West regards as superstition: ghosts (*bhuts*), sorcery (*tuna*), and the evil eye (*nazar*). In order to cope with these they turn for help to the Brahmin or to an *ojha* (exorcist) or a non-Brahmin priest. Their gods or goddesses are more likely to be local heroes and worship can take place anywhere. They strive to survive, accumulate merit, follow their dharma, and end the cycle of rebirth. The lower classes are mainly occupied with surviving and hoping they will get a better rebirth in the next cycle, but the higher classes aim at bettering their dharma by acquiring spiritual merit and reaching forward to the transcendental salvation. Of course motives overlap and in worship, making a vow, going on a pilgrimage, acts of charity and so on, there is both a practical and a spiritual purpose. Thus E. B. Harper advocates an integrative approach for all the diversity so that religious activity is viewed as inseparable from a Hindu's secular life. His approach differs from the 'fragmentary' method favoured by M. N. Srinivas and McKim Marriot by which such religious experience can be pigeon-holed into different categories.[4]

But Hinduism is such a diverse religion that it is able to encompass any experience that life provides. A major determining factor is caste, but despite government opposition to it the belief continues. We have noted its effect earlier, but how did it arise? According to legend it was due to the divine creation of Manu, the first man, from whose body the classes emerged. From his head came the Brahmins, the priests who perform the Vedic rituals, from his hands came the Kshatriyas, warriors and noblemen, from his thighs the Vaishyas, merchants and farmers, and from his feet the Sudras, the lowest class of servants and labourers. The system was imposed by Aryans who conquered the country and reflects the thinking of Plato, the ancient Greek philosopher, who taught that there were men of gold, silver and brass.

The *Bhagavad gita* describe the duties: 'Brahmins, Kshatriyas, Vaishyas and Sudras differ by the characteristics of their action which are related to the modes of appearance of their material nature . . . Peacefulness, self-control, continence, wisdom and piety are the characteristics which govern the actions of the Brahmins. Courage, strength and resolution, skill, fearless in battle, generosity and the capacity to react are the characteristics which govern the actions of the Kshatriyas. Agriculture, cattle-rearing and trade govern the actions of the Vaishyas, and the task of the Sudras is to perform physical labour and provide other services.'[5]

But the classes are subdivided into *jati* (castes) and there are also the *pariahs* (outcastes) who were excluded from the above classes. Many of these originated from unlawful mixed marriages or from neglect of rituals or did work which was considered unclean. They were not allowed to live in villages, to use the common wells or to share food with members of the caste system. Ironically they maintained caste-like ranking among themselves. Mahatma Gandhi called them Harijan, 'God's people', and wanted to make them part of the *Sudra varna* or lower class. In 1950 equal status was given to all by the government, but they are still oppressed and have organized themselves (Dalits) to fight for equality. It is the karma that is formed in a previous life which determines what caste one is born into and there is no escape from it in this life.

It was in the Upanishads that *samsara* (reincarnation) appeared regulated by the law of karma, basically meaning that what you sow in this life you reap in the next. Every Hindu has a general dharma which includes the usual prohibitions but also a special dharma depending on caste. Thus in the *Bhagavad gita*, the warrior Arjuna hesitating about going into battle, is told to do his duty as a soldier and not to worry about killing the enemy since they are destined for rebirth! The story is not to be taken literally but regarded as the internal struggle between good and evil in our hearts. Arjuna chose selfless duty but others, usually in the last stage of life, become *sannyasi* or earlier become *sadhus*. Gandhi (1869–1948) was a *sadhu* but did not withdraw from life in the world since he maintained that the road to salvation is in service of one's country and of humanity.

Thus in a diverse religion various ways (*moksha*) are put forward to end *samsara* or transmigration either by devotion (*bhakti*) or ritual (action) or knowledge (*jnana*). The latter means recognizing Brahman as the only real entity, in opposition to *maya*, which deludes us into thinking that the world and material goods are reality. Such knowledge is more like insight than that gained from information or sense experience. But the path of devotion (*bhakti-marga*) has become the predominant way for many in Hinduism which means an inner surrender to God or performance of rituals before an image and pilgrimages to holy places. The spiritual master or Guru assumes a leading role as a mediator of God's saving grace. This is evident in the theistic traditions such as Vaisnavism, Saivism and Saktism. Vishnu, for example, became a personal saviour, granting grace to the one who followed him. Dancing and chanting became popular, with scriptural study not regarded as so important. This spirituality followed Kabir, who influenced Nanak, founder of Sikhism, and criticized religious practices because they failed to recognize that Brahman was within.

But liberation depends on how we view the relation of the deity and us. The classical philosophers disagreed about it. Are we really united already with God and only need to realize it?

Shankara said: 'That is the real, that is the soul. That art thou.' But Madhva maintained that there was a great gulf between God and humanity which requires an act of grace to bridge it. Perhaps the truth lies somewhere in between as Ramanuja asserted. He maintained the principle of identity-in-difference. We are like Brahman yet unlike Him, He is in us but also beyond us, therefore not identical, and immortality will not be absorption in Brahman but an eternal individual existence in communion with God.[6]

Hinduism does raise the question: If all souls are equal why the inequalities of the caste system? Probably the Hindu would answer that souls have got bad karma attached to them so pay for it in the life cycle. But there does seem to be a great difference between the philosophical systems such as Vedanta and 'the down-to-earth' religious practice of Indian villagers. Shankara regulated these practices to a low level and distinguished between different levels of truth. But Ramanuja opposed him, arguing that worship could not be put on the lower level, it was essential for the salvation of the soul.

Gautama was the son of the ruler of the Shakya tribe in Nepal, and after his enlightenment became known as the Buddha.[7] According to the stories he had a miraculous birth and left home when twenty-nine years old seeking an answer to suffering. He did not find help in asceticism as we mentioned but achieved enlightenment through meditation. Like Jesus who was tempted by Satan, he was tested by Mara, the personal symbol of evil. The Buddhist writings have all kinds of gods, spirits and demons, so that while the faith transcends the worship of gods it does not deny them. There is a spiritual dimension. But the Buddha is above the gods who are mortal and look to him for help to escape rebirth. Having assembled the sangha or group of monks, he taught the four noble truths and the eightfold path. We have mentioned these before but it is important to remember the four noble truths: suffering (*dukkha* or *duhkha* which can mean unsatisfactory), the cause of suffering, the cessation of suffering and the eightfold path that leads to its cessation.

The early form of the religion, Theravada, believed that the Buddha was infallible and a channel for the spiritual force of dharma (teaching). Hence the dharma is more important than the historical Buddha who confirmed it by saying: 'What is there . . . in seeing this vile body of mine? Whoso sees the spiritual Law or dharma he sees me, whoso sees me sees the spiritual dharma.'[8] The Buddhists in Asia described themselves as followers of the dharma and it is the core of all their teachings. It means one ultimate reality underlying all things and in all things, and should be manifested in righteousness and virtue. Just as the scientist sees behind the world invisible entities understood by mathematics, so the Buddhist says that our view of the world is appearance only. The centrality of dharma would seem to indicate that this is religion for them. Salvation is by self-effort, for the individual must work out his own salvation. The Buddha said: 'Be, each one of you, your own island, your own refuge; do not seek another refuge. It is in this way that you will reach the high place of the Immortal.'[9]

But the greater vehicle of Buddhism, the Mahayana, saw the need for saviour figures and introduced the bodhisattvas who have attained enlightenment but postpone entry into full nirvana in order to help others. Indeed there are many Buddhas who appear from time to time and a future Buddha is expected. This greater vehicle of Buddhism opened up the way for the laity to experience nirvana and departed from the self-help of the Buddha. A technique called 'skill in means' was developed which sought to find ways to accommodate the teaching in difficult circumstances and changing conditions. Another variation of Buddhism, Vajrayana, which reverences the Dalai Lama (regarded as the reincarnation of the Bodhisattva Chenresi), has a strongly devotional practice and seeks to classify the deities beginning with the Buddhas.[10]

In any assessment of the status of the Buddha the boundaries of master, model and saviour are blurred and there are many difficulties in sorting out the different perspectives. But his message is clear. He related suffering to desire. We continually desire power, money, wife, children and these attachments lead to pain. All is impermanent and yet we treat the world as permanent, and everything is decaying, yet we think life will go on forever. Buddhism differs from other religions in that it denies the self (*anatta*) or soul. If all things are impermanent (*anicca*) and insubstantial, how can a self exist? It is an illusion (*maya*). We are simply a collection of mental and physical qualities (*skandhas*) and if there is no ego, nothing can belong to it. It is foolish to say: 'This is mine.' To understand this eliminates desire, for it is connected with the ego. Lack of knowledge makes us feel that the world and self are permanent entities and that we can find happiness by indulging our senses and pleasing our egos. Ignorance, hatred and greed are three fires that threaten to destroy us, and sensual desire, ill-will, sloth, restlessness, worry and doubt can only be dealt with by the study of the dhamma or dharma.

Buddhism joins Hinduism in arguing that it is liberation from ignorance that we need, whereas the Semitic religions insist generally that it is disobedience to the commands of God, but also in Judaism it is asserted that an ignorant man cannot be pious. The denial of the self is also a problem and it is interesting to note that within the religion itself there were those who were not certain about the belief. They were known as the 'Personalists', a philosophical school who contended that there was an ego or person who provided a structural unity for the elements or aggregates. But the Buddhist goal for the individual is similar to other religions: generosity, morality, renunciation, wisdom, energy, patience, truthfulness, determination, loving kindness, equanimity. These are cultivated by the Bodhisattva.[11]

How then can we end the cycle of rebirth? Not by religious rituals or belief in the supernatural but by following the middle way between self-indulgence and asceticism. As we said earlier, it is by the eightfold path. The Buddhist believes that we are composed of five aggregates: matter, feelings, perception, mental formations, consciousness. What is strange is that consciousness or the mind is not given the central role that appears in other religions but is just another element. Yet the mind in Buddhism has a leading role in meditation, so should it not be more central? The goal is nirvana which is peace and insight in this life and after death freedom from rebirth. But nirvana is not easy to understand and there are both positive and negative views. How can the individual survive after death if she is simply a succession of mental and physical states? The Buddha was ambiguous about it and did not like such questions! The root meaning of the word is 'to blow': blowing out or extinction of self. There is an affinity with Christianity with its denial of the self or death to it.

But the self or soul is illusory in Buddhism so what is reborn is the web of karma in its causal connections. Just as one flame is passed to another or a billiard ball striking another stops dead but the other ball moves on, strikes another and itself stops dead, then a third continues the process, the Buddha moved beyond karma as action to intention which underlies the action. Another explanation is to see that the *skandhas* relate to each other according to patterns which are reproduced from one moment to the next and provide the continuity of the person. Death interrupts, but the *skandhas* form new patterns which are not identical to the old but connected with them. Thus the new being that is born is not identical with the old but not completely different. Karma ensures the causal sequence.

The Buddha denies both the permanence of the soul and any immortality of the gods or God. How, then, can it be called a religion? Scholars say that it differs from modern atheism by its renunciation of worldly values and the need for liberation from attachment which are common religious ideas. The one permanent thing is nirvana which is the extinction of the fires of greed, hatred and delusion and the delusion that we have a permanent self. Once attachment ceases nirvana is attained. It can be attained in this present life as is shown by the Arhats, worthy persons, but there is an ultimate nirvana for the Buddha spoke of 'another shore', 'a deathless realm, unborn, uncreated . . .'[12] While all other things are caused or conditioned, nirvana is unconditioned. Philosophers continue to debate whether it is positive or negative, but perhaps the best view is that nirvana is not a place but a state and since it belongs to the area of the absolute it cannot be described, being without properties.

But there does seem to be a problem about nirvana as the unconditioned. According to the philosophers the world has no inherent existence: it is empty, meaning arising only from certain conditions. Nirvana is not like this, being unconditioned, hence it must be beyond this world. But if this is so how can it, the permanent, be experienced in a world which is impermanent? If it belongs to the world of the Absolute then some way needs to be found to have nirvana transcendent and immanent as God is in other religions.

The monks are at the centre of Buddhism and the lay person in Theravada hopes to be reborn as a monk. Women from the villages consider it a privilege to cook their food, for such a service acquires merit. The monks spend much time in meditation and strictly following the Vinaya or disciplinary code. They must attain knowledge (*jnana*), mental peace (*samatha*) and insight into how things really are, which leads to enlightenment. Meditation is more than thinking, it is freeing the mind from things of sense, it is concentration, contemplation, and engaging in various physical postures. The Mahayana sutras are used not simply as conveying information but as an aid to meditation. Yoga, which is now popular in the Western world, teaches relaxation, motionless controlled breathing, and the shutting out of the world. Thought is concentrated on a single object until consciousness itself disappears before the experience of ultimate reality.

The Yoga sutras call for a quieting of the mind and the setting aside of ignorance or the illusion that the transient is real. Attachment to anything must be relinquished and a dietary life embraced. Breath control is essential, as are concentration and contemplation, leading to a trance-like state. Clearly a teacher is required for such a difficult process. Zen Buddhism in Japan uses this technique together with *koans* or riddles in order to show the limitations of reason. The resulting states are variously described as loving-kindness, compassion, sympathetic joy and even-mindedness. But Zen differs about enlightenment in that meditation is engaged in not to seek it but to realize that we already possess it. The idea is based on the view that all possess the buddha-nature which is concealed from us so we need to be awakened to it. We suddenly become aware of it, it is not a gradual cultivation.

Bhakti developed in Buddhism and the cremated remains of the Buddha were interred in stupas and attracted worshippers. Personal devotion to the Buddha developed and in many countries great statues of the Buddha were erected. In Mahayana there is Amitabha, who is the transcendent Buddha of Infinite Light: the personification of infinite mercy, wisdom, love and compassion. Also, Avalokitesvara is one of the greatest of the Bodhisattvas, the Lord who lowers his gaze towards humanity in compassion and the wish to help. A future Buddha is expected, Maitreya, who will bring peace to the world. All of which shows that a religion beginning with self-help developed saviour figures. Heavenly Buddhas entered Buddhism with compassion and grace and with the Bodhisattvas an accumulation of merit that could be shared with all. In the Lotus Sutra the Buddha carries the Buddhist to the other shore.

Guru Nanak (1469–1539 CE) was the first Sikh Guru and founder of the community. He grew up in the Punjab, an unsettled country which had experienced many invasions and was at that time governed by Islam. He had an enquiring mind, declined the Hindu sacred thread because it was a caste symbol, and at thirty years of age had a religious experience. The result was a belief in God and the conviction that there was neither Hindu nor Muslim, which encourages some people to think that Sikhism is a combination of both.

These influences can be detected but the faith has its own uniqueness. Influenced by the Indian bhakti movement, he travelled widely, criticizing those who without the right conduct offered prayers, pilgrimages, giving of alms, and the use of images. The Sikh scripture contains the hymns which he composed and other sources relate stories about him. One day he joined a group of pilgrims standing in a river and offering water to assuage the thirst of their deceased ancestors. Turning to the west, Nanak began to throw water. Asked what he was doing, he said that he was watering his fields in Kartarpur. They laughed at the ridiculous belief that water could reach fields so far away. Nanak replied that it was just as stupid to think that water could reach souls no longer on earth and who had no physical wants or needs. He opposed magic, superstition and idol worship throughout the country.[13]

The uniqueness of Sikhism stems from the teaching of its founder and succeeding gurus and its opposition to caste. Nanak attacks the external paraphernalia of religion in favour of inner personal devotion and has been understood as a charismatic figure who offered a new revelation. Brotherhood was stressed and community kitchens were founded. They were forerunners of the *langar* that was institutionalized by

Guru Amar Das, the third Guru, to provide food for all. His followers became known as Sikhs from the Sanskrit word *shishya*, which means student or disciple. The title, Guru, appears in the hymns of Nanak as identical with God but he did not claim it, being given to him by his followers. They apply it to God, the scriptures, human masters and the community. There is no doctrine of incarnation in Sikhism but the community believes that Nanak was sinless and like other Gurus became perfect through obeying the will of God. However, the Guruship of Nanak is derived from God and they think of Nanak as a boat transporting them across the ocean of existence. It implies a saviour as well as a guide.[14]

The place of the scripture is unique and there is the distinctive nature of the Khalsa Brotherhood. Sikhs agree with the other Indian religions that man's plight springs from ignorance not disobedience. It arises by aiming at the wrong goals in life and being waylaid by desires which make us self-centred. The Sikhs summarize the situation in one word, *haumai*, meaning not only egoism but self-reliance. There is a strong doctrine of predestination in Sikhism, as in Islam and Calvinistic Christianity, which appears to make God responsible for bad deeds as well as good. But the Sikh scripture states that past actions determine our garments.[15] A solution is that God wills the salvation of all but permits the law of karma to operate so making us responsible. The key term here is permit rather than determine. A person who does not do the will of God is *manmukh*, while those that obey are *gurmukh*. The world deludes us (*maya*), but it is a delusion rather than an illusion. It deludes us into embracing lust, wrath, avarice, worldly love and pride.

The cure for the disease is meditation on the word of the Guru, making us conscious of God who dwells within us. In particular, by meditating upon the name of God, *nam simaran*, which summarizes His being and nature, the Sikh hopes to be filled with God just as in the secular sense our interest in work or home or hobbies may fill our whole lives. A further step to liberation is knowledge (*gyan khand*), reliance on the grace of God, duty and effort. God is understood in various ways through the word (*shabad*), name (*nam*), divine preceptor (*guru*), divine order or will (*hukam*), truth (*sach*) and grace (*nadar*). For Nanak, grace means revelation both in nature and through the prophets and without it we cannot know him.[16] Salvation is not by our own efforts or ritual.

Nam Japan, remembering the name of God, must be repeated in a thoughtful way and the five adversaries lust, anger, greed, attachment and pride are only kept in check by concentration on this word of God.[17] Union with God is not complete identification but similar to the union of bride and groom (*sahaj*). Salvation is not obtained by withdrawing from the world but living the life of the householder (*grhastha*) for God is present in the world. Like Judaism, liberation applies more to the community than the individual. Thus a Sikh is any woman or man whose faith consists of belief in God, the ten Gurus and the teachings of the Guru Granth Sahib, and who professes no other religion.

In conclusion we note with respect to a definition of religion that the Buddha stressed the dharma or dhamma: a popular Buddhist affirmation is, 'I take refuge in the dhamma', meaning his teaching. It is, according to the Buddha, more important than his person, so it is the main characteristic of the religion. Both the Buddha and Nanak react against the gods, sacrifices and rituals of Hinduism. But as we said in Chapter 3, we cannot do without some kind of ritual and is Nanak's call for naming and remembering God not the development of a ritual? We recall too that in Hinduism dharma means duty or right conduct or way of life, which is also reflected in all the Semitic and Indian religions, for there is no separation between the secular and religious. The early Christians were marked out by their lifestyle and were called the people of the way and dharma for the Sikhs is a religious duty expressed in the code of the Khalsa.

Religions believe that there is a need to be saved from something but also to something: a new lifestyle and mindset not only for the individual but also for the community. The stress on the kingdom of God or nirvana or brotherhood upon the earth is a worldly goal but there is also the other-worldly: heaven or paradise or ultimate nirvana or . . . where the righteous or the enlightened will dwell in a state of bliss. There are different ways of reaching these goals but, in general, apart from early Buddhism, aid is sought from God so one of the marks of religion is reliance on His grace.

It is no surprise when we consider the number of people involved in the religious quest that divisions should develop between religions and within religions. We shall look at both these matters in our next chapters.

8 Divisions within religions

There are many differences between religions but also divisions within them. In the latter case it may happen when the founder of a religion dies and there is debate about his successor or dissension regarding the interpretation of scripture or conflict over belief or rituals. In a limited way we will consider some of the divisions in this chapter.

Most Jews are descendants of the Sephardim, those who originated in Spain and Portugal, or the Ashkenazim, those from East and Central Europe. The sharpest division in the faith is between the orthodox and the progressives. As we recall, the ultra-orthodox believe that the Torah was written by Moses and the oral law interprets it. They keep a strict observance of the Sabbath (from sundown on Friday until sundown on Saturday), when no work is done, and of the festivals and the dietary laws (kosher). They believe in the coming of a Messiah (anointed one): a son of David to usher in the messianic age. Boys are instructed in the faith but girls are trained to become mothers and homemakers. Marriages are arranged by the parents.

The ultra-orthodox are called the *Haredim* and are influenced by the mystic kabbalah tradition which contains a lot of speculation about God and mankind. They oppose historical criticism of the scripture, and have various views about the messianic age determining their attitude to the state of Israel. Within the group there is the hasidim who believe in a personal God and have a veneration for their *zaddikim* or *rebbes* which is not in accord with Jewish democracy. One section, the Neturei Kara, are anti-Zionists believing that the state of

Israel should not have been inaugurated until the coming of the Messiah. Thus they accept the claims of the Palestine Liberation Organization (PLO). But others, the quasi-Hasidim Gush Emunim, accept the state of Israel, adopt a more aggressive stance to the Palestinians, and believe that the redemption of the land has begun since messianism is confirmed by the victories over the Arabs.[1] No land must be conceded to the Palestinians and territory gained must be occupied by Jewish settlers. They have resorted to terrorism against the Muslims in the hope of a massive attack by the enemies of Israel when God will intervene to save them.

One of the best-known Hasidic trends is the Lubavitch. In the 1980s Menachem Mendel Schneerson announced that redemption had been accomplished and implied that he was the Messiah. The claim earned the condemnation of Rabbi Schach, a non-Hasidic, who argued that the coming of the Messiah was delayed because of the impact of modernity on the Jews which meant that they had failed to obey the Torah. Another Hasidic group, called the Satmar Hasidics, condemned Lubavitcher messianic claims, as well as Zionism, for setting up a state without waiting for the Messiah.

The Haredim are conspicuous because of their black coats and homburgs, observance of the *Shabbat* and early marriage.[2] But among their opponents are the Mitnaggedim who say that the Hasidics are ignorant of the Torah and give too much veneration to their rebbes. Another group, the Traditionalists, are not so strict, taking into account changing circumstances. They do not separate women from men in their synagogues, and women have been allowed to take part in the services without allowing them to become rabbis. In these Traditional synagogues there is Bat Mitzvah for the girls and they can attend the schools with the boys.

Progressive Jews have different labels: Conservative, Liberal, Reform and Reconstructionist. They have replaced the personal Messiah with the idea of a perfect age which will gradually unfold. Israel will play a large part in the new development, so they have discarded prayers for the rebuilding of the Temple and the restoration of the sacrifices. They look forwards rather than backwards. Conservatives interpret the Torah in the light of modern historical knowledge and Liberals encourage families to sit together at their services. There is organ music and a choir and only part of the ritual is in Hebrew. The laws concerning food are obsolete and not relevant to modern conditions. Reform accepts converts who are born of a Jewish father. Women can be cantors and rabbis.

Among the Progressives there are differences about God. Is He personal or impersonal? Is He dependent on our cooperation or is His power unlimited? Is there continuing revelation? Should the Jewish laws not be reformulated? These questions are debated among them, but the New Union Prayerbook produced in the 1970s eliminated sexist language and has a diversity of forms of service. The stress is on conduct rather than creed. It is difficult to get agreement, however, about God's action or miracles or life after death or that a future Messiah will come or about how the law is to be updated or whether conscience is a sufficient guide for the individual. The Conservatives do not accept the Reform view that the Torah is due to human creativity, but they do accept the ideals of Zionism.[3]

The Zionists are political and national, denying that Israel was a people solely on the basis of its bond with God. The liberation of Israel will come in a natural manner, not by any supernatural intervention. These are the secular Zionists but among them are those who think that religion can play a big part in a free state. The first conference of Zionism was held in Switzerland (1897) with Theodore Herzl as leader, and it paved the way for the founding of a Jewish State in Palestine (1948). Today the largest concentration of Jews is in Palestine, about three million, and in the United States of America, about six million.

Reconstructionist Judaism, founded by Mordecai Kaplan (1881–1993), comes nearest to Humanism, denying a supernatural God and insisting that such a concept means a complex of forces in the universe which ensure salvation. When we ask 'What is religion?', Kaplan takes a Durkheim view insisting that it emerged from the development of Jewish society. Religious worship is the release of emotions so that people become conscious of the power within them. Judaism is an evolving civilization, not a people elected by a supernatural God. Decisions are reached by consensus, women have equality, and intermarriage between the races is acceptable.

But the question arises: Can a non-supernatural interpretation do justice to the history of the Jews? Would a reformulation of Jewish theism not be better than complete rejection? Kaplan has confidence in human potential despite the horrors of the Holocaust. A group originated in the United States in the 1960s and declared that humanity could solve its own problems. It asserted that the Bible is full of myths, including the Exodus, and any history that might be retained must foster humanistic ideals. The deity is an infantile projection rejected by reason and the Torah is an unreliable guide, but the commands against stealing and murder need to be retained. Festivals and life-cycle events can be retained when they express humanistic values, but death is final for there is no eternal life.[4]

Many Jews who have problems with traditional Judaism would not agree with these proposals, but there is among them a search for a new spirituality which has reference to God. They do not believe that their history is simply due to natural causes. Dan Cohn-Sherbok writes: 'In all the major branches of contemporary Judaism there is a general acknowledgement that human history is in some way shaped by divine providence however understood.'[5] Yet his proposal for an open Judaism seems to suffer from the same kind of diversity and subjectivity that he has criticized. There is uncertainty about the nature of God, nothing definite and final in religions, with each religion simply one way among others, and there are no heretics since no-one knows what the truth is. All is relative and subjective. Scripture, election, covenant, the Messiah, after-life, and so on, have no certainty attached to them but are tentative hypotheses. Everyone formulates his own personal interpretation of Judaism, but it means defining religion as a private affair without reference to the beliefs of a community.[6]

In Christianity there is also a diversity of belief and divisions. In the early centuries disputes arose about the status of Christ and various heresies such as Arianism (*c*. 250–336 CE) were condemned. Arius believed that the Son was created and was not of the same substance with God. He was condemned at the Council of Nicaea (325 CE) which had been summoned by the Roman Emperor Constantine (247–337 CE). The doctrine of the Trinity also posed a problem, seeming to imply three gods. But it was eventually decided that the Godhead had three persons in one substance. Today there are various views about it. Some argue for a social Trinity meaning that there are three minds acting in a unified way but having different roles to play. They mutually indwell one another (*perichoresis*). Others, stressing the unity of God, believe that there is one centre of consciousness and the persons are eternal modes of being. But these aspects or modes do not fit easily with any modern definition of a person. What the doctrine seeks to do is to show the activity of God in creation, incarnation, and the power of the Spirit. Its formulation caused dissension with the Unitarians and they separated or were excluded from the mainstream. The doctrine is opposed by both Muslims and Jews.

Christianity experienced three major schisms in the fifth, eleventh and sixteenth centuries. The first occurred because it was alleged in the East that the Syrians and Copts did not have the correct view of Christ and the second occurred between the East and West over the Headship of the Church. The Greek Orthodox Church maintained the headship of the Patriarch at Constantinople but the Latin Church at Rome recognized the headship of the Pope. The Patriarch said that the Pope was only a bishop which resulted in the latter excommunicating him as a heretic! The result was the division of the Church in 1054 CE into Orthodox and Roman Catholic. But there were other disagreements about the date of Easter, the Eucharist, the celibacy of the clergy and theology. The East believed that the Holy Spirit proceeded from the Father through the Son, while the West insisted that the procession was from the Father and Son. Critics laughed at the debate about a Greek diphthong, but to say that the Spirit proceeded from Father and Son did, according to the Western view, give more significance to the divinity of Christ.

The Orthodox and the Catholic Churches have seven sacraments: baptism, confirmation, confession, matrimony, ordination, anointing the sick, and the Eucharist or Communion. Easter is celebrated at a different date in orthodoxy and the resurrection is the focal point of belief. A wooden screen (*iconostasis*) is usual in the churches and the priest is concealed behind it for most of the service. There are candles, icons or pictures of a holy person painted on wood and figures of

Christ, Mary and the Saints. Their use was authorized by a council in 787 CE. Priests are allowed to marry but bishops are not. The Catholic Church believes that St Peter was the first Bishop of Rome and the Pope (papa or father) is Christ's representative on earth. In this capacity he is infallible when he speaks *ex cathedra* (from the chair with authority) on matters of faith and morals. Certain regulations govern the conduct of members: they must attend Mass on Sundays and Holy Days, present themselves regularly at confession, keep feasts and fasts and refuse meat on certain days, support the church financially and not marry someone of another faith. Nowadays this latter requirement is not generally observed.

In ecumenical dialogue it is said that only two items of disagreement remain between East and West: the teaching concerning the Holy Spirit and the limits of papal power. The East believes that all believers are entrusted with the power of guarding the true faith and preserving the sacramental order of the church, whereas in the West the Pope exercises the power, having jurisdiction over the entire episcopate.[7] Both churches do have a similar government of bishops, priests and deacons.

The Catholic Church has always tried to enforce strict control over its members and at one time established an Inquisition to censor books and try heretics, but was unable to prevent the call for reform in the sixteenth century. It is said that the Protestant reformation was due to various political, national, economic factors and the Renaissance. A German monk, Martin Luther (1483–1546), was concerned with the way the Church financed itself, particularly through the sale of indulgences, remission of punishment for sin, and its doctrine of salvation. The debate centred around the question of how a person is justified or made righteous in the sight of God. Luther insisted that justification was by faith alone and accused the Catholic Church of teaching faith and works. The protest raised questions about the sacraments, priesthood and the central role of the Church. Luther contended that the people could read the Bible for themselves and form their own private judgement about it and that scripture justified only two sacraments: baptism and the Lord's Supper. He proceeded to translate the scripture into German so that all could read it. The protest hit at the heart of the system, for if faith was personal, why the need for the intermediary office of the priest? But it is asserted that Luther or John Calvin (1509–1564) did not exalt the right of private judgement and the Reformers retained a professional ministry. It must be informed judgement requiring education. Splits, however, were soon to develop in Protestantism.

Ironically, the Reformers disagreed over the meaning of the Mass (derived from the closing words of liturgy, *Ite, missa est*) or Eucharist which was one of the reasons for their protest about Catholicism! John Calvin stressed predestination, original sin and total depravity, and it was reflected in the outlook of Baptists, Presbyterians and the Reformed Churches of France, Holland and Switzerland. Another Reformer, Ulrich Zwingli (1484–1531), in Switzerland denied purgatory, praying to saints and the creation of monasteries. He, like Luther, rejected the authority of the Pope, the sacrifice of the Mass and clerical celibacy. But he disagreed with Luther over the meaning of the Eucharist. Luther contended for some kind of bodily presence of Christ, Zwingli said that it was only a memorial and Calvin held that there was a spiritual presence. All denied the Catholic doctrine of transubstantiation, the turning of the elements into the body and blood of Christ. Calvin believed in authority and established a theocratic state in Geneva (1541) which ruled both church and city and imposed a ban on most forms of entertainment. The city council expelled him for this puritanical rule but the people, with the restraint removed, went to the other extreme so that eventually they had to bring Calvin back!

More radical reformers divided into anabaptists, spiritualists and anti-Trinitarians. The first were the forerunners of the Baptists who insisted on the total immersion of adults, not the sprinkling of infants, as the rite of entry into membership. The second led to churches that stressed the experience of the Spirit and the third anticipated the development of Unitarianism. While the reformation in England was political, Thomas Cranmer gave the church two magnificent books of Common Prayer (1549 and 1552) and the Forty-Two Articles of Religion (1553). These are the basis for the present Thirty-Nine Articles of the Church of England. In 1570, Elizabeth I was excommunicated by the Pope, arousing controversy in the

Anglican Church. Edward Pusey (1800–1882), who did not cross over to Rome when John Henry Newman did (1845), contended that such excommunication was an error and proceeded to deny the authority of the Pope. He claimed Apostolic succession for the Anglican Church and the 'power of the keys': the Anglican Church was the Catholic Church in England. He was also not happy about the veneration given to the Virgin Mary. The response of the Catholics to these and other protests was to declare that Anglican orders were invalid and they alone had the Apostolic succession. We can imagine what the reaction to this was in the Eastern Church, for they also claimed Apostolic succession!

The Catholics responded to the Protestants with their own reformation. It stressed the centrality of the Church, outside which there was no salvation, and elevated the Mass as the source of the grace of God. Private interpretation of scripture was ruled out; baptism removes the guilt of original sin, the Virgin Mary is excluded from it; human nature is not as corrupt as Luther thought; and justification is not independent of morality. The Jesuits, the Society of Jesus, played a leading role in the reassertion of Catholicism. Formal approval of the order was granted in 1540 which engaged in missionary and educational work and vowed absolute obedience to the Pope. The first Vatican Council (1869–1870) asserted that the existence of God can be known by reason and that the Pope is an infallible head of the Church in the succession to St Peter. The doctrine of the Immaculate Conception of the Virgin Mary was declared because of her role in the work of redemption.[8] The Catholics contended that if every person has the right to interpret the Bible for himself then Protestantism will split into many denominations, and they were right. Some see it as a good thing since it caters for individual variety, but others regard disunity as a weakness and engage in ecumenical discussion.

The nineteenth century, on the one hand, was the century of doubt with the assault of higher criticism on the scripture and the problems raised by Darwin's *The Origin of Species* (1859), but on the other hand it witnessed the greatest missionary outreach of the Church since the first century. Evangelism and Revival occurred in Britain and America with the Americans Moody and Sankey and the founding of the Keswick Convention. The social problem was addressed by the Churches and the Salvation Army (1878), but gradually the state and the trade unions took control of welfare and the rights of the workers. Religion was beginning to be pushed to the periphery of life.

The Second Vatican Council (1962) showed a changed attitude to Protestantism, recognizing the integrity of the Reformers and proposing a vernacular liturgy and a greater role for the laity in the Church. The existence of Protestant churches was recognized and the need for unity emphasized. But on ethical matters there was condemnation of any form of artificial contraception, celibacy was endorsed, and the marriage bond considered indissoluble. However, despite its stand for priestly celibacy the Church allowed the Anglo-Catholics, who left the Anglican Church because of its decision to ordain women to the priesthood, to bring their wives with them. Celibacy was only introduced in the middle of the fourth century, and while the Vatican wants it maintained, there is the possibility that time will bring a change.

The reconciliation of the Churches took a step forward in 1910 with the Edinburgh Missionary Conference, leading to the World Council of Churches (1948) which has held conferences in various places up to the present time. The Roman Catholic Church sends observers, but so far has not joined the organization. Doctrines such as the Immaculate Conception and the Assumption of Mary (1950) and reaffirmation of transubstantiation with regard to the Eucharist are theological problems for Protestants, apart from the more practical matters of organization and worship. An advance was made at the Second Vatican Council when it was conceded that other Christians were in communion with the Catholic Church even if imperfectly! Authority in the Catholic Church resides in the Pope, but orthodoxy is more democratic, asserting that it should reside in the whole body of the faithful. In this they are close to Protestantism. The Presbyterians, Congregationalists and Churches of Christ have gone forward in the United Reformed Church and there is much cooperation with the Methodists. There was also the union of the Anglicans, Methodists, Congregational and Presbyterian Churches in India to form the Church of South India (1947).[9]

Doubts, however, about the role of the Church in the modern world had been expressed by Dietrich Bonhoeffer (1906–1945) who became involved in the bomb attack against Hitler and was executed. He insisted that Western society had rejected Christianity and nothing was to be gained by the Churches withdrawing into an ecumenical fortress. Christianity needed to dissolve itself into this secular culture, 'making the secular a mode of the transcendent, giving up traditional forms of piety, organisation and priesthood'.[10] Bonhoeffer defined religion as 'inherited metaphysical notions expressed in formal propositions and combined with individualistic piety'. He was attacking the Lutheran Church of which he was a member because it emphasized church activity and individualistic piety and did not interfere in the affairs of the state. He opposed religion as formalized religious occasions, but believed in it when it was sincere, prayerful and strictly disciplined. Christ was the man for others and the Church should sell her possessions and give to the poor. Clergy should continue but take secular jobs. The Church must be the people in the world.

The proposal is interesting for our attempt to answer the question 'What is religion?', for here is someone who has had remarkable influence, speaking of a religionless Christianity. It has echoes in Guru Nanak's call for the abolition of religion, and it cannot be denied that Christianity in its traditional forms is failing to capture the attention of the masses. One way forward may be the enthusiasm of the new religious movements which have sprung up everywhere, but currently it is too early to judge their influence. Personally I do not think we can dispense with the traditional forms, but we might accommodate them more to the age in which we live as some Churches are doing. In any case the World Council of Churches has ceased to expand and plans for the reconciliation of the Anglican and Methodist Churches in England has so far failed to succeed.

In Islam, when the Prophet died division ensued as to who should be the successor and as a result two groups emerged: the Sunni and the Shi'ah. The Shi'ahs thought the successor should be Ali, cousin of the Prophet and husband of his daughter Fatimah, and after him his grandsons, Hasan and Husain. But Abu Bakr, father-in-law of the Prophet and one of his closest friends, was elected. He in turn named Umar Khattab as his successor to be followed by Uthman. Under these Caliphs, Islamic conquest was very successful, but the Shi'ahs remained dissatisfied until 'Ali at last became the fourth Caliph. Unfortunately he and his grandsons were killed: Husain at the battle of Karbala in 680 CE, forever sacred to the Shi'ah, and Hasan by poison. The hatred and strife generated continues between these main divisions until the present time. The Sunni are followers of the *sunnah*: the right path or the path of tradition. They profess to follow the example of the Prophet, hold to the consensus of the community and believe that the imam should have no authority except to lead public worship. They reject temporary marriages and have a much more tolerant attitude towards customs and tradition.

The Sunni are the majority but the Shi'ites have always been prominent, especially in Iran. They differ from the Sunni·in contracting temporary marriages for short periods, or better; and their worship and ablutions before it take a different form. Karbala is more important than Mecca and the battle that took place there is commemorated annually in the Passion of Husain. His sorrow was redemptive, a vicarious merit that is remembered when pilgrims go to Karbala. They hold that their leaders, the Imams, are descendants of the Prophet through his daughter Fatimah and possess infallible authority and super-human powers. Hence what they say is more important than the consensus of the community.

One particular revolt against the Sunni is significant. It was led by Muhammad ibn-al-Hanafiya, a son of Ali by a wife other than Fatimah. He died in the battle, but afterwards a rumour circulated that he had simply disappeared or concealed himself and that he would return to restore justice and peace. He is now thought of as the Madhi, the rightly guided, and regarded as divine. The idea of the hidden imam who will some day appear has led to a number of pretenders proclaiming that they are the expected one. But the two groups of Muslims have in common the Qur'an and some traditions.[11]

The Shi'ah have split into various sects with regard to doctrine and who should be the imam. There are the Isma'ilis in Egypt, the Assassins (Persia and Syria), the Zaydis (Yemen), and the Twelvers, who accept a line of twelve imams as distinct from the Isma'ilis who believe in only seven. The Aga Khans belong to the Isma'ilis. The Sunni have persecuted these over the years and in reply the Shi'ah have ritually cursed Abu Bakr, Umar and others and celebrated the murder of Umar.

As well as the Qur'an there are Hadiths that record the *sunnah* or customs of Muhammad and provide direction and moral guidance. Within the Sunni tradition, six collections of Hadiths have reached canonical status, but Shi'ah recognize sources independent of these. The Shi'ah insist that many Hadiths support their position; for example, the Hadith of Ghadir Khum, where it is stated that on his return from his final visit to Mecca, Muhammad clasped Ali's hand in his and told the crowd: 'For whomever I have been a protector, Ali is his protector.'[12] The Sunni accept the Hadith but believe that Ali is named an authority in only a limited way. The Shi'ah have other Hadiths that contradict the Sunni view of events; for example the Nahi al-balagha, comprising sayings and sermons attributed to Ali.

The Sunni are the majority, but the Shi'ahs have always been prominent and today they are the majority in Iran and Yemen and the largest minority in Iraq. They hold the five pillars with the Sunni but differ in adding to the first pillar, 'There is only one God and Muhammed is His prophet', the words, 'And Ali is the vice-regent of God'. We now look in a little more detail at militancy in Islam. The Shi'ah have been violent over the years not only in Iran but also in Lebanon. Much of their history shows a rejection of worldly power and stress on martyrdom. In Iran the Shi'ah wanted shari'ah law to rule, but it was in conflict with the modernizing of the country as undertaken by the Shah and his son which affected law, dress, pilgrimage and clerical representation in the government. Ayatollah Khomeini (1902–1989) was very outspoken about it and was exiled in 1964, but it led to a coalition of Shi'ite clergy and politicians who deposed the Shah in 1979. They saw the return of Khomeini as the revealing of the 'hidden Imam' and the vindication of their faith. The clerics insisted that it was another example of the Shi'ah suffering under oppression.

In more recent times, since the death of Khomeini, a liberal attitude has been shown by his successors and there is now more hope of better relations with the West. But again Islam is divided for the Sunni see such a state as an elitist theocracy, a hierarchy of Shi'ite clerics which opposes their beliefs. Khomeini is reported to have criticized them, saying that with the Shi'ah there is rebellion against bad government but with the Sunni there is obedience. This is overdone because there have been rebellions also by the Sunni.[13] Some thought of Khomeini as the hidden Imam, but he believed that he was simply his representative. A moderate, Muhammad Khatami, was made president in May 1997 and the *fatwa* against Salman Rushdie was lifted, but Khatami is likely to encounter difficulty with the more conservative clerics.

There has been a resurgence in fundamentalist Islam throughout the world. Usually this term refers, as we mentioned, to those who in different religions stress the fundamentals of the faith and interpret their scriptures literally. While these elements are present, the modern rise of Muslim fundamentalism has taken a political stance and been engaged in militancy. In Palestine they have not been happy with the PLO because it is secular. Hamas (1989) repudiates this and demands that there be a holy war with Israel and agrees with Islamic Jihad and Hizbollah in their opposition to the United States. They were encouraged by the success of the Afghan Muslims, the Mujhadin, against the Soviet Union in 1992 and want to export the militancy to other countries.

Commentators debate the impact of both Islam and nationalism/socialism on Al Quaddafi in Libya. He did reject the *sunnah* as a legal basis for his government and he restricted the power of the *ulama*, the Islamic doctors of theology who are the custodians of the teachings. Religion is not supreme but allied to socialism and communism. The ideal is to raise the standards of the poor and free them from the injustices of capitalism. Islam stresses that the rich have got rich by the levying of interest on the needy which is forbidden in the Qur'an.[14]

A third division in the faith is Sufism, who are mystics. The name means 'wool' and was applied to ascetics who wore wool against their skin. They reacted against Islamic legalism, the worldliness of money-loving Muslims, and sought union with Allah by practices similar to the Indian religions. They enjoyed an ecstasy of the love of God and sought to escape the illusion of the self in order to achieve union with Him. Many converts were made as they exhibited missionary zeal. Some claimed to have achieved complete unity with Allah, which was treated as blasphemous by the Sunni who punished or executed them.

One noted scholar who was influenced by the movement, Al Ghazali (1058–1111), demonstrated that the emotion of Sufism was in conformity with traditional Islamic faith and practice. He could point to Muhammad who was a mystic and received his revelations in solitude. Sufism founded monasteries and today there are many centres throughout the Muslim world. Nevertheless, the Sunni have always been suspicious of the movement with its spiritual interpretation of the Pillars. The Sufis could say of pilgrimage, if Allah is everywhere why travel long distances to sacred places? They rejected the external forms of the religion and longed for direct experience of God. Mystical interpretation is applied to the Qur'an and the same authority reserved by the Shi'ah for their imams is granted by the Sufi to the founders of their orders. Both Sufism and Shi'ism infuse the law with spiritual meanings and seek to establish avenues to illumination inspired by love of Allah rather than fear of punishment.

This limited look at the divisions in Islam raises a point that appears in other religions. Is God on the side of the big battalions? Does success in war (*jihad*) mean that God endorses the faith? The Sunni thought so when Muhammad was victorious over his enemies, and some Jews in modern times feel assured that God is on their side because of their victories over the Arabs. But the peaceful ways of the Sufi and the command to love your neighbour in Judaism and Christianity, call into question the use of force. faiths can defend themselves as a last resort but what they preach about love and compassion does not equate with wars of aggression.

Hinduism, though having a multiplicity of gods and diverse approaches to them, has not divided into the clearly defined divisions of other religions. But the Brahmanical religion present in the Upanishads led to the worship of the two great gods, Shiva and Vishnu, and there are followers of each. They show tolerance to one another, with worshippers at times alternating between the gods to get the best of both worlds!

Vishnu is the god of the most popular scripture, the *Bhagavad gita*, and Shiva is associated with asceticism, yoga and contemplation. Vishnu, with the incarnation in Krishna, is more personal than Shiva and has many incarnations (*avatars*). A future one is Kali, who will destroy the wicked and bring the age to an end.

There are six philosophical divisions (Darshana):

1   Sankyha: Dualistic and atheistic, teaching about the nature of *purusha*, self or spirit, and *prakriti* or matter.
2   Yoga: It concentrates on the spiritual discipline that is needed for the self to attain liberation.
3   Mimamsa: The importance of *dharma* or right action.
4   Vedanta: The end of the Veda focusing on the Upanishadic teaching regarding Brahman.
5   Nyaya: Logic will lead to liberation.
6   Vaisheshika: an analysis of *dharma* and other elements.

As we mentioned, philosophers such as Shankara (788–820 CE), Ramanuja (died 1137 CE) and Madhva (thirteenth century) differed in their views about God and His relation to mankind. Shankara followed Shiva and identified *atman* (soul) with Brahman who is the reality, not this world of sense perception (*maya*). To realize it and our identification with Brahman means liberation. But his doctrine of the two levels of truth meant that while on the higher level the world is illusory, on the lower level of our experience it is not. Hence the worshipper can see Brahman as personal (Upanishads have both a personal and impersonal Brahman), but he must go further beyond such ideas to the higher level of impersonality. Such teaching implies that religion can belong to the lower or higher levels, scripture reflects both levels, and so does Brahman. Worship must give way to meditation and contemplation.

Ramanuja, however, denies the identifying of the *atman* with Brahman and the relegating of the personal in Him to the lower level of reality. If Shankara was right, worship would be the worship of ourselves! Just as the soul is in the body so Brahman is in all things, the world is the body of Brahman. But if the world is an illusion then Brahman is. He opposed any idea of the individual being eventually absorbed into the deity and endorsed the *bhakti* of Vishnu. Madhva (thirteenth century), who was probably influenced by Christianity, went further and taught a greater gulf between the soul and Brahman which placed a stress on the need for the grace of God to liberate us.[15]

Hinduism has had its reformers. Ram Mohan Roy (1772–1833) founded the Brahma Samaj and called for the end of *suttee* and of polytheism. Sri Ramakrishna (1834–86) initiated a Hindu renaissance and founded the Ramakrishna Math and Mission. He was open to the influence of other faiths and experienced states of ecstasy. Swami Vivekananda (1863–1902) was his disciple and founded the Ramakrishna monasteries and missions dedicated to social work. He taught universalism but based it on Hinduism. We have mentioned Mahatma Gandhi (1869–1948), but Sri Aurobindo (1872–1950) was a pioneer in initiating a synthesis between Hindu ideas and evolutionary theory and proclaimed a new yoga which did not encourage asceticism. He founded an *ashram* or spiritual community which attracted people from all over the world and it continues today.[16]

Buddhism divided into the Theravada or Hinayana or Lesser Vehicle, which is the southern school and is found in South-East Asia (Sri Lanka, Burma and Thailand); the Mahayana or the great vehicle adopted by the majority of Buddhists and is in China, Nepal, Korea and Japan; and Vajrayana in Tibet. Theravada focused on the monks (*bhikkus*) in monasteries, with strict rules, stress on meditation and reading, and a retreat from the people. The asceticism which the Buddha had rejected in favour of the Middle Way asserted itself so that the only logical Buddhist was the monk. It is sometimes asserted that Theravada, using the Pali texts which are the earliest scriptures available, is the true Buddhism while Mahayana is regarded as an erroneous development. It is an imbalance which recent scholarship has corrected. It is now pointed out, for example, that the world view of both Theravada and Mahayana is the same and that faith, devotion and meditation are present in the former as well as the latter. The divisions are not as sharp as in Christianity but they are distinct forms.

Mahayana had much greater appeal since it held out the possibility of the lay person becoming enlightened as well as the monk, and it spoke of divine help and grace. Compassion or devotion (*bhakti*) is extended to all. In this division the historical Buddha was elevated to divine status and there were many Buddhas for different times and places. The Buddha lives on in the dhamma, and the aim is to become a Buddha so there are many Buddhas. The Theravada, however, believe that there was only one historic Buddha for this age, but the tendency to devotion was there with his remains, so stupas were built. The Buddha was more than a man as he himself said after his enlightenment. Hence the Mahayana developed the three-body (*trikaya*) doctrine of the Buddha. His human existence was his 'transformation body', but in his celestial existence he appears in his 'enjoyment body'. However, the ultimate basis of his Buddhahood is his 'truth body' which unites all three bodies, which is identified with ultimate reality. It appears to imply that the historic Buddha was a manifestation of the heavenly Buddha and thus we have a parallel with what Christianity believes about the Word (John 1:1f) which became incarnate in Jesus Christ.[17]

There is also the compassionate Bodhisattva whom we have mentioned, whose desire is to lead others to the enlightenment which he possesses. Unlike the *arhat*, worthy person, who some say seeks nirvana for himself or herself, the Bodhisattva reaches out to help others. It does seem to be contradictory to think that the *arhat* is selfish since enlightenment is the realization that there is no ego. However, the concept of Bodhisattva is a broader concept embracing both monks and lay persons motivated by the desire to communicate enlightenment to all. When the conditions are right and there is the aspiration, Bodhisattva vows are taken and the path of the six Perfections is followed: generosity, morality, patience, energy, meditation and wisdom. These lead to nirvana. The distinguishing marks are compassion and wisdom.

There are heavenly Bodhisattvas: Avalokitesvara, though male, is usually depicted in female form in China and Japan and is the Lord who looks down with compassion. Tara is female and is popular in Tibet. Wisdom is represented in a third Bodhisattva who is called Manjushri. Offerings and devotion are given to them.[18]

There are various schools of philosophy: the Yogacara, who

were idealists, teaching that mind is what exists not the external world, and Madhyamika, which revelled in showing that there is a self-contradiction inherent in any fixed view of reality. It was stressed that words only pointed to the truth but did not express the highest reality which was an experience. Madhyamika is interesting because of their development of *shunya*, meaning empty. Everything is empty because it arises from conditions and we understand one empty thing by another. To be empty is to know that there is no self or permanent nature. Everything changes so there cannot be a permanent essence in anything, even the teachings of the Buddha! This, as might be imagined, has caused a great deal of debate.

Despite the varied nature of Mahayana, both in doctrinal and philosophical ideas, it prospered and became the state religion in Japan and was only removed from the position when Shinto, a form of ancestor and nature worship, was re-established in 1860. Buddhists spread their faith usually by peaceful means, but some Japanese groups were militant and developed power and wealth. In general, benevolence and compassion were prominent and meditation continued with stress on yoga and Zen, which looked for an inner enlightenment without reliance on external authority or scripture or religious rituals or the supernatural. Side by side with it was the devotional current with its worship of the godlike Buddhas that reached its fullest development in Japan.

In Tibet, Vajrayana, Thunderbolt or Diamond or Tantra Buddhism used meditation, ritual dancing, incense, music, hand movements and prayer mills, and developed the worship of many gods and goddesses. In some cases Bodhisattvas became more important than the Buddha. During the long tradition of Buddhism in Tibet, monks were rulers up to 1951. Sexual activity, as long as it was not lustful, was useful for spiritual fulfilment, with the union symbolizing the coming together of the human and the divine. Tantric practices moved away from despising the body and believed that only the improper use of pleasure was wrong. The tantras texts are difficult and must be carefully interpreted if they are not to be misconstrued. But it is a new body of literature for the elite, not linked with the historical Buddha but originating from some mythical Buddha of the past.[19]

Buddhism takes into account the changing environment, and 'skill in means' is used to make Buddhism relevant to the hearer. A more flexible attitude to the precepts of the Buddha is seen in not telling the truth in an awkward situation: a father may have to tell his child a lie to get him/her out of a burning house, or in a country where only meat is eaten, a monk for whom this diet is forbidden may eat it in order to win people to the faith. Vajrayana does encourage practices that violate the usual precepts. Killing is possible to prevent someone committing actions that would send him to hell, stealing to stop another stealing, adultery to provide better rebirths for the recently deceased, and so on. Vajrayana was influenced by Nagarjuna, founder of the Madhyamika philosophy, and Asanga, founder of the Yogacarin school. Some think that these developments were an excuse for immorality, but others maintain that they were a sincere experiment.[20]

In Tibet the Dalai Lama is the head of the most famous Tibetan school, the Gelugpa or Yellow Hat school.[21] It is a reformed Tantrism and differs from the Red Hats who produced the Book of the Dead. In 1969 Communist China invaded the country and within days of the departure of the Dalai Lama the Chinese bombarded his palaces and the government of which he was the head was dissolved. In the years that followed, about 90 per cent of the monasteries were destroyed and thousands of Tibetans followed the Dalai Lama into exile in India where under his leadership Buddhism flourished again with the building of monasteries, libraries and medical institutes. The exiles raised cattle, cleared the forest land and wove carpets for export. The Dalai Lama travelled widely in the world, preaching peace and brotherhood and arguing that religions were not meant to compete with one another but to enrich human experience and bring peace. In Tibet itself communism is now showing a more human face and exiles are welcome to return, including the Dalai Lama who was awarded the Nobel Peace Prize in 1989. But the Chinese, while allowing him a visit, would not agree to his settling there because Tibetan religion and politics had been so interwoven with state affairs.

In general we may say that Buddhism worked actively with

the state and in certain countries did become the state religion. But the influence of politics on the religion and the ready acceptance by Buddhists of other religious rituals and practices moved it away from many of the original insights of its founder. The result of communism has been the extinction of the faith in Outer Mongolia, the destruction of monasteries in China with monks called upon to work for the state, the dismantling in Tibet, and much loss in Burma and Thailand. The bombing of Buddhist strongholds in Korea, Vietnam, Laos and Cambodia by the Americans also damaged the faith. But in Japan, Zen, and Soka Gakkai have flourished. And Buddhism has revitalized itself in its continued spread to Western countries. All the divisions hold the three jewels: the Buddha, the dhamma and the sangha.

In Sikhism there have been a number of power struggles, usually over the control of the *gurdwara* or temple. But fortunately, Nanak named Angad as successor before his death in 1539. His spirit, it is said, passed to Angad and to the later Gurus. He was a pious man whose poetry is included in the scripture and during his time Kartarpur, which had been the centre of the faith, was replaced by Khadur. A succession of Gurus followed – Amar Das, who condemned *suttee*, advocated monogamy and widow remarriage. Ram Das came next and developed a settlement, later to be called Amritsar, which came to be famous in the faith. The next Guru, Arjan Dev, was a good poet, faced opposition from his own family but overcame it and composed an anthology. He incurred the wrath of the emperor, Jahangir, and was tortured to death, becoming the first Sikh martyr.[22]

Har Gobind followed and he replaced non-violence with active armed resistance and constructed the Akal Takht, the seat of Sikh authority. He was imprisoned, but on release secured the setting free of other prisoners and travelled back to Amritsar at the time of the Hindu festival Divali which became special also to the Sikhs. Har Rai, gentle by nature, succeeded him and he was followed by Har Krishen, who was only five years of age. But dispute erupted with other members of the family who had been passed over in the succession. Har Krishen behaved wisely, was deeply spiritual, and died helping people suffering from smallpox. His successor, Teg Bahadur, was also devotional but experienced the opposition of the Muslim emperor and was executed in 1675.

Guru Gobind Singh, the final Guru, composed the Dasam Granth, refused any aspiration to be considered divine, accepted the use of the sword in the interests of self-defence and justice, founded the Khalsa, and engaged in battle with the Mughals. He died on 7 October 1708. His founding of the Khalsa set aside caste, giving everyone including women equal rights, and he declared that the Guru henceforth would be the Granth Sahib. The authority would rest on it, and the Panth or community. It was thought that the physical presence of the Guru was no longer necessary but could be mystically present when a group of faithful devotees gathered to sing the hymns of Nanak, and that any decisions reached at these communal meetings, provided they were made in the presence of the sacred scriptures, would be acclaimed the will of the Guru. These assemblies became known as the Guru Panth. In due course a Sikh kingdom was established by Maharaja Ranjit Singh.[23]

However, groups have arisen due to tension between the nature of Sikhism in its original form and the development of a warlike spirit which arose out of the need for the Sikhs to protect themselves. The militancy showed when the Sikhs proved themselves to be good soldiers in the British army. But it is difficult to reconcile the trend with a peaceful founder, who spoke about the delusion of worldly values and the need for a quiet and patient meditation upon the Name of God. Perhaps it was due to the Jats who were very warlike and who soon came into conflict with the Mughal administration in the seventeenth century. The brotherhood of the Khalsa, with its 'Five Ks', suited the martial Jats, but there is a group of Sikhs who do not belong to the Brotherhood and try to follow the peaceful way of Guru Nanak. They are the Sahajdhari, who continue as if the changes which took place in the seventeenth and eighteenth centuries had not occurred. It is impossible to determine their number and they do not have the stability of the main body under the Khalsa code.

Then there are the Namdhari, founded by Baba Balak Singh (1797–1862), who believe in the tradition of the living Guru and were not happy with the replacement by the Adi Granth.

Some of them became political and were involved in the struggle for independence against the British. Another group is the Nirankari, founded by Baba Dyal Das (1783–1854), who seek to counter ritualism with an insistence on conduct. The opposition to the place given to the scriptures is seen in the Radhasomi movement, founded by Baba Shiv Dyal (1818–1878). They do not install the Adi Granth in their *gurdwara*, oppose caste, and attract many untouchables.[24] The vegetarian lifestyle is acceptable to them, and they do not distribute *karah-parshad* at the conclusion of their services or remove their shoes or wear a headdress. During the movement's second generation the two disciples of Shiv Dyal organized separate branches, one of which was on the banks of the Beas river in the Amritsar District. It was led by Jaimal Singh, a Jat, and when he died in 1903 he was succeeded by Sawan Singh. A line of Gurus had been established.

There are other Sikh sects in North America but the unorthodox practices and beliefs of the Namdhari and the Nirankar, later known as the Universal Brotherhood, led to violent confrontation. Both groups had amended the Ardas, the prayer commemorating Sikh martyrs, and the Nirankaris replaced God's divine titles with their own name. They wore Sikh dress but ignored the Khalsa code. As we noted, in 1978 Sant Jarnail Singh Bhindranwale embarked upon a campaign of armed violence. It was against the Nirankari. There was much unrest which included the assassination of the Indian prime minister Indira Gandhi by her Sikh bodyguard and the resultant backlash claimed the lives of 3000 Sikhs.

It is estimated that there are eighteen million Sikhs, many of whom are farmers, but there are many soldiers, artisans, carpenters, and metal workers and mechanics in industry and the the fine arts. Many educated Sikhs are in the professions.

In conclusion we have seen that the problem of who is to succeed the founder of a religion often leads to major disruption, as in Islam. Sikhism avoided this because Nanak named his successor, but it raises the question of whether spirituality can be passed on. According to the view of Max Weber (1864–1920) about charisma, Nanak would qualify as a charismatic leader whose teaching and personality attracted the people, but he did not think that such charisma could be passed on. Sikhism asserts that it was also seen in their Gurus, but they have sometimes displayed a spirit which would have been alien to Nanak. The criticism could also be applied to Christianity with its doctrine of apostolic succession. As successor to St Peter, the Pope is believed by Roman Catholics to be the vicar of Christ on earth, but some have engaged in wars and lived in a style contrary to the teaching of the faith.

Nanak, as we noted, called for the abolition of religion in the sense that he opposed pilgrimages, ritual bathing and the giving of alms, and saw holy persons as being spiritual and not practising rituals. He attacked images that portrayed the bodily parts of God and incense, etc. Religion for him was the direct vision of God, the ecstasy of being caught up into spiritual contact with the divine. It was a personal experience of God and he dismissed the trappings of religion which kept Muslims and Hindus apart. There would seem to be some parallel with Dietrich Bonhoeffer and his 'religionless' Christianity. But a faith needs an organization even though it may contain elements that do not reflect what the founder did and said.

In the light of this discussion concerning divisions within religions, it seems unlikely that religions could be united, but this question is worth discussion in the next chapter.

9   Why can religions not unite?

If religions point to the same God under different names, why can they not get together? Does the disunity arise because of the variety of beliefs, practices and cultural differences, or are there other reasons?

In the preceding chapters it is clear that religions do differ internally and it extends to differences with other faiths. There are differences in various ways: Jewish males cover their heads, Christians do not; Sikhs refuse a haircut, Buddhists shave their heads; some have women ministers, others not; some offer the deity flowers, incense, fruits, others sacrifice animals; some worship standing, some sit; some are silent, others dance and sing; some see the world permeated by the sacred, others separate the secular from it; some are theistic, others not; some believe in reincarnation, others not; some hold a creator, others not; some have a saviour, others rely on self-help.

But there are similarities. The grace of God is offered in Mahayana Buddhism, Sikhism and Christianity, mysticism is widespread with a love of God and the neighbour, and in most there is monotheism and a desire to change the world. The incarnation doctrine of Christianity is unacceptable to Jews and Muslims, but it does not perturb the Hindus for they have the concept of avatars. The Christian doctrine of the Trinity has a certain similarity with the Hindu triad, Brahma, Vishnu and Shiva, and in Mahayana Buddhism there are the three manifestations of the Buddha as dhammakaya (eternal teaching), nirmanakaya (historical Buddha) and sambhogakaya (transcendental Buddha). The Christians, however, believe that in Christ there is a unique incarnation and there are three eternal entities in the Godhead which goes beyond the conception of other religions, but they do not find it easy to explain the doctrine.

Sikhs deny incarnation and any threefoldness in the Godhead. The Muslims accept both the Torah and the Gospels and number the Jewish prophets and Jesus among their holy men, but it is asserted that the Qur'an completes and corrects other scriptures. Muslims do not refer to Allah as Father, for they believe that they are His servants not His offspring, and to contend that Jesus is the Son of God is blasphemy. Strangely, having said that, Muslims accept what some liberal Christian theologians deny, the virgin birth of Christ, and consider Mary his mother to be one of the three holy women of Islam, the others being Khadijah, wife of the Prophet, and Fatimah, his daughter. Furthermore, for them Jesus is the Messiah of the Jews, something which Judaism denies. But Muslims argue that Jesus did not die on the cross, being rescued by his disciples and eventually ending his life peacefully in India.

The Jew is not a missionary for he believes that there are many ways to God, but there have been converts over the years. Christianity has always been missionary-minded and it created tension with the other faiths, but in the nineteenth century some Christian missionaries were affected by the vitality and spirituality of the Hindus, Africans, etc. Some religions were classed as primitive, but others, like Hinduism, were recognized as complex. There were tensions between the missionaries and British rule in India because of their calling for conversions, and the government went as far as blaming the missionaries for the Indian mutiny. But it was difficult for a Hindu to convert to Christianity since it meant that he would be disowned by parents and friends.[1]

In Britain the loss of belief in the doctrines of Christianity encouraged learning about other faiths. Some Christians saw shadows and images of Christ in other religions and used the concept of logos, the word of God, as present in all faiths. Others contended that all religions contain a common truth and developed the evolutionary approach to religion. Religions should be studied objectively and attempts at conversion should be stopped. Liberal Christians saw religion as stemming from human emotion and reason rather than revelation, and called for a revision of Christian doctrine.[2]

At the end of the nineteenth century there was a variety of attitudes. The interest in the academic study of religion continued but it failed to change the attitude of church members. In general, people resisted any attempt to convince them that they should seek to understand the culture and faith of 'foreigners' because of imperial attitudes and the continued belief that Christianity was the superior religion. Free thinkers, who were largely agnostics or atheists, did not agree and cynically dismissed all religions as having failed to bring peace to the world.

In this present century there are three approaches: exclusivist, one religion is best or the truest; inclusivist, salvation in all religions but needing fulfilment in Christ; and pluralism, all religions are valid and none superior to another. There are variations on these. Many liberal Christian theologians assert that Christianity is one way of salvation among others and the traditional doctrine of incarnation is an obstacle to a global faith and must be reformulated. They think of God as being at the centre of a circle with all the religions on the circumference, pointing to Him. The incarnation of Christ should be understood mythically, meaning devotion and commitment to Him. Hence there is no ontological claim that God has revealed Himself uniquely in Him. All religions have their saints so religion is reduced to morality, and salvation is from self-orientation to God-centredness.

There has been a lot of criticism of the above proposal which was put forward by John Hick. We have raised questions about myth, incarnation and pluralism elsewhere, but for our present purposes it is significant to note that some of the critics assert that Hick and other writers make the assumption that there is an essence of religion which is the common characteristic of all religions. If this is so it undermines their proposal, for it is generally accepted that though religions have the characteristics of religion, there is no common essence. Some of Ninian Smart's dimensions may be missing, but if a faith has a spirit of reverence, morality, rituals and beliefs, then we are entitled to think of it as a religion, for example Buddhism.[3]

One can enter into dialogue with other faiths without relativism by simply believing that there is more to truth and wisdom than one's own tradition, which is far from thinking that one has the absolute truth. The one absolute is God, according to our investigation of the faiths, and what is common to the religions is that we cannot describe adequately or fully what He is like for we see 'through a glass darkly' (1 Cor. 13:12).

Apart from the mythical view of Christ and the relativizing of Christian claims about him, there are also those who embrace a Spirit Christology where Christ is so filled with the Spirit of God that he can be regarded as unique. The uniqueness, however, is one of degree, not that of kind which historically emerged in the Chalcedon formula (451 CE). Christ was both human and divine, though the human mind did not have full access to the divine. The Catholic Church and other Churches hold on to the tradition and have been influenced by Karl Rahner, who contended that God had revealed Himself to all people so they are 'anonymous Christians'. The salvific grace is conveyed without a confrontation with Christ. It was the case with Israel before Christ appeared in the flesh and other religions have provisional revelations which mediate such grace. The approach has a resemblance to the logos doctrine mentioned above.

Islam has a final revelation – Muhammad – and is not likely to accept that it is provisional! Historically, Islam has not got on well with either Jew or Christian. The Jews opposed Muhammad and he confiscated their property in Khalibar, which is not far from Medina, and he was quite prepared to kill those who stood in his way. But Islam insists that it has never forced conquered people to convert, and it can coexist with other faiths. In particular those who possess the scriptures are asked only to pay tribute.[4] Today the tension in the Middle East continues, with Muslims accusing Israel of being favoured by America which rushes to their defence when problems with the Arabs or Saddam Hussein arise. But Israel replies that they are only defending themselves and point out that liberal Jews are willing to surrender land to the Palestinians if Israel's security is not threatened.[5]

There are some signs in Islam of the recognition of pluralism and that there are various paths to God. Michael Cook points to one thinker, 'Abd al-Karim Surush, who, though he works in Iran, acknowledges that the Qur'an speaks of 'a straight path' (Islam) but not 'the straight path'. If this is the case then liberals in Islam could engage in dialogue with other faiths without seeing their religion as superior.[6]

Conversations between Jews and Christians started with the founding of the Council of Christians and Jews in Britain in 1942. The Christians have expressed regret for their attitude to the Jews over the years and shown that the tragedy of the Shoah (Holocaust) has had a big impact upon them. The World Council of Churches (WCC) in their discussions acknowledge that Christian opposition to the Jews played a part in laying the foundation for Nazi persecution, but it insists that Christianity never officially backed the genocide of the Jews. In 1965 the Catholic Church and other Churches rejected the view that the Jews had killed God in the death of Jesus and pointed out that trying to convert the Jews undermines trust between the faiths.[7] Jews are attached to their land which identifies them and is essential to their survival, but Christians focus on the heavenly Jerusalem.

In a review of Jewish–Christian relations over the years, Jewish participants in the dialogue point out that Jesus was a Jew but he was not their Messiah as he failed to set up the kingdom and deliver them from their enemies. The Christian scriptures are anti-Semitic, stating that the Jews had killed Christ (Matt. 27:25; Acts 2:36; 1 Thess. 2:15–16), and the charge of deicide was levelled at them in the second century. Subsequently, any disaster that occurred was blamed on the Jews. They were depraved, conspiring to take over the world, harder to convert than the devil, and parasites, yet Christian scripture admits that God has not rejected them (Rom. 9–11). Forced conversion to Christianity continued until the Council of Nicaea in 787 CE allowed Jews to practise their own religion. After the foundation of the state of Israel in 1948 the Church renounced the teaching that God had rejected the Jews and was willing to trust and cooperate with them.[8] The experience of the Holocaust convinced the Jews that they must make every effort to survive so that Hitler will not have a posthumous victory. The basic question that arises out of the

Shoah is: Where was humanity and where was the Church? Could it happen again? Jews and Christians share such fear in the light of anti-Jewish propaganda, the rise of neo-Nazi groups, and historians who deny that it happened.

The Jews were to be a light to the Gentiles (Isa. 42) and they were missionary-minded, but now believe that attempts to convert implies that other faiths are inadequate. Election by God does count in their favour and some think that the concept of a Messiah is not crucial as long as there is the presence of God. Church statements do not reject all mission to Jews but the World Council of Churches in 1988 repudiated anti-Semitism and announced the 'double covenant': Judaism and Christianity are two parallel and legitimate ways to God. For the Jews the land of Israel is very important – 'the holy land' given by God to them – but it is recognized that it is also holy for Christians and Muslims. Christians tend to be pro-Jewish or pro-Palestinian. Both religions in the dialogue plead that Arab and Jew in the conflict will listen to one another and meet to share their religious and political views. The country is the natural homeland of the Palestinians and with this in mind the Catholic Church did not recognize the state of Israel until 1933. But the fact is that 90 per cent of Jewish Israelis have never met a Christian and meetings to discuss ways forward have little effect on the rank and file. So far it has been expatriate theologians and scholars, mainly Christian, who have initiated dialogue.[9]

In these discussions the question of the status of Jesus is prominent. Jews treat him with respect and while it is recognized that his teaching has parallels in the Talmud, it is admitted that he taught directly on his own authority. He was a prophet and could be accepted as a son of God. But Jews believe that Paul created the uniqueness of Christ, developing a human messiah into a divine figure. A question that is raised many times is: How can Jesus be the Messiah when the Jews expected a warrior king? The Christian answer is that he came to create a spiritual kingdom, but Jews fail to accept this. They go on to contend that the doctrine of the Trinity did not develop until the fourth century and point out that today Christian scholars question the divinity of Christ. The Jews also argue that they did not reject Jesus but it was the High

Priest who represented Roman interests that did. He was not the supreme Jewish religious leader but only had the status of scholars like Hillel and Gamaliel. However, it is evident to all in the dialogue that Jewish scholars admit that when the myths and legends about Jesus have been removed, there still remains an irreducible reside that resists demythologizing, a certain something, which, as Martin Buber says, gives Jesus a great place in Israel's history, a place that cannot be described by any of the usual categories. In the end it shows the mystery of Jesus.[10]

Christians share with Jews persecution over the years. In the early years they were tortured, ridiculed and killed under the Roman emperors and in the twentieth century a determined atheistic drive by the Russian communists closed churches, persecuted priests, disbanded synods and removed rights of protest. The Orthodox Church lost at least 50 per cent of its churches, and other religious groups, including Buddhism, were relentlessly pursued. Some contend that the Church should have mounted active resistance rather than passive acceptance, but the Church replied that martyrdom was at the heart of its tradition. Critics have left it contending that it had compromised itself under communistic rule. Ironically, orthodoxy today has restricted the freedom of other Christian denominations including the Catholic Church.[11] Often in the history of Christianity, the persecuted, when they have overcome, become the persecutors and try to convert by force, killing heretics and censoring any kind of criticism.

Hinduism has always been regarded as tolerant. Raja Ram Mohan Roy (1772–1833) was one of the first to enter into dialogue with Christianity and thought that the moral values of Christianity would improve the social needs of India, but his movement, the Brahma Samaj, has little influence. Sri Ramakrishna (1836–1886) and Swami Vivekananda (1863–1902) produced a 'Hinduized version' of Christianity and at the Parliament of World Religion in Chicago (1893) Vivekananda extolled the virtues of holiness, purity and charity, characteristics of good people of all religions. His universalism was based on the catholicity of Hinduism, but pays eloquent tribute to Jesus Christ. The Hindu finds it difficult to think of one incarnation since he believes in many and is inclined to see divinity in all things. Mahatma Gandhi (1869–1948) hoped for reform of Hinduism and showed friendliness to Muslims and Christians. But he remained a Hindu and declared that his religion was that of humanity, 'the best of all religions known to me'.[12]

The history of interfaith dialogue has had its ups and downs. In 1995 there was a global meeting of the World Conference on Religion and Peace in Italy which degenerated into a power struggle and ended in the appointment of twenty-eight presidents of the organization. Conflict was also seen in 1993 at the Chicago Parliament of the World's Religions when disagreement became heated regarding the parliamentary procedures. More rational discussions are evident when scholars get together because competition is not so prominent. Recently the proposal has been put forward for a group of religious leaders drawn from all the faiths to give advice to the United Nations on global problems, but representation will be a problem.

Hans Küng is trying to get agreement on the basic ethical principles that all religions preach, which would assist any declaration of human rights issued by the United Nations. Attempts have also been made to engage in interfaith worship at conferences with greater success and there are interfaith chapels for non-sectarian worship at international airports. Mary Pat Fisher, who lives in India and has written about such dialogue, also draws attention to the spiritual communities in India called Gobind Sadan (the House of God). They are composed of members of the religions which we are considering. The birthdays of the prophets are celebrated and their lives and teaching emphasized in contrast to the religions institutionalized in their names. It is taught that all the prophets came from the same one light which has been given different names.[13]

These efforts are praiseworthy, particularly in India which is a secular state. Many there are questioning sterile religious dogmas and practices and asking how relevant religious values are: for example, the withdrawal of the ascetic when there is much work to be done in society. Nationalists have reinterpreted the *Bhagavad gita* as an action manual in their fight against oppression. Individualism, karma and caste are being questioned. Despite the efforts mentioned above, many do not think that Hinduism and its unification with other faiths would solve the varied economic, social, and political problems that are confronting the nation.

Despite the differences within religions, some attempt to revive the concept of logos or word used by the writer of the Fourth Gospel. The early Church called the principle 'spermaticos' which, like a seed, is and was everywhere in the world since the beginning. Revelation and salvation were always operating even before the embodiment of the logos in Jesus, so there is the universality of Christianity. Justin Martyr in the second century wrote: 'Those who live by logos are Christians even though they have been considered atheists such as among the Greeks, Socrates, Heraclitus, and others like them . . . so also those who lived before Christ and did not live by logos were useless humans, enemies of Christ and murderers of those who lived by logos.'[14]

The Sikhs refer to the word *sabad*, a form of divine self-expression which is eternal so God from the beginning revealed Himself to people before the coming of Guru Nanak. Sikhism shows the way to inclusiveness by including Hindu and Muslim writings in the Adi Granth. There is also the symbol of light found in religions which indicates a revelation of God everywhere and at all times: There is the 'light that lighteth every man that cometh into the world' (Job 19). It is the response to the light received which is crucial since Christianity has often been judged by the work of the Spirit in other religions producing people like Gandhi who have lived up to the highest ideals of the Sermon on the Mount.

But there is great benefit in understanding the beliefs, customs and culture of others, and it becomes essential in a pluralistic society and global world to educate children about these. As we know, dogs bark at strangers, and it is natural for us to view with suspicion those who differ from us. Hence conversation, working together and brotherhood must be fostered, rather than hatred and racialism. It is unlikely that doctrinal differences will be resolved even within religions, as the last chapter showed. Some scholars have tried to reduce the claims of a faith in order to make it more palatable to others but this would lead to further divisions internally. The Unitarian strain of Christianity would applaud the monotheism of

Islam and most Christians would appreciate the work of Ram Mohan Roy because he opposed polytheism and idol worship, but Trinitarians would reject any proposal based on a monotheism that did not take into account the belief that God is three in one.

The religions do place stress on ethics and beliefs for a religion will only appeal if it results in good lives. Intellectual belief in God is insufficient for according to Christian scripture even the devil believes (James 2:19). In the same Epistle religion is defined in terms of relieving the orphans and widows and not doing evil. According to Matthew's Gospel humanity will be judged not on belief but on behaviour towards the needy. Judaism, which has no official creed, would agree.

Hence more agreement might be reached in ethics, mysticism, religious experience and monasticism. Every religion has experiences of the divine in dreams, visions, imaginations, the numinous, prophetic utterances, and so on. The change that occurs is not only in external behaviour but in the inner life. The religions can contend for peace among the nations, support the fight against crime, argue for a just distribution of resources to the Third World and cancelling their debts, demand world egalitarianism and toleration, human and animal rights, and the ending of world pollution. The West can learn from the Indian religions how sacred nature is. The religions in dialogue can deplore their history of conflict with one another and pledge that it will cease in the future. They can take encouragement from a history that shows that religion has contributed much to the world: Islam brought learning to the Mediterranean area, Buddhism contributed art and architecture to China, and medicine, education, famine relief and more to Japan. Hinduism and Christianity brought literature and learning to their specific spheres of operation. The objective of the dialogue is not to find a common essence of religion upon which all would agree, but fellowship and the planning of the contribution that they might make in a troubled world.

Each faith has something distinctive to offer and every person has the right to look at the religions which emerged and make their choice. No-one is prevented from arguing the case that his or her faith is best, but the arguments must be coherent and rational. All religions make absolute claims, it is one thing that they have in common! None is likely to retract their claims for the sake of a quick reconciliation, but reformulation could take place as the dialogue proceeds. Understanding can be expanded but it must be done in openness and affection. Dialogue explores common ground, keeps the conversation going, and shows the participants that their faith has limitations. It may even lead to a transformation of what one believes and an inducing of humility because there is the realization that we are dealing with an ultimate Reality that surpasses all that we can think and say.

In the following chapters we consider the impact of science on religion and how the latter has reacted and modified some of its beliefs as a result.

10 Confessing a murder

Science in the developed world controls and guides most of what we think and do. When a crisis hits the nation it is to the scientists that governments turn, believing that they will be presented with the facts and the remedy in a way that religion cannot do. One of the reasons is the tremendous advance of science in the centuries preceding our own and the development of technology as a result of its research. Religion has to take into account what science is saying about the creation of the world and mankind because its assumptions about these crucial matters have been challenged in the past and continue to be today. In the next chapters we will see some of the implications of scientific research for what we are and what we could become, but in this one we want to understand how scientific knowledge replaced religion in understanding how the human race originated and developed. Religion permeated every aspect of life in nineteenth-century England, so the impact of Charles Darwin's work was devastating on a society which prided itself in being superior in every way to the animal kingdom. We need to discover how this happened.

There was a measure of accord between science and religion prior to the nineteenth century. Newton was a Christian and the clergy were involved in science. God was the grand designer who had made the world and humans according to a purpose. Though there had been trouble with Galileo, he held firmly to the revelation of God in the book of nature and the book of God. It was Darwin who 'set the cat among the pigeons' with his evolutionary theory about the origins of life, the status of mankind, and relation to God. His theory of natural selection explained the development of life forms in a mechanistic and naturalistic way without the need for supernatural intervention. A year after the voyage on the *Beagle* he wrote: 'I am almost convinced (quite contrary to the opinion I started with) that species are not (it is like confession to a murder) immutable.'[1]

He had intended entering the Church but gladly accepted an offer to travel round the world to observe and collect plants, birds, animals and fossils. At this stage of his life he was religious, reading the Gospels and thinking about religion, much to the amusement of the crew of the ship. But gradually he began to criticize the Bible because he thought its history was false and its picture of God tyrannical.[2] Darwin interprets the accounts literally, which was odd since he had studied theology and must have been told that the scriptures were full of allegory, myth, metaphor and symbol. He had a poor view of the natives in the lands that he visited and he regarded the Fugians in particular as miserable barbarians who could not be changed by civilization. But he praised the missionaries who tried to introduce them to the ethics of Christianity.

He observed variation among the species and the struggle to survive and saw that some variations were more advantageous than others and helped them to reproduce. He realized that most properties of a species were inherited, being passed on from generation to generation. Hence species modify towards these favourable characteristics that would enable them to survive and reproduce. Nature would select those with the best characteristics and new species would emerge. Evolution would be a slow process instead of the instant creation mentioned in Genesis and species would change. Humans were part of the animal kingdom, not being distinctive because of a soul or in the image of God. Mind itself evolved. The whole process was random and due to chance and appeared wasteful and cruel. How could it reflect the purpose of a good God? Those who successfully adapted to the environment would survive and variation and natural selection replaced any divine design.

Darwin had been influenced by the Reverend Thomas Malthus and his *Essay on the Principles of Population* (1798), which dealt with how populations increased if unchecked by

early death rate, disease, war, lack of food resources and contraception. Being a cleric he could not advocate the latter. It
was during the casual reading of Malthus that Darwin got the
idea of natural selection and that those who survived would be
the best adapted to nature's demands. While breeders of horses
or greyhounds would knowingly select to improve them, there
was no need for nature to 'know' which variations are best to
make selection work. A bird with a longer beak means more
food so it is more likely to survive and pass on the tendency to
the next generation. The inheritance of characteristics which
enable animals to adapt to the environment plus blind chance
explains evolution by natural selection. Darwin's book, *The
Origin of Species* (1859), was an instant success and sold out
on the first day of publication.

Darwin spent a lot of time with breeders of birds and mar-
velled at the way they could be changed by selective breeding.
Nature which replaces God in his scheme would, over a vast
period of time, create a new species. He knew that the fossil
record was incomplete but there were signs of the process
occurring, such as a reptile becoming a bird, and there are
organs in species which resemble one another: the embryos of
mammals, birds, lizards and snakes in their early stages are
very similar. 'Fittest' does not mean strongest, but ability to
breed and the traits that led to reproductive success will
increase in frequency from one generation to the next and will
remain in a population.

But how do we define a species? One definition is that a
species is a group of actual or potentially interbreeding populations that are reproductively isolated from other such
groups. Darwin's finches are an example, but another would
be the squirrels in the Grand Canyon. They live on opposite
sides of the Canyon, having divided as the great chasm
developed. Following their own evolution they are now quite
different and unable to interbreed. Different environments
cause populations to diverge, but species can become more
alike so there is also convergent evolution. If the environment
does not change the species remains the same: the Lingula has
survived unchanged for 500 million years so the theologian
who denies that species change can find some comfort here!
The eye which had been accepted by Newton as showing the

design of God was seen by Darwin as developing by gradations. In brief, the survival of the fittest in a context where more organisms are produced than can survive, inheritance and the ability to adapt, plus variations which confer an advantage, lead to a new species. The modern emphasis is more on reproduction than in Darwin who tended to see 'fitness' as some feature possessed by an organism which enable it to adapt and increase survival chances; for example, birds possessing wings.

At one stroke Darwin had challenged religious beliefs about the authority of the Bible with its doctrine of creation by God, the dignity of mankind which had been made in His image, the Fall into sin, and a world made by a designer. If there was no Fall of mankind then human nature could be regarded as good and moving upward both physically and morally. Original sin could be dismissed. The theological response assumed a variety of forms. Some theologians replied that the Bible must be accepted literally, thus setting up a conflict, but others insisted that historical and literary criticism had shown that the creation narrative could be interpreted in a non-literal way. After all, *Essays and Reviews*, which contained the writings of Anglicans, interpreted the creation stories in a poetic and symbolic way and it had been published a year before the *Origin*. It might be that evolution was God's way of creation.

Darwin had mentioned God as creator at the end of the *Origin* but in his *Descent of Man* (1871) He is left out. Darwin insisted that brain and mind gradually evolved and moral qualities were derived through natural selection from lower forms. On a visit to the zoo in London he had been impressed with the behaviour of Jenny the orang-utan with her intelligence, affection, passion, rage and sulkiness. Comparing her with the savage who roasted his parents and was naked and artless, he pointed out that Jenny did not suffer by comparison! Yet he did admit that there was an immense difference between the mind of the lowest man and that of the highest animal, since the latter could not reason or reflect on life and did not have the language which has enabled humanity to make such striking progress. Basically he was arguing that while there is a difference between us and the animals it was a matter of degree, not a unique one of kind due to a creator.

With regard to design that would reflect a designer, Darwin explained apparent design by arguing that adaptation did not mean purpose but was a response to the environment. The chance variations enable life to survive in a hostile context so that birds evolved wings which gave them a decisive advantage. He contended that birds did not evolve wings in order to fly, which could be seen as purposive, but by enabling them to fly the wings were a major contribution to survival. Yet he said that he could not believe that the universe was the result of blind chance and thought that design could apply to the whole process rather than the details. Why should God interfere with nature every time a new species was created? It is better to think of God as the framer of the laws of evolution. At least that was his opinion up to 1850, but he fluctuated throughout his life with regard to his beliefs. His problem was that if God determines all things then He would be responsible for bad variations as well as good ones. He could not think of God being good if He had designed a nature 'red in tooth and claw'.[3]

But theologians were inclined to fasten on the laws of the universe and see design in them through which life emerged. Design was overall rather than specific, with the Creator building it into the structure of the process. T. H. Huxley, 'Darwin's bulldog', admitted that the Darwinian view had to assume an initial molecular arrangement in order for things on earth to evolve and that means that the biologist is always at the mercy of the theist who asks him to disprove that such an arrangement was not intended. The design argument for the existence of God returns in this shape as we will see in the next chapter.

Darwin taught that all living things are descended from one form which shows how closely related we are to the animal kingdom. The reaction of many Victorians was to hope that the theory was not true but if it was that it would not become widely known! They found some comfort in Darwin's contemporary, A. R. Wallace, who arrived at the theory of evolution at the same time as Darwin. Wallace disagreed with Darwin. Unlike him he had been poor and had no university education. In his travels he was impressed with the natives because they were obedient, had an affection for children, did not quarrel, and were hard-working. Education, he thought, would benefit them and they could be civilized. They had good qualities, better in many ways than the civilized nations but Darwin got the opposite impression and thought that they might fill the gap between humans and animals.

Wallace pointed out that they had the same kind of brain as civilized people and they had language which is a distinctively human characteristic and differs vastly from animal signs. Natural selection could not account for higher mental faculties or artistic or ethical or musical capacities. Some higher agency had come into play to develop the higher intellectual and spiritual nature of mankind so he saw a difference in kind rather than degree between humanity and the animals. There was divine direction in the progress to the human.[4] Wallace was pessimistic about the moral progress of humanity and Thomas Huxley agreed that ethical standards could not be derived from the struggle in evolution but by combating it. We have concern for the weak, so Huxley repudiated 'the gladiatorial theory of existence'. As far as he was concerned science had no objection to a theology which insisted that God had set the progress going. But this cannot be sufficient for a theology which postulates not only a God who transcends the process but is involved in it. Otherwise we have deism, belief in the existence of God but not in revealed religion or personal providence. This kind of theology was widespread in England in the seventeenth and eighteenth centuries before Darwin came on the scene.

Christianity found itself fighting on two fronts. There was the external attack of science with the theory of evolution but also the internal assault on the authority of scripture in *Essays and Reviews*. The *Essays* interpreted scripture in a non-literalistic way and accepted the findings of geology regarding the age of the earth. Darwin needed this in order for the process of evolution to reach the human. But it opposed any calculation like that of Bishop Ussher who arrived at the conclusion that the earth was only a few thousand years old. The writers go on to argue that revelation should not be restricted to Christianity and its relation to reason should be examined. Blind faith is not acceptable. It is evident that nature can evolve, and the miraculous cannot be taken for granted. With regard to the Bible it must not be regarded as so special that higher criticism is ruled out and it must be interpreted like any other book. The writers generally equate religion with feeling and experience. Bishop Wilberforce, however, took a more orthodox stance and led the defence against evolution in debate with Huxley at Oxford. Details of it are well known and we need not go into them but the conclusion was that Huxley got the better of the encounter.

The Essayists were attacked not only by orthodox Christians but by Agnostics who said that they were presenting a view that was not Christian and they ought to resign from the Church. Other critics were more moderate, seeing value in the *Essays* as representing a modern understanding of the faith.[5] Darwin said that he did appreciate such writing which insisted that the Bible contained revelation or witnessed to it rather than being equated with it.

Religion pervaded the whole of life in the Victorian age and any factor that questioned its authority was viewed with dismay. Darwin continuing to say that he thought he was committing a murder for his work affected the central doctrines of Christianity. Asa Gray (1819–75), the American biologist, reasoned with him, arguing for design to be applied to the total process and Revd Charles Kingsley impressed Darwin with his argument that God could have created animal forms capable of self-development rather than divine intervention to create distinct species. With Kingsley's permission, Darwin included it in the preface to the second edition of *The Origin of Species*. It was this method of creation with God designing things to make themselves that has continued to appeal in later thinking about the problem.[6]

The Church did point out what they saw as deficiencies in the theory of evolution: that the earth was not old enough; there was a lack of fossil evidence; how could such slow stages lead to the wonderfully designed things that we see around, and so on. The first has now been resolved with the earth viewed as much older than in Darwin's day and neo-Darwinians argue that we would find the fossils if we could locate the right place! The debate about the mechanism, slow or fast, is still going on but the theory itself is not denied. It is evolution by natural selection that is debated, not evolution. There may be other additional mechanisms that needed to come into play to lead to humanity. Gradually the Church came to accept the theory, with a group of Anglo-Catholics publishing *Lux mundi* (Light of the Earth) and trying to accommodate Christian doctrine to the new dynamic view of nature. With many, the authority moved from scripture and reason to religious experience. Friedrich Schleiermacher equated it with a feeling of absolute dependence, a sense of finitude before the infinite. The Bible records the religious experience of Israel, Christ and the early Church and such feelings can be experienced by all. Immanuel Kant was not impressed and jested that if religion is a feeling of absolute dependence then Schleiermacher's dog would be more religious than he since it was more dependent! For him religion equated with practical reason based on conscience and judgements of value. But his view separated religion and science into the subjective and objective.[7]

In the nineteenth century there were many freethinkers and scientists who contended that science would explain everything and generate progress while preventing the retarding effect of religion. Science was the high priest of the future. One of them, W. K. Clifford, professor of mathematics at London University, denied the separate existence of a mind or soul for which immortality might be claimed and contended that morality was due not to any divinely imparted conscience but to the social instincts bred in mankind. Another, Professor J. Tyndall, declared to the British Association for the Advancement of Science in 1874 that science would wrestle from theology 'the entire domain of cosmological theory' and all schemes and systems which seek to infringe upon science or control it must not only be stopped but realize that science controls them.[8] In other words, areas that once were considered the province of theology were now open to science which had the last word. It would include the mind or soul, the creation of the earth, and the origin of life.

Herbert Spencer sounded the optimistic note predicting that humanity would move upwards morally and let 'the ape and tiger die'. Evil was an evolutionary hangover that would disappear. Neither Darwin nor Huxley shared his optimism. The fact is that scientific progress does not guarantee the moral, as the twentieth century demonstrated. The countless millions who experienced how inhuman those who participated in two world wars could be, find it difficult to believe that some nineteenth-century scientists could have been so dogmatic and optimistic. It is a cautionary word to those biologists of today who extend their scientific views into an overall world perspective.

But some more religiously inclined commentators of the century thought that science would serve religion so the master idea was on both sides of the divide. What is clear is that a different way of looking at humanity had emerged and the scriptures were seen in a more metaphorical and mythical way. It now became clear that the biblical writers had a pre-scientific view of the world and that different writers were involved in writing both the Hebrew and Christian scriptures. But Catholicism condemned the theory of evolution and did not take a more positive view until the twentieth century.

Hinduism would not have been so worried as Christianity in this new context for it pays little attention to history, has a closer link between the animal kingdom and humanity, and the concept of the universe is much larger than the traditional Hebrew/Christian view. Both Hinduism and Buddhism see time as infinite and divided into moving *kalpas* or ages, and believe there are many universes.

Certain problems remain. We are basically interested in surviving but we have mental and spiritual powers that are not necessary to survive. Can these simply be regarded as a by-product of the struggle because we have more than what is needed? Does continuing creation embraced by nineteenth-century theologians replace instant creation or can both be held? How is altruism in nature and mankind to be explained? Can we accept the view that God has given to the world and humanity the capacity to make themselves and does not interfere because of a respect for our freedom? Can a case be made for a real distinction between the human and the animal kingdom? Are religion and science not seeking to answer different questions? Science is concerned with how things have developed but religion asks 'Why?' The latter is more concerned with meaning and purpose.

Darwin described evolution as random and a matter of chance but theologians asked why God would not work in this way. After all, Darwin could not give any satisfactory answer regarding variations with simple statements about 'chance' and 'accidents'. Biology cannot be divorced from physics and we will see that physicists are impressed by the order, fine-tuning and mathematical elegance of the universe which reflects design. The biologist focuses on waste, random change and violent suffering in the story of evolution. But some physicists do speak of the world as 'an accident' or in the well-known words of Bertrand Russell, 'an accidental collocation of atoms'.

With regard to Darwin's personal views of religion he moved from the belief that the Creator had impressed laws on matter to a gradual loss of faith and ended his life as an agnostic. He did not deny the existence of God.[9] After Darwin, theologians, apart from those who are now designated as creationists, were willing to accept that evolution was the method of creation but that God was still the designer of the whole process. There is order and intelligibility in nature and creativity and contingency which are not dependent on seeing God in particular gaps in the scientific account. Darwin did say that natural selection is one explanation of the evolution of conscious, rational beings but not the only one, which allows the theist to speculate on the role of God in the process.[10] He could use natural causes to perform His purposes in the world.

Darwin did not know much about inheritance, not being aware of the work of the monk Gregor Mendel who was experimenting with peas about the same time as Darwin published his *Origin*. The work of Mendel enabled genetics to test the inheritance of variations so that evolution came to be seen as a change in the frequency of genes in populations. But it was only in the twentieth century that the genetic code was understood with the identification of DNA. Genes and mutations were shown to be the reason for variations. Mutations can be harmful but those that indicate tiny random changes in the DNA mean that one individual may have at least one characteristic which differs from that in her parents. It will be passed on and may mean an advantage in the struggle to survive. Critics argue that mutations are rare, too small to cause alterations, and are random.

There has also been the development of palaeontology, with

a rigorous study of fossils and population studies showing that a species is a group of interbreeding animals or plants within an isolation boundary. But the fossil record is imperfect, there is no smooth transition from one species to another, and the missing link between animals and humans has proved difficult to find. Different candidates have been put forward – Neanderthal, Java, Piltdown, Nebraska, Peking, Nutcracker and Lucy – without any definite proof. An attempt to answer this is punctuated equilibrium developed by Niles Eldredge and Stephen J. Gould which envisages sudden leaps in the process of evolution resulting in new life forms. Hence, the debate arose in biological circles between gradualism and the new burst of life.

Confidence was the hallmark of many scientists in the nineteenth century and some thought that they had done it all and there was nothing left to discover about the world and humanity. John D. Barrow mentions the apocryphal story of the patent office whose director made an application for his office to be closed at the end of the century because all important discoveries had been made. Somewhat ironic, considering that Einstein worked in a Swiss patent office! In the next chapter we consider if there is any evidence for the universe being designed, before going on to ask about the implications for us today of evolution and genetic engineering.

11 Is the world designed?

Science has proved to be a two-edged sword bestowing good and bad gifts. In the twentieth century it created weapons of inconceivable destructive power but advanced the understanding of the immensity of the universe with its millions of galaxies governed by mathematical laws. It promises to be able to alter the human genetic make-up, relieve diseases, and inform us about the brain and its relation to mind. For many, science has become the new saviour of mankind and presents problems for religion in at least three areas: is the world the result of an accident or designed; are we simply material beings without spiritual aspirations; and if there is a Creator how does He act in the world? In the last chapter we saw that Darwin's work challenged the concept of a designed universe but perhaps physics today can provide some evidence for it. We begin by trying to understand how it all began.

It might be useful in considering the origin of the universe to think of the questions 'When?', 'Where?', 'How?', 'Why?', 'Who?', asked about any event. The answer to 'When?' is 12,000 million years ago which will surprise anyone used to the time-scale of the Hebrew/Christian scriptures. With respect to the evolution of mankind it took place about 100,000 years ago. Hence, in order not to conflict with the scientific account, most theologians today interpret the Genesis creation stories in a non-literal way. The Big Bang, the singular event of infinite density from which the universe originated, and its development, is sometimes explained by the inflation theory but it and other theories are not certain. What needs explaining is how everything was so finely tuned for expansion. If the mass density had been greater than the critical value it would have moved to a Big Crunch, or if the mass density had been less than the critical value of gravity it would not have been able to stop the expansion. The remarkable fact is that the mass density is equal to the critical value so that it expanded just fast enough not to collapse. There was a delicate balance between the law of the fundamental forces of nature and the circumstances in which the world emerged from the Big Bang.

Science cannot explain its own laws and evolutionists simply assume right conditions for life. That there was a beginning is in agreement with the Semitic religions but there is another possibility which is consonant with the Indian viewpoint. It is possible that the Big Bang was really a Big Bounce: one of many with the universe being reprocessed in each Big Crunch and a new start made. There are multiple bangs in successive cycles. In Hinduism we have an oscillating universe with time and history regarded as cycles of creation, deterioration, destruction and recreation. Unlike the Semitic perspective, the Hindus have believed in a universe that accords with the scientific, being vast and immense. But currently science prefers a beginning and an ending since there is not enough material to bring everything back together again.[1]

The second question is 'Where did it happen?' Like most events we are inclined to answer, 'in space of course', but at the moment of the Big Bang there was no space or time. Theology was in advance of science here for St Augustine in the fourth century recognized that time was created with the universe. The third question: 'How did the universe originate?' caused conflict between science and religion. The Semitic religions and Sikhism believe in creation whereas Hinduism thinks of emanation and the Buddhist dismisses a belief in a creator. Many scientists would side with Buddhism believing that we can dispense with the theological hypothesis. Accounts of creation in the scriptures are rejected as mythical conflicting with scientific understanding. But myths convey meaning and in this case spiritual truths of a divine purpose for the universe. Theologians today argue that if we want to know how the world began then we turn to the scientific account of the Big Bang and its prediction of the Big Crunch, but if we want to know why we are here then it is the religious narrative of purpose that we consult.

But some scientists think that the universe created itself, it arose spontaneously out of nothing. If that is so there is no need of a creator for it was due to quantum fluctuations in a vacuum: a 'chance' event. But if the universe makes itself, how did it get 'the astounding capacities to transform its nothingness into something'.[2] The properties of helium, beryllium, carbon and oxygen were available but the slightest change in these would have made life impossible. Quantum physics shows that energy comes in quantum packets and deals with how matter behaves on the small scale. It is likely that this is what we were encountering at the instant of the Big Bang, for at that point the universe was an infinitesimal point and the uncertainties would have been enormous, so that starting with nothing, quantum fluctuations may have produced something. But if this was so, and it is highly debatable, quantum mechanics is governed by statistical laws. Where did they come from? The theist points to a law giver, otherwise we have no explanation. It is not sufficient to say that once there were quantum laws the universe became inevitable and try to explain everything by chance, randomness or an accident. Chance itself would allow anything to happen. The theist argues that the Spirit of God was active in creation, bringing order out of chaos.

But if there was no time, how can we speak of cause and effect? And how can we think of a creator who at some point in time decides to create the world? Stephen Hawking refers to the universe as self-contained, having no boundary or edge without beginning or end, so there is no need for a creator. But he rests his argument on imaginary time, a mathematical concept, which is divorced from the time we experience. In the latter, real time, the universe would have a beginning and an end and there would be a creator. He said: 'All that my work has shown is that you don't have to say that the way the universe began was the personal whim of God. But you still have the question: Why does the universe bother to exist? If you like, you can define God to be the answer to that question.'[3] Most agree that Hawking is ambivalent in his answers but he is willing, unlike some scientists, to reflect about the question. Physicists prefer real time, for Hawking is verging on the Platonic idea that real time is a shadow of the original time. But language itself fails, for how can we talk of 'before' when time as we know it did not exist?

The theist argues that God is the ontological ground of the universe which does not depend on any temporal relationship. He, unlike the scientist, is concerned with the intentions of the creator: the purpose and goal of creation. Russell Stannard makes the point by a clear distinction between origins and creation. How everything started relates to origins, why is there something rather than nothing refers to the ground of all creation. For religion, then, what happened or whether there was a beginning is immaterial.[4] The world makes itself, matter being fertile, so there is no need for a creator to mould pre-existing material, and the objection that the existence of suffering shows the imperfection of creation is countered by saying that it is the cost of a universe allowed to make itself.

This position departs from the special creationist picture of God involving divine acts. It contends that the universe cannot organize itself. Objectors concentrate on it, saying that they cannot believe in a God who continually intervenes in His creation. But modern theology dispenses with continual divine intervention and has picked up the point made in the last chapter that the universe has been given the ability to organize itself into more and more complex forms. But more is needed, as we said, if we are to escape Deism, hence the theological view of providence or continuing creation by God or sustaining the universe. God has given the world and us the gift of independence.

The fourth question is concerned with 'Who?' is behind the universe. Its order and intelligibility appears to point to a Mind. Sir James Jeans referred to God as the great mathematician. Since the Hebrew/Christian tradition insists that we are made in the image of God, our minds reflect the mind of the creator. Intelligence meets intelligence as we use mathematics to analyse patterns in nature and draw a map of the world. As John Polkinghorne says: 'The reason within and the reason without fit together because they have a common origin in the reason of the creator who is the ground of all that is.'[5] But mathematics and physics are incomplete, as Kurt Gödel showed in 1930, so there is a limit to our understanding. Some mathematicians accept the Hindu belief that the world is illusory, for the beautiful world of equations which so perfectly mirrors the world is much better than the fitful, unpredictable world in which we live. The ancient Greeks did not accept knowledge gained through the senses because it was based on our world, and the philosopher Plato argued that true ideas or forms resided in the mind of God with our world containing only shadows of these. This is not acceptable today but what we might say is that the Platonic world provides the structure of the cosmos so that we are dealing with both the abstract (mathematics) and the concrete (the physical world). To accept the Platonic view, and not all mathematicians would, could mean viewing the patterns or forms as the divine design.

Stephen Hawking thinks that by studying the order in the world we can read the mind of God. He says that only a finely tuned universe is capable of producing systems of the complexity and fruitfulness which we observe and the right kind of laws are required so that change can take place. Evolution itself needs the right kind of environment if life is to emerge. Fred Hoyle commented: 'I do not believe that any scientist who examined the evidence would fail to draw the conclusion that the laws of nuclear physics have been deliberately designed.'[6] To call upon the inflation theory at this point would mean replacing one anthropic condition with another for the laws of nature would still have to take a certain form.

It is the anthropic principle (derived from the Greek word *anthropos* meaning man) which helps to bring design back into the world. It means that the possibility of life on earth depended upon a delicate balance of the basic forces of nature and on specific initial conditions. But if there were many universes, as some physicists believe, then it is more likely that by chance one would have the right conditions for life so a designer is not required. But how do we know that these universes actually exist? And would they have life? The speculation introduces a complexity to explain the universe but the scientists like a more simple solution. The idea of a designer supplies it and if design is then based on the order of the universe it is immune from Darwinian assault. The most extensive discussion of the anthropic principle has been undertaken by Frank Tipler and John Barrow who argue that the structure of the universe is such that life was always a possibility, that the strong anthropic principle cannot be disproved, and that the theory of many universes places too much stress on accident.[7] The principle does not give us proof of the existence of a Creator but adds to the cumulative evidence that we will discuss in another chapter.

What is the purpose of creation? According to the religions it was to create creatures who could behave morally and love their creator. Evil was always a possibility and it is realized by choice resulting from free will. Otherwise it would have been necessary to create robots programmed to obey the Creator. The choice of good is what God intended for humanity but it involves discipline, resistance to temptation, courage and self-sacrifice. Is there not some other way to realize these values without suffering? Apparently not, since these qualities are evident in the founders of religions, Bodhisattvas, saints and martyrs. Since the choice of evil was so fascinating and we are unable to reach these virtues unaided, a saviour was required, as we noted in the chapter on liberation. But, alternatively, science today offers a human solution to our salvation by dealing with defects in our genetic constitution and the culture of which we are a part. We consider this later.

Why did God create? Hinduism has the belief of Brahman bringing the world into being as a kind of sport. But the Christian tradition insists that God created because He valued the world, loved His creatures, and when they fell into sin wanted to redeem them. By His grace we can realize the values of goodness, beauty and truth. Creation was a good thing but went wrong because of disobedience, according to the Semitic tradition, or through ignorance as the Indian religions insist.

All of the questions that we are raising so far are connected, and despite the theological view that the how and why of creation are separate, there must be a connection. I want to read a book. How? By switching on a light and making sure that my glasses are not steamed up! Why? Because I want to learn more about science and religion. How has humanity originated? Evolution. Why? Because God chose this method of creation. Hence the scientific account explaining the how complements the religious belief focusing on the why. Stephen Hawking is seeking a complete scientific theory which will explain the universe and thinks that it will answer the Why question as well as the How. He writes:

> If we do discover a complete theory, it should in time be understandable in broad principle by everyone, not just a few scientists. Then we shall all, philosophers and scientists, and just ordinary people, be able to take part in the discussion of the question why it is that we and the universe exist. If we find the answer to that, it would be the ultimate triumph of human reason – for then we would know the mind of God.[8]

Hawking differs from other physicists in moving away from the view that the Big Bang was an expansion from a singularity which is an edge or a boundary to spacetime. He wants to use a quantum theory of gravity and dispense with singularities because of his investigation concerning black holes in which they occur. There are difficulties with his proposal because how do we apply a theory of sub-atomic particles to the entire cosmos? As Paul Davies points out they are the behaviour of component parts of the universe and it is unlikely that a relatively non-quantum world would emerge out of a quantum. Quantum fluctuations occur at certain positions in spacetime but there was no spacetime to begin with. Davies thinks that if the view of a singularity is retained then it is the nearest thing that science has found to a supernatural agent.[9]

Science has difficulty in coping with predicting how the smallest units of matter behave. An electron is a particle, a minute portion of matter with a negative charge of electricity. When it is looked at under a microscope with light focused upon it, the light disturbs both its direction and speed. To use low-frequency light does not help, for then there is only a poor determination of its position. If the scientist knows the speed he or she does not know the location and vice versa. These unpredictable particles form the foundation of the universe and affect it on the micro-level. Quantum theory has given us lasers, nuclear power, the electron microscope and the transistor. They affect the sort of events which go on in the nerves and the brain and in the molecules which determine the qualities we inherit. Heisenberg believed that such uncertainty was a built-in feature of the universe, but others, including Einstein, argued that it was due to ignorance or the imperfection of the instrument used. But we do know that the observer disturbs the situation and decides whether the electron will behave as a wave or a particle. Thus the decision is made to measure position or velocity. But uncertainties occur when nothing is being done to disturb the system. Two points can be made when all of this is considered: knowledge of the world is obtained by interaction with it and we can only describe the behaviour of the world, not what it is in itself. Later we will discover that there is a parallel here with God, for revelation is interaction with us and we cannot know what God in Himself is like. There will also be mystery in this connection.

Quantum mechanics show that inital conditions involving the very small are difficult to predict because of Heisenberg's uncertainty, but there is also the chaos theory, a sensitivity to circumstances which affect a system. We see it with the weather which is difficult to predict. Clouds are not clocks, but amid all the freedom and openness displayed they are able to form patterns. Order emerges from chaos.

Scientists in the twentieth century were surprised by nature, as we will see in our next chapters, for the unpredictable behaviour of the very small is so different from the predictable world which we deal with every day. It has been said that if you know where an electron is you do not know what it is doing and if you know what it is doing you cannot know where it is! It would seem that if there is a creator He is full of surprises.

We now turn from the world and its creation to continue what we began in the last chapter, the question of how we orginated and what the future holds for us. The genetic revolution has occurred and opened up the possibility of changing the pattern of evolution itself. What it means may have its dangers as well as benefits, as we will see in the next chapter.

12 What are we?

The objections raised in the nineteenth century to a designer God, biblical accounts of creation, and the uniqueness of the human mind and soul have continued until the present time. Evolution wedded to genetics has raised questions about the nature of humanity and has posed problems for ethics by germline engineering, therapy and cloning. Science in this area has become involved in issues which call for ethical and religious judgements since they concern not only where we came from but who we are and what we might become. The relation of mind and brain is important since some scientists think that the latter is a kind of supercomputer and certain conclusions have been drawn from it. We will consider this in Chapter 13. Religious responses to these developments are considered throughout this chapter and the next.

Development of Darwin's theory

Darwin's theory was evolution by natural selection: the environment selects those forms that are best suited to survive and breed. Today, species is seen as a group that interbreeds and produces fertile offspring. Cooperation rather than competition is given more stress and some palaeontologists think that evolution proceeds not by slow steps or stages but by sudden leaps (*saltus*). The process is so complicated that a slow process could easily go wrong, so punctuated equilibrium is suggested. It is confirmed by the fossil record which for long periods shows little change and is then followed by rapid speciation. Neo-Darwinism replies to the criticism by trying to combine the slow with the fast, for Darwin had said that his theory would fail if the slow was not accepted. They suspect punctuated equilibrium, for it might let the theist argue that God could have given impetus to the process.

Chance is emphasized which appears to oppose any thought of planning but theists argue that in an open and dynamic world it is used by the Creator for order eventually to emerge. If the cosmos is making itself, having been given the potentiality to do so, chance can be viewed as the world exploring possibilities. Chance and unpredictability operate at both the micro- and macro-level as seen in quantum and chaos systems, so there is openness, novelty and spontaneity. But chance at the micro-level leads to regularity at the macro-level. In brief we have a world in which there is both chance and necessity. Such a view opposes a world which is determined completely by God, or one in which we have unlimited freedom. It is an open world where there are many causes, not restricted to one as in the Newtonian machine-like picture.[1]

Are we distinct from the animals?

Darwin's theory of natural selection cannot be tested for evolution is unrepeatable and opinions vary as to how life began, but it is accepted as the best theory that we have. One implication is our kinship with advanced primates such as chimpanzees. Various experiments have been carried out with them to try to see how much they understand. One called Vashoe could use signs and knew their connection with objects. Others in the group, Sarah and Lana, were more advanced, being able to distinguish between coke and water. When given a sign Sarah understood and Lana could communicate by pressing keys on the computer. Further experiments showed that chimps are like five-year-old children in being able to understand words, stories, and so on.[2] We share 98.5 per cent of genes with chimpanzees but are unable to discover why the difference makes such a difference!

We have a biological continuity with the animals but there is something special about us. We develop concept formation and complicated social relations and show a sophistication that animals do not possess. We have symbolic language, an ability to transmit advanced information to future generations ensuring rapid change, a distinct self-awareness, a larger brain, the ability to develop tools and the use of fire, abstract thought, creativity and morality. By way of contrast, instinct and conditioning are the source of animal cooperation. We live for more than survival: we have music, art, religion, astronomy, philosophy and science, and strive to attain ideals. The characteristics of being human are developed self-consciousness, relationships and emotion, language and symbols, ethics and responsibility, the making of meaning, and soul. Theists argue that these qualities point to being made in the image of God who has set ideals before us of what we might become. Evolution in that sense does seem to have direction and purpose. However, what is not denied is that humanity has a propensity for religion and the evolutionary approach to it speculates that the burial sites of Neanderthal man confirm an early origin. Religion stems from the search for meaning within the cosmic scheme of things, the awareness that we can choose good or evil, and are responsible for our actions.[3]

Neo-Darwinists exclude purpose from their study of nature and speak of adapting to the environment. According to Richard Dawkins religion is a virus, a meme or a unit of cultural inheritance acted upon by natural selection. What is meant is that it spreads through the population like any other aspect of culture and is not questioned properly but accepted on the basis of custom. In the early chapters of *The Selfish Gene* (1989) he placed the emphasis on the genes but he then moved to see the impact of culture on the organism. Religion has had such a pervasive influence on the culture of all places that he sees it as a disease which must be eradicated. But where does the virus come from? What is its root? In the evolutionary approach which we considered in Chapter 2, it goes back to 'primitive' man and seems to have some root in his constitution as well as his experience of the environment. Does this mean that there is a religious gene? Something which we possess and the animals do not?

We have noted in examining religions the great variety which springs from the cultural environment, so we can agree with Dawkins that this is the way religion develops. We learn about it by experience and receiving information from others. But this understanding is different from saying that the culture determines religion. We know that as persons we rise above both our genes and culture and Dawkins acknowledges that we can rebel against our selfish genes. If so, it is likely that we can also transcend the culture context. Religions point to individuals and communities that did not accept the values of their society but protested about them. They were inspired by faith in God as the writer of the Epistle to the Hebrews points out (Heb. 11). People in the same culture make different choices and while animals adapt to their environment we change nature to conform to our wishes and, unfortunately, while it has brought benefit it has also resulted in vast pollution. Dawkins is using virus in the sense of indoctrination and it must be admitted that it takes place in many cultures as well as the massive advertising of products! But in modern societies the individual exercises the right of free choice.

DNA and the human genome

As mentioned in Chapter 10, what gave the study of genetics a great impetus was the discovery of deoxyribonucleic acid, DNA. It was one of the most exciting discoveries of the last century and helps us to understand who we are. It contains two chains of molecules which are linked to one another in base pairs. Without going into detail about these we can say that genes, the meaningful sentences, are made up from a letter sequence. There are 100,000 genes or coded messages which govern our physical characteristics and genetic behaviour. The Human Genome Project has sequenced all the base pairs, sorting out which sequences apply to the different genes. The aim is to locate genes that cause diseases of various kinds. Physically, we are dependent on the genes which are transmitted to us, but in the copying mistakes can happen, hence offspring are not exact replicas of parents. It is these variations that result in different physical characteristics and traits. Nature selects those that have the best and enable us and the animals to survive. The process seems random but nature is involved in selection so order enters in as well as chance. Since both physical characteristics and inherent behaviour traits are passed on, we have some support for the doctrine of original sin. Richard Dawkins records that after he had written *The Selfish Gene*, he received letters from the clergy congratulating him on having confirmed it!

But again we are only confronted with survival and the problem remains: Why do we value things that do not contribute to it? Why are we concerned with the needs of the weak since any unfit creature would not survive in evolution? If we are composed of selfish genes why do self-sacrificing ideals attract us? What is the source of altruism? It has been detected in animals with mothers caring for their young to the point of sacrifice. One of the difficulties here is that animals who did this in the context of the survival of the fittest run the risk of failing to survive.[4] It happens in close kinships and is more difficult to apply to the group. Altruism among humans is sacrificing without any hope of being repaid and is done not only for individuals but for the nation in time of war. It is a genuine concern for others, without biological advantages. Some see the root of this morality in the religious gene and the imprinting of God's image upon us, but the whole matter is debatable.

The mapping of the human genome was hailed as a turning point in history. It reveals the genetic material in each cell and identifies the three billion letters or bases which make up the thousands of genes. Such information is staggering and enables us to guard against defective genes and treat them before they can cause damage. Faulty genes could be replaced in unborn children and germline therapy could give us designer babies. Some place stress on genes as determining our behaviour but others contend it is the environment, hence the old nature versus nurture debate has returned.

Genetic engineering

With regard to work on genes there are various views. Gene therapy is generally endorsed, for if disease and disorders can be prevented, why not? But there are risks in the removal of genes since other combinations may be created that could cause harm. How genes interact with one another remains a puzzle. Some fear that trying to produce the perfect human being is likely, with the creation of an elite that would gain greater benefit in the allocation of resources than the genetic underclass. Then there is the necessity to safeguard privacy and rights. Should a doctor reveal a person's defective genes to prevent crime or prevent him or her being insured? It has been reported that the current government intends to take DNA samples from innocent members of the public and detectives will no longer be obliged to destroy genetic samples taken from suspects if they are cleared. Civil rights groups were outraged at this enlargement of the DNA database and the amount of money involved: 143 million pounds over several years. It goes against the decision made in 1994 that only convicted criminals would remain on the database.[5] Complaints have also been registered by the public about insurance companies using information about defects in their genes as a reason for not giving life insurance.

Genetic research should benefit the community and not be done simply to satisfy scientific curiosity or make life more difficult for us. But are we not playing God by tampering with genes? An answer to this might be that God has created us with enquiring minds so scientific experiment is justified. But we need to emulate the moral qualities of God – compassion, understanding and love – in dealing with the benefits and dangers of such work. Genetic modification started with mice and has continued with experiments on monkeys. In 2001 it was reported that the first genetically modified monkey had been produced at the Oregon Regional Research Centre. Scientists inserted a fluorescent 'marker gene' found in jellyfish into the unfertilized eggs of rhesus monkeys. The eggs were then fertilized and implanted into the womb of a surrogate mother monkey. Andi was the only one of the three monkeys born which responded to the integration of the marker gene into his genetic blueprint. There was an outcry by protesters who pointed out that it was being done on humanity's nearest relatives and that it was the first step in rearranging the building blocks of humanity itself.

Cloning has increased fears. The report of the cloning of Dolly the sheep and carbon-copy mice was followed by the announcement that a human had been cloned in South Korea, but the embryo was destroyed after six days. It has been banned in Britain and other countries but we do not know what might happen in China, Russia or America. On 19 December 2000, Parliament, with support from the BMA, voted to allow scientists to clone human embryos, but protests followed from the Archbishop of Westminster and other church leaders and Buddhists and Hindus who saw it leading to the slippery slope of human cloning. The government denied that it would happen for they were agreeing to therapeutic cloning which would use embryo stem cells to cure crippling diseases.

Therapeutic cloning of human embryos creates body tissue such as skin, muscle, nerve or brain cells and they could be transplanted into patients. Embryonic cells would supply transplant tissues. Stem cells have the potential to become any type of tissue but embryo cells are more effective than those taken from adults. The embryo could be cloned from the patient and would be genetically identical, preventing tissue rejection. The cells would then be used to grow tissue compatible with the patient. The technique is the same as used with Dolly the sheep when scientists extracted DNA from the cell of an adult patient and inserted it into a hollowed-out donor egg. The egg is jump-started with electricity and an embryo is created and implanted into a surrogate mother. The scientist removes stem cells from the embryo and uses them to grow replacement tissues required for transplant. The law now allows experiment on embryos after fourteen days but pro-life groups argue that the embryo is a form of life and a rogue scientist could produce a cloned baby. It was reported by the media in March 2001 that Professor Severino Antinori intended to clone babies for infertile couples. Some Mediterranean country had given him permission to do this but he would not reveal which one. The House of Lords confirmed the government's decision to allow research to proceed but stated that they continued to oppose human cloning.

The debate, however, continues among philosophers, scientists and theologians. It is important to remember that the distinction between sexual reproduction and cloning is that the latter means that all the genes come from a single parent using tissue cells rather than a germ cell, so the usual mixture of two parents is not present. Critics see problems here. The technique is still in its infancy and some see it as unsafe and inefficient since it required 277 attempts to produce Dolly. It would involve a waste of embryos and how would cloned children be treated by other children?[6]

Those for cloning argue that if we did it to animals, who are our cousins, why not to humans? If parents have the right to abortion, why not designer babies and cloning? Compassionate reasons are put forward: a woman who had lost her two-year-old to leukaemia asked if her child could be brought back; and a couple in which the male partner was infertile wanted to clone the male; and in a marriage where one partner had a severe genetic disease the couple wanted their own child and wished to use the other partner's genome. It is difficult to say that in these cases and others it is unethical or contrary to human rights or dignity. But Ian Wilmut points out that cloning means a new and different individual who may grow in a different way and become a different sort of person.[7] Parents may not be too pleased with the result! The whole debate, just like the ethical issues surrounding abortion, suicide, euthanasia and capital punishment, centres around human rights. We have gone into this elsewhere[8] but note here that while the rights of the individual are important, we must take into account those of society and the nation.

But what is clear, as Richard Dawkins points out, is that a revolution is taking place which will affect evolution itself. Evolution means change and it has occurred over the centuries, but the process of evolution itself has been much the same process. Now artificial genetic revolution seems destined to change the very pattern of evolution for human interference is possible. Natural selection works on a short time benefit for a species or for its extinction, but now we can plan for a long time ahead. We can, by using genetic engineering, plan both the mutational phase of the Darwinian process and the selectional phase.[9]

Such power has been given to humans by God, who has relinquished absolute power as we think of it and reveals Himself in Christ in the power of weakness, suffering, compassion and forgiveness. He has limited Himself but it is a self-limitation which does not imply an imperfection. But the danger of giving power to creatures like us is that it can result in control and domination. Religion today encourages scientific development as long as it will benefit mankind and not be governed by profits or other doubtful motives. Science will need to be controlled not only by the professionals and government but also by widening the public understanding of what is going on and what genetic engineering can lead to. In any case, we remember that we are more than just vehicles for transmitting genetic information from 'one generation to the next, and that human life is more than just the expression of some computer program written in the biochemical language of DNA'.[10]

In the next chapter we take up the debate about mind and brain which is still puzzling scientists and philosophers. Are they identical, so that we are simply material entities, or different? The answer will help us to understand what we are.

13 Mind and brain

In this chapter we continue the theme of what we are by considering mind and brain. The materialist argues that we are nothing but a collection of interconnected brain cells that opposes the concept of soul and mind, which philosophers such as Descartes (1596–1650) understood as two substances, with mind dominating the body. Today the materialist view has many followers, contending that it is more reasonable to think of one material entity, and conscious events are complex arrangements of low-level particles. But without the organization of such arrangements thought would not occur.

The brain is so complex that there is little understanding of its operation and the same applies to mind. While thought is dependent on the brain, it seems to go far beyond it and there is also the unconscious mind. Consciousness is possessed by animals but self-consciousness makes us aware of our difference from them. Only a very primitive form of self-knowledge is found in the chimpanzee. It may be that once we became fully aware of ourselves and the environment, the capacity gradually emerged to make moral decisions and plan for the future.

But some biologists believe that the workings of the brain, with its billions of nerve cells (neurons) and molecules, will explain the psychological elements of reason, emotion and desires. Basically we are like computers, but even if we accept the similarity it can be maintained that the software is the mind and the brain the hardware. Without the former, the latter would not work, and vice versa. Consciousness could be a particular form of organization, a whole, in contrast to the brain that has many areas or parts. It is consciousness that gives meaning to occurrences in the brain. An analogy might help. I am watching a drama on TV with different parts and varied characters, so it is difficult to make sense of it. But when it is finished the various parts fit into the whole and it becomes clear. Only when the parts are brought together by the emerging factor of organization do I understand it. In the brain there is communication between different parts, with a web of chemical and electrical activity, but consciousness is the organization of the whole.

Of course when injury affects parts of the brain it has an effect on our consciousness. A disintegration of personality is displayed when cells die in the front lobes, and disorders such as epilepsy result in a different perspective on the world or even religious visions. Researchers in Canada stimulated temple lobes and patients had the feeling of not being alone in a room, but no spiritual experiences were recorded. We know that the brain stem controls breathing and sleeping, the cortex is linked to reason, and that there are lower and higher structures. Emotions and thoughts are intertwined, with the latter triggering the former. Fear has a specialized region, making it difficult to forget horrific experiences: a soldier who fought in the Vietnam War could not forget his experiences and still feels depressed and suicidal.

Terror can change the structure of the brain and wear a deep groove in it. The damage may affect everything. A woman who had experienced a stroke could not detect motion and had difficulty with moving staircases and traffic. A man could not form words or understand what he read. Others were able to detect individual features of the face but not its totality. If there is damage on the left side of the brain, difficulties arise because other areas have to take over the job. But it is now believed that the left and right side of the brain function together to some extent and are not separate. There are at least thirty-two visual areas in the brain with information flowing in and out. In dreams our senses are suspended, the brain makes images, creates reality and projects outwards, hence in a sense we create our own reality.[1]

A brain can be understood as information processing. But we are more than receivers and communicators, for unlike a computer we have different feelings about information received by the brain. The mind is the intellectual capacity that we possess, but what about the soul? The religious concept of the soul was regarded as more than the intellect, for it has the meaning of 'living being' in the Genesis account and in the philosophical debate Descartes included feeling and will. The soul in the Hebrew Bible is *nefesh* and comes from and belongs to God. It indicates that the self is a moral entity in relation to others and God. Perhaps we should return to the view of Aristotle and Aquinas who thought that the soul was the form or pattern of the body. It is that which actuates a body and has certain characteristics which convey personal identity.

Hinduism teaches that souls are immortal which reflects the Greek view, but in the Semitic religions stress is not on the soul. We are a psychosomatic unity, hence it is the resurrection of the body, the total personality, that is important, not the survival of the soul. Scientists think that the soul may be the dynamic pattern in which the atoms of the body are organized. These atoms are changing all the time but it is the pattern which provides continuity. In other words it is the soul which is the software running on the material body. It may be, in connection with an afterlife, that God could remember the pattern which is the real person and recreate it in the resurrected body.[2] This would be Christian belief but in the context of the Indian religions there would be its insertion into another material body for a future life here. The idea of patterns also emerges in Buddhism, as we mentioned.

But the materialist returns to the attack by arguing that every mental state corresponds to a physical one in the brain. However, she is unable to prove it for we cannot directly observe memory, imagination and reflection. Thoughts are unpredictable and do not follow general laws, but when I think of some object I have sensations, perceive certain things and have feelings towards it. The mental causes physical events: I can decide to stop writing and turn my attention to other things. It is 'top-down' causation. The mental emerges out of and is dependent on the brain, but seems to develop a life of its own. It again is understanding the whole as more than the parts: holistic properties which are not due to direct causal influence of any of their parts. There are physical examples of patterned behaviour where the patterns clearly emerge from the total system which are not found in the particles individually. Molecules in a hexagonal 'cell' move with a common velocity whereas before they had random motion with respect to each other. The constraint of the whole makes them behave differently than in isolation.

'Bottom-up' causation may be explained by receiving sensations. I am near a bakery and the smell of hot bread causes me to enter and buy, but 'top-down' occurs when I am at home and the thought of the bread causes me to head for the bakery! The message started not from the external environment but from the imagination and in the mind.[3] By analogy we can postulate divine action on human agency. Just as the mental causes changes in the physical, so God could bring about changes in the world if He is related to the world in a way similar to the relationship of mind to bodies. We will discuss His relation in a future chapter.

We cannot observe the workings of God but then we cannot observe what is going on in our unconscious mind. If we could observe it, it would no longer be called the unconscious! Freud insisted that the unconscious was behind actions: hidden motives, desires, etc. Psychoanalytic theory still follows this basic point but it has been challenged by brain and genetic study which seeks to explain abnormality by biological factors. Drugs can change the personality so that a frivolous person can become serious or vice versa. We live in a pill age as the humorist says: 'Will I take a pill and go to the party or will I take one and go to bed!' But biological explanation leaves out the effect on personalities of bad parental and educative environments. The psychological, sociological and biological factors need to be taken into account to effect a cure for abnormality, though some people may be affected by one more than the other. Biological accounts of the brain require investigation of beliefs, desires and feelings as well as neurons, synapses and serotonin.[4]

Consciousness appears to be an emergent feature of the brain and in the human searches for meaning. Richard Dawkins, however, is suspicious of any organized complexity that has any source other than the evolutionary development from primeval simplicity. The theist replies that he or she is accepting the evolutionary development of consciousness or mind but that Dawkins is not taking into account what we have seen in a previous chapter that the laws of nature had to be just right in order that such complexity might occur. The universe had to be finely tuned for life to emerge. If it is reasonable to assume that God was involved there, then why exclude the divine influence in the development of mind? Furthermore, if mind is simply the product of the random forces of evolution, how can it as it were stand outside the process and both describe and judge it? The mind does appear to be a type of activity which, though related to the physical, is distinct from it and requires different predicates to describe and a different type of explanation.

Matter has many levels and has been compared to peeling an onion, so that some think that while quarks and leptons may be the ultimate constituents more may be discovered. Some reductionists (bottom-up causation) try to explain things by the lower level rather than taking into account what emerges at a higher level (top-down). We noted in Hinduism that Shankara thought of understanding in terms of levels and applied it to scripture and God. He did not ignore the lower but argued that progress would only be made when we rose to the higher. In science, while the micro- or lower levels of organisms do affect the higher, they cannot explain fully what happens at the higher. The levels of knowledge are illustrated by Michael Polanyi. He uses a building example. The art of making bricks depends on raw material made at a lower level, then on another level is the architect with his plan, and on the final level the town planner. There are rules applying to each level. Physics and chemistry govern the raw material of bricks, technology prescribes the art of brickmaking, architecture teaches the builders, and the rules of town planning control the town planners.[5]

With regard to the analogy of the computer it is evident that it is an amazing aid in gathering information, storing and performing operations that we cannot do. It is much better than we are in performing mechanical operations and daily a writer, among others, gives thanks for this technological miracle. But my computer, unfortunately, will only process the words of this book, it will not write it for me! It is automatic and pro-grammed and the experts on artificial intelligence have not so far remedied the defect. The problem is that neurons in the brain are not the same as chips and circuits. The neurons are indeterminate and require a principle of organization which supplies predictability at the higher level of mind. It is a ques-tion of understanding, so that while a computer can play chess as well as the human and sometimes even better, it finds diffi-culty when the unexpected happens. It happened to the super-computer, 'Deep Thought', at the chess game which failed to report why it had made its blunder although the programmers knew.

The mind would seem to be a global attribute of the brain and not a local product of any of its parts. Computers compute but the mind has an awareness, insight and creativity that programmes the mechanical computation. After an exhaustive survey of computers, the mathematician Roger Penrose concludes that 'mere computation cannot evoke plea-sure or pain or poetry or what we feel looking at the beauty of an evening sky or the magic of sounds or hope or love or despair'.[6] Brains and organisms which they inhabit are not closed systems but in continual interaction with the world and brains are capable of modifying their structure and have the ability to make judgements. A computer is a dead storage system but the brain is living and dynamic.

But if the materialist point of view is taken as the norm, there flows from it certain theories concerning our actions. We mention briefly two: sociobiology and behaviourism. Socio-biology emphasizes the genes and if they survive in our off-spring then our behaviour pattern becomes the norm in society. But Richard Dawkins is aware of the disadvantages of a society based on the selfish gene: it would be a nasty one. To counter this he advises teaching generosity and altruism because we are born selfish. Religions would agree and go further, inculcating values that oppose the sociobiological view that behaviour is directed towards the survival of our genes through reproduction. As we have seen, Buddhism advises us to lose the illusion of self and other religions call for its denial or death. Helping others to survive is more important than one's own survival. This is very difficult but it is put forward as an ideal to be realized. And, it has been pointed out, cultural systems develop in ways that do not contribute to the transmission of genetic material. In the religions we have examined, celibacy can be a value and indeed in some cases is prized above the married state.[7]

Behaviourism adds to the mechanical view of humanity with an attempt to relate behaviour to external stimuli. It is training that is important. Well-known work in this area was conducted by Pavlov (who can forget his dogs!) with his unconditioned reflexes. It results from previous experience, so if food is placed in a dog's mouth, it salivates. J. B. Watson and B. F. Skinner accepted this and contended that the right training would produce any kind of individual. Behaviour is determined by reward and punishment which is true but does not explain originality or purpose, nor did it explain how children learned languages so easily. Noam Chomsky pointed out that they managed to acquire a language at a very early stage without much instruction. The brain seems to possess a genetic ability, a built-in framework, that enables us to master a language. Behaviourists did not give sufficient attention to the workings of the mind.[8]

The study of the brain does not tell us what it is like to be a person. But that we are persons, and more than the material elements of our bodies, is something that the religions hold firmly on the basis of soul or mind. The latter's distinction has been held by many philosophers: Bishop Berkeley (1685–1753), Georg Hegel (1770–1831), Bertrand Russell (1872–1970), J. S. Mill (1806–73) and A. J. Ayer (1910–89). It was Berkeley who contended that 'to be is to be perceived', Russell who believed that the physical world was constructed out of the 'sense data' of perception, and Ayer who argued that consciousness builds reality. G. Ryle (1900–76), however, moved more to the materialistic position with his view that the mental is really a disposition to behave in a certain way. Currently scientists are pursuing a theory of consciousness, but so far they have not been able to find an answer.[9] Many think that it will never be solved, but science has solved mysteries in the past and it may come up with an answer in the future.

In conclusion we note that religions stress the value of the individual in the sight of God. Man may be a little lower than the angels but he possesses reason and creativity, searches for meaning in life, has the ability to make moral choices and is accountable to God. The evolution mechanism of natural selection does not favour the loving person that is the ideal of the religions. The value of love opposes the world of the survival of the fittest, yet there is something in human nature which responds to it especially when we see acts of self-sacrifice. Religions do not deny that we come from the dust of the ground and that evolution could be the Creator's way of creating humanity, but they also point to the *imago* (image) of God that all possess. There is no proof that this is so but it is a perspective that cannot be overlooked when we consider what we are and what we can become.

Finally, with respect to the scientific viewpoint that we have been considering in this and previous chapters, we need to mention that today science has to face the challenge of post-modernism. It contends that science, like other disciplines, is riddled with personal and communal values and preferences. There is no monopoly possessed by science on truth for other disciplines have to be taken into account. It is an interpretation of the world and ourselves but not a total explanation. Physicists, despite all the success that they have had in opening up our understanding of the world, do seem to recognize their limitations by insisting that they know how this mysterious world behaves but not what it is in itself. Perhaps biologists could learn something from this humility, particularly when they try to extend their boundaries beyond their discipline and believe that they can explain both our origin and our behaviour.

In the next chapter in our search for the characteristics of religion, we consider secular beliefs which have many of the trappings that we have observed when considering the six religions. Is it possible that they are quasi-religions or surrogates for religion?

14 Other belief systems

Today we have a global variety of beliefs, including some that are religious and others that are usually viewed as secular but could be considered religious if a broad and flexible definition of religion is used. We start with what are called new religious and New Age movements but have been called neo-pagan by mainstream religion.

New religious movements developed in the twentieth century with a blossoming of cults. Some of these are Scientology, Krishna Consciousness, Children of God, Jesus People, Divine Light Mission, Transcendental Meditation and the Unification Church. They may affirm the world or deny it and are often influenced by psychological ideas. Scientology, founded by L. Ron Hubbard in 1949, stresses the elimination of trauma and fears and being successful. Without much attention to belief in God, Hubbard recognized the immortality of the soul and sought to combine religion and science. There were clashes with the state in various countries but the movement attracted film stars and other notables. It is recognized as a religion in the USA for tax purposes and has upwards of twenty million members.

The Unification Church (1954) is known as 'the Moonies', after its founder Sun Moon, who made messianic claims and said that he was establishing a new religion centring on himself. But he had to spend some time in prison, having failed to answer charges of disorder, tax evasion, bigamy and adultery. The Divine Light Mission was founded in 1960 and now claims five million followers. It, together with the International Society of Krishna Consciousness (Hare Krishna), reveals the influence of Hinduism and the appeal of the *Bhagavad gita* for many young people. Krishna is recognized by the devotees as the supreme God. In these movements there is a tendency to pantheism and polytheism.

Other cults come under the umbrella of the New Age Movement and dabble in myths, shamanism, messages from the dead, crystals, and so on. They are 'green' and vegetarian, viewing the earth as a personal living thing. Stressing self-improvement, they appeal to the middle class and profess beliefs about the supernatural, aliens and the end of the world. Near-death experiences are recorded, as well as alien abductions, flying saucers and UFOs. Transcendental Meditation has an Indian background and was led by Maharishi Mahesh Yogi as he came to style himself. His activity became widely known because he attracted the Beatles who must have seen the need to withdraw from the public and engage in the meditation techniques that he offered. When the movement centred itself in the United States in 1959 it applied to be exempt from tax but was turned down in 1977.

Members of the religious traditions warn against neo-paganism in these movements but they show that mainstream religion often does not appeal to youth and they witness a spiritual sensibility. The fact that they have beliefs in the supernatural and rituals would seem to bring many of them under the umbrella of religion, but often they turn out to be humanistic with self-worship. These movements usually call for total commitment, display opposition to society, have no professional clergy, and are inspired by a charismatic leader. In the UK there has even developed a cult of the late Princess Diana where respect gives way to reverence. In addition there are many people who do not belong to any faith but say that they are religious. There is a believing without belonging.

In a global society without the constraints of culture and close social ties, these movements show that people are aware of the opportunity of a much greater choice of what to believe in. They have what has been called a 'pick and mix' choice in the world's supermarket. Sociologists debate why they are attractive and think that it is due to the desire to become a better person, or achieve success, or wanting to follow an inspired leader, or an aversion to scientific rationalism and an attachment to older forms of understanding. Mysticism, individualism, living in touch with earth, astrology, palmistry, Tarot reading, and the cult status of such TV programmes as *The X-Files* are characteristics of such movements.[1] But most have no central organization and without it they are not likely to survive for a long time.

While many would say that the cults are religious or quasi-religious, the two main belief systems, Marxism and Humanism that we discuss below, have been traditionally considered anti-religious. Karl Marx (1818–83) was born in Trier, Prussia, the son of a Jewish father and Dutch mother. He had a good education at the Universities of Berlin and Bonn and obtained his Ph.D. degree with distinction. One of his first jobs was writing articles for a radical newspaper which were critical of the government and he was expelled from Germany. He tried living in Paris and Brussels, but eventually settled in London, until his death in 1883. Among the influences on the young Marx were the writings of Ludwig Feuerbach and G. F. Hegel (1770–1831). Marx criticized Feuerbach but agreed that theology was anthropology. The mistake that theology makes is to refer to some transcendent being instead of seeing the truth and divinity of human nature. Feuerbach defined religion as the dream of the human mind, but even in dreams we find ourselves on the earth. God is really the consciousness of humanity, and when we understand it the projection of deity is not necessary. Religion is a distorted perception of the world, riddled with contradictions, and makes God in our image. The objectification results in self-alienation, for we think we are alienated from a divine being which is resolved by realizing that the divine is simply the consciousness of our own nature.

Some of these ideas appear in Marx as he objects to religion. Man, he says, has looked towards heaven and seen only his own reflection, he makes religion which is the spiritual aroma of society, the state, the human world. But it is an expression of real distress and a protest against real despair. It is the sigh of the oppressed creature, the feeling of a heartless world, the soul in a place without a soul. It is the opium of the people. Religion creates illusory happiness about a condition which requires illusion. Once we have got rid of religion we will see reality in a rational way as human self-alienation. Instead of thinking of alienation from God or the Mind (Hegel), we realize that we are alienated from one another by the possession of private property which reduces us to less than human beings. As Marx proceeds, the criticism of heaven is transformed into the criticism of the earth, the criticism of religion into the criticism of law and the criticism of theology into the criticism of politics. Religion is a compensation, justification and concealer of exploitation. It is an ideology like nationalism and democracy which enforces the idea that inequality is justifiable and that the capitalist power is God given.[2]

But somewhat illogically Marx says it is a protest against such conditions. If it is a protest, how can it be called a deadening drug? Perhaps he would have answered that the protest was so weak that it could not be heard! Religion in the nineteenth century supported the status quo and did very little to reform politics. But there were protests such as the Christian Social Movement and a reaching out to the poor in the work of the Salvation Army. If Marx had lived to see the vigorous protest of the Catholic Church in Poland against communism, Liberation Theology in Africa and South America, and the stand of Martin Luther King in America and Gandhi in India, he might have changed his mind.

If we accept that religion must include what Marx calls an other-worldly reality, then his movement cannot be a religion, for the supernatural dimension is evident in the religions that we have reviewed. According to Marx, religion is a symptom of the ills of mankind but it cannot deal with the disease from which man must be cured. As opium, it is taken to deaden suffering, but pain relievers do not cure diseases.[3] What was needed, he argued, was an analysis of society and the breaking of the economic chains that dominate the work force.

Looking at history, Marx pointed out that it had passed through various stages – Asiatic, antique, feudal and modern bourgeois – and each stage had been determined by how wealth is obtained. Thus in the feudal stage wealth is obtained from ownership of land, in the bourgeois period it is derived from ownership of factories, mines, and so forth. It is the class struggle that causes change. In feudal society there were the lords and the serfs but it was the middle class (the bourgeoisie) who led the struggle to overthrow the aristocracy. In the capitalist period, the bourgeoisie struggles with the working class or the proletariat. The revolt ensues when new productive forces conflict with existing class relations as in the industrialization of nineteenth-century England. Marx saw in the new machine age the ripe conditions for an overthrow of the bourgeoisie.[4]

He was influenced by Hegel but turned the idealist on his head! Let us put simply what Hegel said in this way. I put forward an argument and you find a contradiction in it; eventually, after a lot of discussion, we decide to bring my argument and yours together to form a compromise. It is called by Hegel, thesis, antithesis, synthesis, and then the synthesis becomes the starting point of another thesis. Philosophers have only interpreted the world in various ways but Marx was determined to change it. Thoughts must spur the feet into action: getting out in the streets to protest. Applying the dialectic to material development, each historical stage contains within itself a contradiction, the seeds of its own destruction, leading to the creation of the new stage. Marx saw nineteenth-century industrialized England through the lens of class distinctions and class struggle. Thus the bourgeoisie had the wealth, the means of production, and exploited the workers using cut-throat competition, free enterprise and a belief in the survival of the fittest.

The worker was treated like a cog in a factory machine and was alienated from his work by long hours of drudgery, monotony and little reward. Before industrialization he had some sense of owning the product but with the mass production of the factory he felt that it owned him. As Marx said, the more objects the worker produces the fewer he possesses and the more he feels under the domination of his product. But once the worker reacts against this slavery he is united with other workers in the revolution. The bourgeoisie has unwittingly produced his own grave diggers. Religion says to accept the situation for there is 'pie in the sky when you die'. The poor will inherit since it is difficult for a rich man to enter the kingdom of heaven. But in the meantime, recognize that it is the divine ordering of society that must not be disturbed. Hence middle-class congregations contentedly sang the hymn:

The rich man in his castle,
The poor man at his gate,
God made them high and lowly
And ordered their estate.

They seemed unconscious, or perhaps they did not have time to think about the criterion of divine judgement laid down by the Gospels, that their belief in God would be measured by how they had sought to alleviate the condition of the poor.

Marx demanded a change in conditions as a way of changing human nature, but religion with its missionary zeal argues that humanity must be changed first and it will then change the conditions. Marx believed that the way forward was the overthrow of the middle class, the abolition of private property and the handing over of the means of production to the people. He did believe that some of the middle class at the time of crisis would go over to the proletariat, just as in an earlier period a number of the nobility went over to the bourgeoisie. Force was needed but unlike most forms of communism he did not rule out altogether a peaceful transition. Marx was the son of a Jewish rabbi and donned the mantle of the Hebrew prophet calling for justice, equality and individual freedom and denounced the pietistic religion which kept out of social and political issues. He pursued the goal of a brotherhood devoid of class, like Sikhism which set aside the Hindu caste system. It was a justifiable protest.

Despite his belief that economics was the determining factor in history, Marx had difficulty, according to his mother, in managing his own monetary affairs and was indebted to his friend Engels for loans. Perhaps that was a starter in seeing economics as the form of alienation! Money is the barrier to human freedom. The more the worker exerts himself, the more powerful becomes the alien objective world which he fashions against himself, the poorer he and his inner world become. Marx did not think of higher wages because they would not restore the workers' dignity, but the abolishing of wages, alienated labour and private property. Marx does not give much detail of a communistic society and would have been discouraged by the eventual outcome in various places. He was idealistic, thinking that once the bad conditions were altered, greed, egoism and envy would disappear in society, with communal property and socially organized means of production. The goal would be the good of all. Individual interest would be replaced by universal interest. The state would wither away as the proletariat asserted itself over other classes. Cooperation would be voluntary with no armed force necessary.

If we define a religion as a group of beliefs held by people in common and providing a rationale for their way of life, then both Marxism and most religions qualify. Christianity has some similarity with communism in its early beginnings. There is a revolutionary sound in the magnificat: 'He has put down the mighty from their seats and has exalted the humble and the needy. He has filled the hungry with good things and the rich He has sent empty away' (Luke 1:52–3). And there was the effect the movement had: 'These that have turned the world upside down are come here also' (Acts 17:6). Again the Marxist slogan: 'To each according to his need, from each according to his ability' would apply to the sharing and structure of the Early Church: 'All that believed were together and had all things common; and they sold their possessions and goods and parted them to all, according as any had need' (Acts 2:44–5). A distribution of property that would please any Marxist.

The *Communist Manifesto* is a surrogate for holy scripture, spelling out doctrines and beliefs. It is not a scientific document for its predictions have not been fulfilled. Like religion it is a faith, with its meetings glorifying its leaders and demanding total obedience. It has high priests and creed, humanistic ethics, missionary zeal, hymns, the Red Flag, and its ultimate goal is heaven on earth. Of course, if we see religion as many do as the worship of a supernatural being above and beyond mankind, then Marxism is not a religion, but if you define religion as the existence in humanity of something which causes aspirations towards an ideal society with justice, peace, equality and freedom then Marxism qualifies. What that something is could be seen as a divine consciousness, but Marx would deny it.

Another point of similarity with religion is division and when we speak of the development of communism we need to ask the question: What kind of communism are we talking about? Mao in China encouraged permanent revolution, considering that such conflict would be creative, but it went beyond Marx who thought of it only in terms of the overthrow of an oppressive society. Scripture appeared with Mao's *Little Red Book*, read and chanted by the workers like the mantras of Buddhist monks. Communism had centralization and control by the Politburo, analogous with hierarchies in religions. It failed in Russia, Yugoslavia, Czechoslovakia, Poland and East Germany, but persists in North Korea, Cuba and China. Much damage was done to religion in Russia and in Tibet, but there is a resurgence of the Eastern orthodoxy in Russia, confirming that religion in the sense of a belief in the supernatural persists.

It was surprising that Marxism and Christianity, being opposed to one another, should unite in Latin America. The reason was a common goal: the fight for justice. From 1964 onwards they collaborated on the basis of practical action, not theories. The struggle was against class privileges and for the poor and the use of the Church to uphold the status quo. The demand was for a new society and new humanity. Revolution was embraced by the Marxists but they did not rule out change by evolution. But how was the new humanity to be created? It is by God's grace according to the Christian, the Marxist disagrees, but both believe that the new person must be free and be a member of a society. The conditions must be changed, religion must get involved in politics and the goal is socialism. Christians argued that the traditional forms of the Church are no longer relevant in such an unjust society but they did not want violence. Only as a last resort should it be used. They criticized the Church which they said had hidden behind vague notions of peace, forgiveness and reconciliation, which in the long run cost more lives than revolution.

In the 1960s the Second Vatican Council recognized collaboration with Marxism for the betterment of mankind and in 1970 the 'Organization of Christians for Socialism' was formed in Santiago, Chile, with the objective of supporting the Marxist, Salvador Alende, as President of Chile. The reason for the link and development of Liberation Theology in Christianity was the continued search for freedom and justice in countries such as Latin America and South Africa. Father

Camilo Torres, a Catholic priest, made a remarkable statement about his decision to join the guerrilla movement in Colombia: 'I have said that as a Colombian, as a sociologist, as a Christian, and as a priest, I am a revolutionary. I believe that the Communist party consists of truly revolutionary elements, and hence I cannot be anti-Communist either as a Colombian, a sociologist, a Christian or a priest.' He died in action and earned the praise of Fidel Castro.[5]

But the history of communism confirms that violence begets violence and there is no guarantee that the men of violence, Lenin and Stalin, would leave it aside when they came to power. Lenin believed in seizing power and holding on to it by any means necessary, for expediency was the only morality in politics. Leon Trotsky (1879–1940) said of Lenin in 1904 that when he spoke of the dictatorship of the proletariat he really meant a dictatorship over the proletariat. Stalin's body was removed by Khrushchev from the Lenin Mausoleum in 1961 but Lenin remained a cult figure for many years with museums housing his writings, effigies, and people filing past his tomb in the attitude of worshippers. Icons of him were installed in their homes, showing that it is hard for the masses not to have a god to worship.

In the light of what has happened to Communism in various countries, the religious person may contend that it is not he who is dreaming but Marx! As we said, the theory is not scientific for its predictions have proved false: proletarian revolts in most industrial advanced countries have not taken place, the gap between worker and capitalist has not increased, wages have not remained at subsistence level and capitalism has not collapsed. Marx was naïve about human nature, failing to see that power corrupts whether it be that of the capitalist or the proletariat. The party will forget they once belonged to the workers and lord it over them. Every system of government, of course, has its defects but democracy seems to be the best that we can find. It was a good protest about the plight of the poor in the nineteenth century and spurred the Trade Union Movement on to get better working conditions for all.[6]

The philosopher Karl Popper engaged in a criticism of Marxism and psychoanalysis and argued that the theories of

Marx, Freud and Adler could not be falsified since they were able to explain everything. A Marxist would open a newspaper and always find evidence that confirmed his theory of history and the same applied to the psychoanalyst.[7]

Marxism can be equated with a form of Humanism because it stresses the ability of man to change his conditions and overcome alienation. Thus Marx opposed not only the alienation of humanity in Britain but commended John Brown in America for his revolt against slavery. Marxism is different from communism which oppressed the people in various countries and denied the Humanists' call for an open society and free enquiry. Humanism advocates a pluralistic society in which no set of values dominate and there is respect for the liberty of others. There is tolerance without a creed and religion because man is master of his fate and must save himself.

Historically it goes back to the ancient Greeks, who claimed that man must use his reason and not depend on the supernatural. The philosophers dismissed the myths of the gods and decried their behaviour. Protagoras (*c.*490–421 BCE) announced that 'man is the measure of all things', he is autonomous and self-sufficient. In the Renaissance the term 'Humanism' was coined, but not all of it was anti-religious. Desiderius Erasmus (*c.*1466–1536) sought to reform the Church as well as recovering the sources of classical learning and has been seen as a forerunner of the Reformation. But rationalism and empiricism in David Hume (1711–76), John Stuart Mill (1806–73), Bertrand Russell (1872–1970), John Dewey (1859–1952) and A. J. Ayer (1910–89) spurred the quest for understanding apart from religion. Humanists were drawn together in societies: the Ethical Union (1896), the British Humanist Association (1963), the American Humanist Association (1941) and the International Humanist and Ethical Union (1952).

Originally Humanism was a revolt against authoritarian ecclesiastical control. Today Humanists place more emphasis on a concern for a just and humane society. There are ethical, scientific and religious groups who are involved in politics, belong to social, educational and charitable organizations and influence events at an international level. If religion is hard to define so is Humanism, because like religion it does not have an essence that can be discovered. It has characteristics such as a stand for human rights, liberty, values, changes in the law with regard to abortion, divorce, and mandatory religious education in schools. Existentialist Humanists such as Jean Paul Sartre (1905–80) asserted that we are made not by genes or environment but by personal choice. Many people who do not belong to Humanist groups agreed with these values and have little use for the organized forms of religion. They contend for the Humanist values of personal rights, liberty and dignity while remaining agnostic about God, and support such organizations as Amnesty International, calling for the abolition of capital punishment, the release of political prisoners, and support for the Campaign for Nuclear Disarmament.[8]

Humanists, though confident about the ability of mankind and its scientific achievement, are worried about the depersonalizing aspects of technology. Creativity and the joy of life is being lost in the consumer-orientated manipulative economic system that exists today. Moving away from the old moral codes of religion is a good thing, allowing an enjoyment of freedom of expression and lifestyle but moral libertarianism has got to be watched. Freedom can degenerate into licence and must be moderated. Tolerance is one thing, approval is another.[9] Other Humanists do recognize man's capacity for 'sin', falling short of 'the highest he has seen'. The highest is the Good, a vision of the moral ideal that will transcend finite ends. Man is 'a spiritual' being and knows both his weakness and his greatness.[10] Religion is usually defined as part of human expression, just like art.

Some Humanists show an affinity with Zen Buddhism since it simply points to the teaching of the Buddha and his enlightenment and aims at freedom of action, the overcoming of self-alienation and alienation with others, and the illumination of the mind without the trappings of scriptures or institutionalism. Both Humanism and Zen pose the question: Who am I? They are more occupied with the answer to this question than belief in God, which both deny. Buddhism is similar to Humanism because it does not have ready-made answers to human nature or ultimates but bids man to save himself. Even in Mahayana it appears at times that the gods are below the Buddha and need to be taught by him. Still Humanism and

Buddhism cannot be equated since the latter has 'cosmic footage' and is designated a religion.[11]

Some Humanists think that there could be more affinity with Christianity. In his book, *Objections to Humanism* (1963), J. Blackham dismisses a negative stance towards religion and calls for the incorporation of good religious insights. He asks whether the Humanist could not have a religious experience without embracing the beliefs that often emerge from it. Pope Paul VI declared in 1969 that Roman Catholicism is a 'Christian Humanism' and that the only authentic Humanism must be Christian. His statement was confirmed by the Second Vatican Council but it was greeted by secular Humanists as ironic since they adopted the name in opposition to a dogmatic Church.[12] Thus Humanism cannot apply to those who still believe in God and would only be possible for those who are atheistic Humanists. It must be naturalistic non-theism. Common values are shared and if religion is defined with only an ethical dimension most Humanists would accept it. Humanists are aware that 'in rejecting religion altogether, they may be throwing out the ethical baby with the supernatural bath water'.[13] But dialogue with liberal Catholics and members of other faiths is not ruled out. What is needed is the substitution of reason and enquiry for faith that is not bound by any ecclesiastical creed.

The Humanists joined with religious groups in producing *A Humanist Manifesto* in 1933 which had fifteen tenets. It was followed by a revised edition in 1973 which dismisses a deity, emphasizes that belief in God is man-made, materialism is accepted, moral values spring from human experience, relativism in ethics is permissible, religious ideas of salvation are illusory, immortality is dismissed, and so on. Despite these beliefs, which oppose what we have seen in the religions, the United States Supreme Court defined such secular humanism as a religion in 1961. The reason given was that although it denied the existence of God, it was a carefully structured belief system. It does have, in common with the religions, a belief in the dignity of the human person and the sharing of other ethical values so that the religions can unite with the Humanist to oppose brutality and injustice wherever it occurs.

A Christian Humanism has emerged in the writing and conferences of the members of the Sea of faith Movement. They believe that religion is something created by humanity and deny a transcendent God. Don Cupitt is the leader and has written many books on religion, but it was the action of the Church of England in excommunicating one of its members, Anthony Freeman, which caused the most stir in the media. It was unusual in a Church of such broad opinions so his beliefs are worth considering.[14]

Freeman contends that religion is a human creation and the supernatural apparatus should be abandoned. He dismisses God as creator and the argument from design for His existence. Revelation does not fare any better because it comes through human beings and is fallible. Religious experience is couched in the God-language which is already known, but people can have such an experience without the traditional idea of deity. Thus he arrives at the belief that God equals the sum of human values. This is his faith and he differs from the secular Humanist in continuing to include the word God and the Christian stories, especially those of Jesus. Religion for him shifts from heaven to earth, from the next world to this one, and from dogma to spirituality and ethics. Such religion, he thinks, still has an important place in human life.

But he admits after a radical handling of the Gospels that Jesus believed in an objective reality when he talked about God and that he was revolutionary both in attitude and teaching. Yet we cannot contend for his uniqueness since it would be denying what other faiths teach about their founders. Each faith has created its own God with some common elements and some independent ones, so we are not forced to call one right and another wrong.[15] Today the Humanist is right to put confidence in humanity, dismiss sin, and look for meaning in this life. Yet Freeman wants to hold on to the Holy Spirit which he sees as replacing a distant God. The Spirit is present in the hearts of all, having been poured out on Whit Sunday (Acts 2). He permeates the world and is particularly present in the sacraments of the Church. In this interpretation, Freeman dismisses the doctrine of the Trinity and concentrates on one of the Persons, but the Spirit is equated with the human spirit. It can only mean for him that the experience described in the Acts of the Apostles was something worked up by the apostles and did not come from any divine source. Eternal life is similarly dispensed with because concentration on this life will make us more appreciative of it and make us realize that we have only a limited time to show our affection.

Freeman is then caught in a dilemma. He has signed the Declaration of Assent at his ordination to the priesthood, which includes the traditional Christian beliefs, but in his attempt at reformulation he is presenting a different faith than his forefathers. How can he remain in the Church? His answer is that practice has priority over doctrine and he values the Christian community and knows that many believe what he believes. But he cannot keep quiet about his doubts while others conceal theirs. He wants to remain in the Church but cannot accept the traditional faith. Secular Humanists will ridicule him because he wants to continue to practise his religion, but he was willing to risk it since he desires to continue in fellowship with the Church. Yet he admits that his Christian Humanism also lacks the certainty of the traditional form of the faith.

The impression that is conveyed by his writing is a confusing one and it is tempting to think that the secular Humanist would repeat the story of the Bishop who, when lecturing potential ordinands, was asked the question: 'Is there a prayer in the prayer book for theological students?' He replied: 'Yes, there is, there is a prayer for those at sea!' For example, how can he interpret the Spirit as Holy yet at the same time equate it with the human Spirit? The passage in Acts 2 which he quotes refers to some external entity, not a surge of the inner human spirit. How can he continue to follow Jesus who, as he says, did believe in God as an objective reality? And how can he deny the eternal life which, according to the Gospels, Jesus spoke about and still remain in the Church? It would seem that the Church of England, which is not noted for harsh decisions but rather attempts at compromise, had no alternative but to excommunicate.

But secular Humanists also admit that their beliefs have defects. One confusing matter is the great variety and diversity of their beliefs about mankind. Some opt for an excessive idealism which relies on reason and good will. Another is the admission that Humanism has failed to grasp the complexity of the soul or self, the power of passion and the depth of alienation. There would seem to be a playing down of the human desire for domination. Further, it is necessary to demonstrate that the practice of humanistic values makes mankind happier and that it can solve the psychosocial and practical problems. A remedy lies in educating the young in humanistic values and starting very early in life so that they will spontaneously choose the good.

In conclusion we note that both Marxism and Humanism deny the supernatural and if a definition of religion requires it then neither can be considered a religion. But having denied the supernatural they proceed to erect idols such as the rule of the party or the individual. If a functional definition is applied then they qualify as a religion for they function in society by calling for dedication and commitment, and give people the goal of resolving suffering, injustice and ignorance. And like religions they form a community and give their members a sense of belonging to a group of like-minded people. Both Marxism and Humanism are praiseworthy and present alternatives to those religions which believe that a substantive definition must include the supernatural dimension.

It is this question of the supernatural or God as a Reality beyond and yet within us which is the subject of debate, hence we consider in the next chapter whether or not there is some evidence for His existence.

15 The existence of God

The religions that we have considered are based on scriptures and traditions which assume the existence of God. Indeed, some go as far as to say that only a fool would deny His existence! However, scepticism, which characterizes our age, demands evidence. We will try and supply some in this chapter by describing the kind of God religions believe in, commenting on some of the traditional arguments put forward for His existence, and discussing revelation. We will ask in conclusion if the existence of evil is the strongest argument against the case for God.

What is God like?

It is clear that if there is a God, He will exist differently from us. Objects in the world, animal and human, have a different type of existence so it is reasonable to think of God's existence as not like ours. It follows that we do not try to demonstrate His existence the way we would that of an object in the world. If there is a God we are dealing with the incomparable and the ground of all existence so it is difficult to establish a proof, and most scholars who try admit that in the end they can only find 'whispers of His ways'. In the Semitic religions, Judaism, Christianity and Islam, the Creator of the world is separate from it but human creation is like Him. Hinduism, however, teaches that the world emerges from the womb of Brahman so the relationship is very close. Just as a child reflects her parents, the world reflects God, so that some theologians, both Indian and Christian, have seen it as the body of God.

Traditionally the Hebrew religion was worried about nature gods and goddesses and opposed any kind of emanation. But now evolution teaches that we have evolved from matter seen as good, so scientifically the distinction between humanity and matter is not so sharp. And even if the child metaphor was accepted it remains distinct from the parent. The model of God as father supports the analogy and there is the mother image (Isa. 49:15; 66:13). Ian Barbour sees the concept of Spirit helpful for it means vitality, creativity, and appears in creation (Gen. 1:2) and in the continuing creation of creatures (Ps. 104:30). The Spirit inspires the prophets, was the inspiration of Christ, gave the early Church the power to witness, and is present today in the community. As long as we maintain the distinction between Creator and creature, the father/child metaphor is useful and has the advantage of a very close relationship between God and the world. Hence it is easier to see God acting in it. In any case both male and female were made in the image of God (Gen. 2), so a likeness between Creator and creature is there.[1]

But Islam does not use the father metaphor, being afraid that it might imply that Allah had offspring. The fear may spring from taking the Christian idea of sonship literally and physically instead of spiritually. Muslims insist that God is king and like Sikhism and traditional Christianity has a strong doctrine of predestination. But the world reflects change and development, so why should we think of its Creator in this static way? And what place does it leave for human freedom, having pictured Him as absolute power? It needs modification, with a stress on Him as the power of love.[2] What we have said about evolution with the role of chance balanced by necessity, fits in to a more dynamic God sustaining the world and continuing to reveal Himself. Perhaps we might think of the Creator giving the world its potentialities and being the activator of them.

All the religions believe in the unity or oneness of God and it is interesting to note that scientists are keen to find a unified theory of the universe. Religions would see this as creation reflecting Creator and the universe would be more intelligible if it was the case. The Semitic religions, while aware of the impersonal nature of the deity, put stress on His personal action whereby He reveals Himself. In Judaism God is creator, warrior, ruler, father, guide and shepherd and a clear distinction is made between Him and humanity. He is called Yahweh and Elohim and the Israelites gradually moved from thinking of Him as a local tribal God to His universality. He is majestic, invisible and immortal, controls the nations and the heaven of heavens cannot contain Him (2 Chr. 6:18). The transcendence of God is complemented by immanence for He acts personally in history and calls for justice and compassion towards those in need.

Christianity and Islam agree with Judaism though there are different emphases: father is mentioned in Judaism, missing in Islam, but given priority in Christianity. All would subscribe to the Islamic sentence which begins each chapter of the Qur'an: 'In the name of Allah, the Compassionate, the Merciful' (Fatiha). Allah is Cosmic, the Lord of Being, Creator (Q 50:38) and is nearer to humanity than the jugular vein (Q 50:16). He demands obedience which is better than enquiring about what He is like. But Islamic philosophers influenced by Greek thought did speculate and arrived at a more impersonal God. Their message never got through to the masses who believed that if there was a God He revealed Himself in time and guided humanity. Some of the philosophers, influenced by Plotinus (*c.* 204–270 CE), believed in emanation rather than creation which has a parallel in the Kabbalism of Judaism. Eventually they agreed that while mankind had only a partial likeness to Allah, personal descriptions were needed otherwise we could not speak of Him at all. The personal is stressed in Christianity with its doctrine of incarnation.[3]

In Hinduism, Brahman, meaning sacred power or energy, is behind all things (referred to as an 'it'), the manifestations are personal and gradually this element became very prominent in Vishnu and Shiva who have incarnations or avatars meaning descent. The view of Brahman went through various stages: cosmic power of the universe, cause of the universe, the one and the many, male and female, and so on. Since the functions of Shiva, Vishnu and Brahma overlap, some have seen a trinity. All forms of life are sacred, for the divine is present in them and the chanting of mantras can bring the deity near. Brahman creates through Brahma; Vishnu preserves, sustains the world, and is loving and compassionate; Shiva is a mixture of opposites, being good and yet behaving in a somewhat irresponsible fashion. The gods have female consorts: Durga, Kali and Sati. Durga is a warrior, mother and daughter, Kali is love and terror and Sati is a virtuous wife.

In Buddhism there are the compassionate Bodhisattvas and the Amida Buddha who is the transcendent Buddha of Infinite Light and the personification of infinite mercy, wisdom, love and compassion. It is also possible to equate nirvana with the concept of God, for even in Theravada it is immovable, everlasting, deathless and permanent, which are predicates of the deity in the theistic religions. It is confirmed by what we understood as the Unconditioned. In Theravada it is usually a transcendent state but Mahayana does identify it with the Absolute and there is worship and devotion. But there is no Creator in Buddhism. Sikhism agrees with the Semitic religions concerning God who is eternal, creator, timeless, self-existent and revealing Himself by grace. He is present as light in every heart whether recognized or not.

Thus the answer to the question 'What is God like?' requires a belief that He is the ground of all existence (all the religions) yet acts in history (Semitic) either through incarnations or prophets or saints. All believe that He permeates all things. In Hinduism the principle of identity-in-difference operates in thinking about God. It is not a question of either (impersonal) or (personal) but both/and. In theological terminology, a dipolar God. It is not a contradiction but a paradox comparable to what the scientist says about light being both a particle and a wave or his understanding of time. We work with one kind of time which flows from past to present and on to the future. But science works with two: our time and static time. For physics all three tenses are there. If you think that is strange, think of the present. How long is it? Is it a second or no length at all? How can I pin the present down? How can I establish a distinction between the three tenses? Is time flowing or static? Which one is true? Most scientists would say both and the paradox has to be accepted.

Some arguments for God's existence

In the history of Christianity attempts have been made to demonstrate God's existence. There are the classical arguments, from the idea of God to its reality, from effect to cause, from the design of the universe to a designer, from morality to a moral law-giver, and from religious experience. I have considered these in some detail elsewhere and only mention relevant points here.[4] None of these arguments proves His existence but they are pointers in that direction. The most criticized is that of St Anselm's (1033–1109) with his definition of God: 'than that which nothing greater can be conceived'. Such a being has all the qualities that we do not possess being necessary. We are contingent: dependent on others for our existence. Anselm's argument was that everyone had an idea of God, but to exist not only in idea but also in reality is necessary if He is greater than any other being.

But Immanuel Kant countered by denying that existence is a predicate or a possession. An idea is a concept, not a reality corresponding to some object, and the properties of a thing do not include existence. I have an idea that there is a lot of money in my wallet but in reality when it is examined I have none. The Buddhist, however, would have some sympathy with Anselm. He argues that some things are real because we can see and touch them but other things like justice are equally real. Why? We cannot see or touch justice. The mind has conceived of justice and can work out if it exists in various countries. The same is true of citizenship and other concepts which we hold dear. Kant, however, produced the moral argument for the existence of God. There is within us a moral law which insists that we ought to do our duty. It is like the dharma which we have noted in Hinduism and it impinges upon us with the force of a categorical imperative. The 'ought' implies 'can' for it would be absurd to feel obliged to do an action if we did not have the freedom to do it. It would be like asking a beggar to donate sums of money to charity! Since doing our duty is often not rewarded here, there must be an afterlife and a law-giver to apportion rewards and penalties. If it could be demonstrated that we have a moral gene, Kant would have some confirmation for his view since he was criticized for not seeing morality as due to nurture. But it is evident that a good environment does not always result in a good person, so our genetic constitution has to be taken into account.

The cosmological argument moves from effect (the world) to God (the first cause), but there is a problem connected with the use of cause in this context. Thomas Aquinas, for example, argues from a sequence of causes to a First Cause: one that contains within itself the reason for its own existence. But we cannot move from a series of finite causes back to an infinite First Cause since we have to leap from the finite to the infinite. How can a series in time give us the infinite? And in any case there was no time before creation. The problem is that when we use the term 'first' we think of 'before', that is, temporal. But time was created with the universe so we cannot apply it to God at this point. Again in speaking of a First Cause we are thinking not of the Big Bang, that is, physical cause, which brought the universe into being, but the reason why we have a universe at all. It is an ultimate explanation, not a cause, and the answer to Hawking's question of why there is a universe, not how there is one. Instead of a causal chain we think of an explanatory one: an ontological ground of all existence.

In a previous chapter we saw that Darwin delivered what many thought was a fatal blow to the design argument for the existence of God. David Hume and Kant had been impressed by it and so was Darwin before he set out on his travels. He had been taught as a theological student by William Paley, whose book, *Evidences of Christianity and Moral Philosophy*, sought to confirm it. But when Darwin saw the struggle for existence in nature and how evolution proceeded by chance and random events with waste and suffering, he gave up any argument for design. However, in Chapter 11 we saw that physics had brought the argument back, particularly with the anthropic principle and the fine-tuning of the universe. How could the Big Bang be a random event or accident and the consequent establishment of order without a designer? Attempts to see it as simply the result of a quantum event have been debated but many physicists find it difficult to accept.

What do scientists say?

Stephen Hawking says that if the conditions and constants in the beginning of the universe and the rate of expansion one second after the Big Bang had been smaller by even one part in a hundred thousand million million, the universe would have recollapsed before it even reached its present size. With regard to biology long before Darwin, David Hume put forward the suggestion that an organizing principle responsible for patterns in nature might be within organisms not external to them. Today it is this which is emphasized: God has ordained nature to make itself through a long history of evolution which looks like design being built-in. Of course scientists exclude teleological causes from their work as serving no useful purpose, but those who on this basis contend that there is no divine purpose in nature, are making a metaphysical, not a scientific, claim. The reason for, or the cause of, an individual thing is not the same as inquiry about the cause of the totality, something which Darwin accepted. To insist that there is no overall purpose is a leap of faith, for it would require an exhaustive and unlimited knowledge of the universe. The theist argues that the interplay of chance and law in evolution allows new forms to emerge and such laws express God's purpose.

Scientists have been impressed with the beauty of the universe and its mathematical laws. Is God the law-giver? Opinions among scientists differ on this difficult point but some of the greatest have believed that He is. The best example we can think of is Einstein, the greatest scientist of the twentieth century. He said that the deeper one penetrated into nature's secrets the greater became the respect for God. Asked if he was deeply religious he replied: 'Yes, you can call it that. Try and penetrate with our limited means the secrets of nature and you will find that, behind all the discernible concatenations, there remains something subtle, intangible and inexplicable. Veneration for this force beyond anything that we can comprehend is my religion. To that extent I am in point of fact religious.'[5] And he went on to deny that he was a pantheist or an atheist. He sees a universe of order and law but we only dimly understand these laws and it is difficult to grasp the force behind it all. Reading the Gospels, he says that he was enthralled by the luminous figure of Jesus and felt that he experienced his presence. He was sure that no myth was filled with such life. But he did not believe in immortality and he had doubts about the soul.

The religion which he experienced in the Jewish synagogue at Munich repelled him so he refused to say that he belonged to a religious denomination but he valued his Jewish origin. As a youth he was a sceptic and a freethinker. But later in life in an article on religion and science in the *New York Times Magazine* (9 November 1930), he noted that there was a higher level of cosmic religiosity than usually propounded by religion. It did not have anthropocentric characteristics and was based on 'the miraculous order that manifests itself in nature as well as in the world of ideas'.[6] He did not think there was a conflict between science and cosmic religiosity but the latter was the strongest and noblest mainspring of scientific research. Einstein saw beauty in the laws of nature but no personified God, rather the guarantor of the laws. In judging a theory he asked himself if he were God would he have arranged it in that way and at times he gave the impression that he had a direct line to the 'old man' as he called Him. But he was a humble man and like Newton in later life expressed that humility: 'There isn't a single concept of which I am convinced that it will stand up, and I feel unsure if I am even on the right road. My contemporaries, however, see me as a heretic and a reactionary who has, as it were, outlived himself.'[7] He was critical and honest and never lost his sense of humour.

Einstein does seem to think that the universe reflects its Creator, though he was inclined to identify the one with the other. The world is intelligible and orderly, it is, like its Creator, mysterious and full of surprises. No one was more surprised and shocked than Einstein when Heisenberg and Niels Bohr emphasized the unpredictability of quantum mechanics, so he spent the rest of his life trying to prove them wrong. The scientist comes with his theories about it and sometimes finds them overturned by what is revealed. More realistic scientists understand that certainty regarding this mysterious universe is a nineteenth-century dream.

The development of science shows how quickly the facts change. Matter for Newton was invariable, but Einstein saw that it was variable and dependent on motion. Causality was deterministic with Newton but probabilistic with Heisenberg. Einstein's theory of relativity opposed Newton. It required a frame of reference, for example a background to show that a train was moving. Remove the background and difficulties arise. How often have we sat in a train at a station and thought we were moving? When we say that the earth revolves around the sun, we use it as a frame of reference: the revolution of the earth is considered relative to the sun. But the sun is moving so we do not know the absolute motion of the earth and the same thing occurs if we try to measure using another star. Einstein persisted with his thought experiments and gave the impression that he was mad when he said that a moving object not only contracts but gains mass as its speed increases. Gravity was equivalent to acceleration and not a force between objects but a curvature of spacetime caused by the presence of mass. Einstein argued that light close to the sun would be bent by the curvature of spacetime and during the total eclipse of 1919 he was proved right.[8]

Revelation

One of the major arguments for the existence of God is that He has revealed Himself to humanity and acts as nature does, providing surprises and complexity. Both the universe and God are mysterious. Mystery does not mean that which the scientist will ultimately be able to dispel but something which lies beyond our comprehension and will always be so.[9] But part of the mystery can be revealed both with nature and God and comes with a shock. We have just mentioned it with the experience of Einstein being annoyed by quantum uncertainty, but then his discoveries also surprised the scientific world. The observer in science interacts with the world and revelation in religion is interaction between persons and God. Of course the psychologist is right when he or she says humanity creates a god in its own image but revelation can upset the idea. Surprise, shock, awe, reverence and consciousness of sin dominate the experience. Arjuna in the *Gita* is terrified by the vision of Vishnu, Isaiah in the Jewish Temple cannot believe in what he is seeing, Saul of Tarsus finds that his ideas of Christianity are overturned, Muhammad thinks that he is going mad, and the people are astounded at the work and words of Jesus.

We do not have direct access to nature and similarly revelation is veiled. No-one has ever seen God as He is in Himself so we see 'through a glass darkly' (1 Cor. 13) or with respect to incarnation: 'veiled in flesh the Godhead see'. Revelation comes indirectly to us through the scriptures and here again there is a problem of oral transmission and editorial redaction. There is diversity and so it is difficult to distinguish between the human element and the divine. Revelation seems to differ from human insight for it inspires an unearthly awe and judges the ideas of the recipient. Karl Barth distinguished between three forms of the Word of God: the written, the preached and the living. The first two pointed to the Living Word (Jesus Christ), so they were not identical with him.

On the other hand, the Muslims claim that the Qur'an is the direct speech of God which is verbal inspiration held by fundamentalists in all religions. Muhammad was inspired (*wahy*), meaning that his powers of thought were suspended, and in a trance-like state he received the word of God. But this verbal inspiration does not take into account the human factor and the freedom given to the individual to interpret what he is being told. Nor does it take into account the role of reason or the impact of the environment or the emotions and decisions of the Prophet. More liberal Muslims, while holding to the divine status of the Qur'an, are moving to seeing it as the result of an interaction between Muhammad and God, and the effect of the environment upon him. The book, for example, does owe something to the Hebrew and Christian scriptures which Muhammad on his travels must have heard.

Revelation means that information is communicated, so we have the creative Word in Judaism (Dabar), the logos or Word in Christianity, the Qur'an as the speech of God in Islam, and Word in Sikhism. Between the two points of view, verbal inspiration and human insight, is the belief that there is an external Reality, however defined, who reveals Himself but it is given to fallible human beings. It appears to be the most reasonable view. The emotions of the recipient are evident as well as the intellect, so there is a recognition that we are more than information processors.

Apart from the written word of scripture, what does Word mean? The Greeks spoke of logos which for them meant the order of the world, the reliable pattern and harmony of all things. It is the principle of rationality and the Greek philosophers were well known for their stress on reason. The Hebrews had a more active view of Word, Dabar, for by it the heavens were made (Ps. 33:6). It was not the inactive God of Aristotle but One who manifested Himself in creation and history. Christianity thinks of both the Greek and Hebrew meanings when it speaks of logos in the Prologue to the Fourth Gospel (1:1–4, 14): the divinely ordained order of the world and the divine activity within it. The picture of God is one of being and becoming. The interpretation goes further and provided a shock for the Greeks because the passage announces that 'the Word became flesh and lived among us'. No wonder the Greeks thought of the incarnation as foolishness.[10]

Such revelation surprises and goes contrary to our ideas of Him and does not equate with understanding religion as a human projection. For example, the Book of Jonah illustrates that no-one was more surprised than Jonah as to what God was like and what he wanted him to do, so he thought that when he was instructed to be a missionary, the best thing to do was to run away! He was even more annoyed when this God, who had put him to so much trouble and distress, refused to destroy the pagan city of Nineveh. Such mercy was not in His lifestyle. The story is not intended to be taken literally but conveys a meaning about God and the reaction of human nature to His commands. Moses, Jeremiah and Muhammad did not want to obey because they knew the kind of scorn they would receive from those who thought differently. When Muhammad stressed the unity of Allah and preached against the current belief in many gods and goddesses, he had to flee to Medina to survive. What he was saying and doing opposed not only the religion of the day but also the economic and social order.

But if God is to reveal Himself in time He must be personal as the scriptures teach. This implies human attributes and involves limitations. Scripture teaches the limitation, particularly with regard to an incarnation (Philipp. 2). But how could the majesty and glory of God be revealed? If it had been without a veiling it would have interfered with individual freedom to choose, being so powerful that mankind would have been compelled to believe. We are persons and it is hardly likely that God should not possess this quality. Revelation is a person-to-person encounter but to understand how God is a person, since He is so superior to us, is difficult to know. We reveal ourselves through information but also by various ways of personal interaction. Even with us there is often a veiling and hiddenness about our intentions. We have seen how this personal centre is rejected by Buddhism but we find it difficult to think of ourselves without it. It is reasonable to argue that we are more than our thoughts, intentions and actions. We do not refer to a person as 'it' so it was an advance when Hinduism moved to the more personal in Vishnu, even though the 'it' guarded the impersonal nature of Brahman.

But a difficult problem has been the invisibility of God in contrast with the visibility of the world which the scientist deals with. Is that still true? A black hole occurs when stars collapse down to a point which does not reflect any light. Scientists cannot see it and only know it is there from the way it swallows up anything that passes too close to it. Physics informs us that there is dark matter in the universe that holds the galaxies together and that there is at least ten times more of it than matter that can be observed. Quarks are a level in the structure of matter and are stuck together by gluons, but no one has ever seen an isolated quark. Do they exist physically or only mathematically? Science relies not only on the empirical but also on the non-empirical: economy, elegance and naturalness. A theory is more likely to be accepted if it has these criteria. John Polkinghorne says that the beautiful patterns of mathematics are those that describe the universe and points to Paul Dirac, one of the founders of the quantum theory who spent his life searching for beautiful equations. It is claimed that a fundamental physical theory about the universe has never been expressed in ugly mathematics.[11]

But some argue that the religions differ in their ideas about God and there are varied interpretations of the sources that purport to tell us what He is like? How can we be sure that we have got the right interpretation? But there are different interpretations of what the world is like. Is it indeterministic (Bohr) or is it deterministic (Bohm)? How do we know that a scientific theory is correct? Karl Popper taught that science stops at the first sign of falsification but Lakatos argued that theories can be accepted even if they do not fit observation perfectly. Michael Polanyi pointed out that science was pursued by persons, based upon personal judgement and commitment to a point of view. Science, he thought, was like a faith community open to the testing of its belief (1 Thess. 5:21).

Scientists must possess faith in their theories despite opposition and the history of science has many examples of the pioneers and how they struggled to overcome their doubts and those of others. faith is an essential commodity with regard to the existence of God. Anselm, in his proof of the existence of God, moves from a faith position. If he had been asked why he did this he would probably have pointed to the statement of the writer to the Hebrews (11:6) who asserts that he who comes to God must believe that He is. The assumption leads to an assurance in terms of not only feeling but also the intellectual quest to find other evidence for the belief. Clearly the converse could occur in that he might find evidence that contradicted it. But he has to take the risk. The scientist assumes that the world is intelligible and orderly and proceeds to discover that it is. There is a risk attached to faith, whether secular or religious, but there is always the hope of being right!

If there is revelation in nature it is asserted that it also occurs in history, moral consciousness and inspiration. There is a general revelation, so humanity in general has some knowledge of God (Rom. 1:19f), but particular revelations, through visions, dreams or events, must be tested by the faith tradition just as the scientific community seeks to judge theories.

Religious experience

Closely connected with revelation is religious experience. Religion is natural to mankind and Sir Alister Hardy at the Religious Experience Research Centre, Westminster College, Oxford, recorded that 50 per cent of people involved in a survey said that they had had some kind of religious experience. Rudolf Otto (1869–1937), as we mentioned, contended that the centre of religious experience is a holy, awe-inspiring being, a *mysterium tremendum atque fascinans.* There is a feeling of guilt and trembling, but also fascination. The experience occurred in early mankind but extended to eminent scientists like Pascal, and writers and poets such as Coleridge and Ruskin. The fear we experience of a tiger springs from the sense of danger, but it does not have the uncanny nature that chills us when we look at a dead person. The numinous that Otto considers has a paralysing effect but also a thrill of excitement for it attracts, fascinates, and draws towards the ideal. He stressed the non-rational, beyond reason, not the irrational – a *mysterium* which transcends normal experience, and he goes on to quote examples from various religions.

But every religious experience is not so spectacular and it may be that it is ordinary experience in depth, so that there is a sense of a presence that disturbs 'with the joy of elevated thoughts'. God is found not in the whirlwind or the fire but in the gentle whisper (1 Kings 19:12). These experiences are not confined to those who are religiously inclined but can happen to philosophers, such as J. S. Mill and A. J. Ayer. The big question of course is, does it alter the way we treat others and make us less self-centred?

The mystic way has appealed to many great scientists: Einstein, Pauli, Schrödinger, Heisenberg, Eddington and Jeans. The sociologist, Peter Berger, believes that religious experience points to something beyond humanity: 'signals of transcendence' as we noted. Perhaps the tests of religious experience resemble more the artistic, for many aesthetic experiences are not naturally shared by a majority and their development requires training. There is no universally adopted testing system for works of art and no sophisticated predication of statements about it. Just like religious experience, the aesthetic cannot be assessed in a quantitative way by measurement but through the study of the great masters. Thinking, listening, absorption in the art form, inspiration and feeling are necessary in music and painting, as in meditation and prayer.

The problem of evil

Even if we could establish that God reveals Himself and that we experience His presence, the problem of evil mitigates against His goodness. As we saw, many Jews lost their faith because of the Holocaust and no final explanation can be found. But if God gave the gift of independence to us and allowed the world to make itself, it was not He who caused such evil but humanity. God, according to the record, did not intend the suffering of Job but allowed evil to have its way to show that Job was faithful. But in that story the figure of Satan is the accuser or tester. He implies that Job only serves God because he gets something from it – but what if he lost everything? Thus the test. In the New Testament, Satan becomes the leader of evil spirits who oppose God, and the name is used to refer to the chief of the devils or fallen angels. The Fall of mankind is also blamed on Adam and Eve yielding to the temptations of Satan. Today such a Fall is seen in our yielding to sin. Of course, thinkers in the nineteenth century, with its belief in the perfectibility of mankind, dismissed these ideas as primitive, but Satan is not only in Islam, Judaism and Christianity; he also appears under the name of Mara in Buddhism. He tries to deflect the Buddha from his aspiration to enlightenment. In Zoroastrianism this evil is on a par with God and a cosmic conflict ensues.

The Qur'an states that God made man from a lump of clay and ordered the angels to bow down to him, but Satan refused and was expelled. It may be that all this is an attempt to personify evil, but it does not take away from the fact that evil on a terrifying scale exists. And can it be ascribed only to humanity or is there some demonic influence? One survivor of the Holocaust said of the German guards: 'These people were not human.' It is a mystery how a people who were among the most civilized and cultured nations in the world could have perpetuated such evil against the Jews, the Russians and others. Evil does not disappear but today continues with genocide in various parts of the world.

The problem of evil is dealt with in Hinduism and Buddhism by postulating karma, which is an impersonal law operating in rebirth so that we suffer because of sin in a previous life. Suffering is a key concept in Buddhism and results from pursuing desires and attachment to material things. Another explanation of evil is that life could not have emerged without suffering. Competition and conflict were inevitable because we cannot have the values of courage and self-sacrifice without suffering. God does not intend the suffering but it is inevitable. What we do know is that God does not willingly afflict or grieve us (Lam. 3:32–3). Pain in normal circumstances acts as a warning in many cases and evokes our care and concern and teaches us compassion in a way that pleasure cannot.

Heaven, paradise and nirvana are offered to those who stand up to the test. But what of the suffering of the innocent? It is difficult to answer this question, but a limited answer might be that undeserved suffering has a tremendous effect on us: for example, the cross of Christ. But it is difficult to apply it to the Holocaust, though some argue that out of it emerged the ardent ambition to found the State of Israel. Suffering can have a bad effect, for the Holocaust caused many Jews to lose their faith. They had called upon God to deliver them and He had not answered. Such a miraculous intervention would have saved them and caused even the Nazis to believe, but God does not seem to work that way, as we mention in connection with miracles.

What about natural evil? Why does God not intervene to stop disasters of every kind? The strange thing is that men and women choose to live in places where scientists warn that earthquakes will occur. They think that it is worthwhile to take risks because of the beauty of the place or the economic gain. As one person said after the flood disasters in England, 'When one decides to live close to a river a risk must be taken.' What we can do is to put more resources into the scientific work of predicting when and where earthquakes are likely to occur so that people can have time to escape. Advice too can be given about building in these areas. It was estimated that in India and El Salvador more people were killed because of the fall of high buildings than in the earthquakes. The world operates by natural laws which we depend upon, so how can God interfere with them?

Representatives of insurance companies suddenly become believers when disasters occur and talk about acts of God! But if He has given the world the potential to make itself then the blame moves from the divine to the human. In evolution there are mutations which are good, bringing new possibilities of life, but there are also mutations which cause malignant cells. It is inescapable in a world making itself. God permits things to happen but does not determine them.[12] If the question is raised, 'Why did the Creator choose such a method?', the answer may be that He wanted to give the world freedom and independence rather than making it like a machine that was programmed and creatures who robot-like always did what was good. God acts by persuasion, giving room for human choice. But given the problem of evil and the injustice that is clear, Immanuel Kant and the religious traditions may be right when they postulated an afterlife where justice will be done. The Early Christians in all their sufferings argued that if they had hope only in this life then they were, of all people, to be pitied, but they endured because they believed that 'the creation itself would be set free from its bondage to decay and obtain the freedom of the glory of the children of God' (Rom. 8:18–21; 1 Cor. 15:10, 32f). The hope is eschatological vindication.

The modern philosophical debate on the existence of God is balanced between those who believe and those that do not. Of particular interest is the influence of Wittgenstein on Norman Malcolm, D. Z. Phillips and Peter Winch. They argue that the existence of God does not need to be justified by philosophy. The task is to clarify what it means to believe in God, for God language is expressive and descriptive, not factual. Anthony Kenny, however, reacts strongly against the use of Wittgenstein's 'language game' as Phillips and Malcolm employ it and asserts that in their hands 'it has become a stone-wall defence against any demand for a justification of belief in God'.[13] Alvin Plantinga, William Alston and R. G. Swinburne vary in their approach but hold that God exists, while Anthony Flew argues that the onus of proof rests on believers.[14] Swinburne tries to supply reasons for His existence and contends that it is probable, whereas J. L. Mackie doubts it.

We conclude that arguments for the existence of God are like His actions in the world, they seek not to prove but to persuade. In so doing they are like the 'paradigms' of science if

T. S. Kuhn is right. In his book, *The Structure of Scientific Revolutions* (1962), he suggested that major scientific theories were due to a change of paradigm, a new picture of reality. Its adoption according to him was not due to proof but to its persuasive qualities. However that may be, perhaps it is best to leave the last word to a scientist. Heisenberg said:

> If from the indubitable fact that the world exists, someone wants to infer a cause of this existence, his inference does not contradict our scientific knowledge at any point. No scientist has at his disposal even a single argument or any kind of fact with which he could oppose such an assumption. This is true, even if the cause – and how could it be otherwise – obviously has to be sought outside this three-dimensional world of ours.[15]

In our next chapter we ask the question, in the light of what we have discovered, of whether religion can be defined.

16 A definition of religion

Having considered the way religion is practised, organized and believed, we proceed to try and define it. Attempts, as we noted in the first chapter, usually concentrate on the functional or substantial aspects. The former wants to draw into the net secular ideologies which have little to do with the divine as understood by the religions we have examined. Questions about ultimacy are rarely answered as the sociologist deals with the function of religion in society, but it is useful to understand how religious organizations and secular movements can be regarded as similar.

The problem of a substantive definition is that it involves belief in the supernatural and raises problems. How are we going to explain it? And in the religions there seems to be such a blend between the religious and the secular, the social and the gods, and the reverence for ancestors and the worship of God, that the supernatural and natural are mixed together. It is difficult for us in a Western tradition, where religion is something distinct, private, and usually seen in state events or funerals or weddings, to understand this. But even where there is a secular government, as in India today, religion permeates every aspect of life. The Muslims insist that religion is Islam and the best state is an Islamic one.

But let us consider some of the elements that could be part of our understanding of what religion is.

An ethical definition?

This seems a good suggestion, for we have seen that good behaviour towards our neighbours and care of animals and the earth is required. Critics are right when they contend that religious members of the faiths have not practised what they have preached, but the ideal is there and needs to be followed. Conduct predominates over creeds in most, and it is interesting that on this basis Humanism was declared by the United States Supreme Court in 1961 to be a religion. The reason given was that though it denied the existence of God, it was a carefully structured belief system and had in common with the religions a belief in the dignity of the human person and the sharing of other ethical values.

By singling out ethics some scholars have sought a unification of the faiths and a reaching out to Humanism. Thus we considered Christian Humanists who reformulate the faith on a human basis. But apart from the criticism directed at them by secular Humanists, we cannot formulate a definition of religion based on only one of its characteristics. Humanists themselves do admit defects in their view of the nature of mankind. They have been too idealistic, believing in reason and good will and forgetting the darker side of human nature. The power, passion and domination of mankind seem beyond our capacity to solve, and some Humanists are not now writing off religion as they did in the past.

In the religions, morality and religion are linked. dharma, for example, in Hinduism has a variety of meanings, but taking it in the ethical sense it points to a religion which is concerned with conduct. It in turn is bound up with caste and social organization, so religion permeates everything. One is born a Hindu just as one is born a Jew, so how does a person separate his or her religion from membership of his or her community with all its beliefs in the gods and Brahman? In Judaism the same applies, so that mitzvah is seen as duty or obligation. It is the moral quality of the religious law. The Buddha's teaching (dhamma) is also basically ethical and in Sikhism it stands for duty.

In Islam, *din* is important, as we noted. It means religion in general and religious duties in particular: the five basic obligations of the Muslim. *Din* has a correlative, namely *iman*, which means faith or the activity of belief. The first pillar is of major importance: faith in Allah or belief in a sacred and spiritual dimension. From this flow the other pillars, stressing what the Muslim must do. Hence the belief in Allah is of extreme significance to Muslims and impossible to omit in any definition of what religion is for them.

Morality, then, must be included, but religion is more than that, so Matthew Arnold's definition of religion, 'morality touched with emotion', is too limited.

A legal definition?

Closely connected with morality is law. Can we define religion as law? Smart refers to the ethical or legal dimension. Islam has been called a religion of law and the Torah is of major importance in Judaism. But it is not only the following of rules or commandments but also the inner condition of the heart which is important. Islam has been interpreted as a religion of law but it has a lot to say about purity of intention in what we are doing and the prophets of Israel, conscious that the people had not kept the commandments because their hearts were far from Him, insisted that God would make a new covenant with them so that the Torah would be written inwardly not externally. (Isa. 29:13; Jer. 31:31ff). Religion can be viewed as the following of external rules, but it is the intention of the 'heart' that is important. In Judaism the motivation for keeping the Torah was the love of God, not for any gain, and in Christianity love of God and neighbour summarized the law.

A ritual definition?

Perhaps if we added rituals to morality and law we would have a definition. In some of these religions rites are essential and convey the sense of the divine. Sacraments, in particular, convey grace and in Catholicism it is necessary to receive them seven. But Islam, Hinduism, Sikhism and Judaism have no sacraments. Rites of initiation, however, are very important and the Eucharist in Christianity has its roots in the Passover celebration of the Jews. As we have said, Hinduism believes that a Brahmin must engage in ritual, and non-performance for one year entails loss of caste. Ritual is essential in devotional Hinduism and tantric since it is thought to be the way of joining the spiritual world. If the ritual is not done properly in the case of death, the soul will be unable to find peace.

Guru Nanak called for the abolition of rituals but he eventually instituted a basic ritual with *nam simran*, remembering God, and *nam japan*, meditation and repeating the name. Ritual re-enacts past events which are crucial to the faith, and with care and attention can foster the inner spirituality of the worshipper. Christians, for example, remember Christ in the celebration of the Eucharist and imaginatively enter into the experience of the disciples on the night when the sacrament was instituted. Whether icons, images, paintings or prayer beads are useful in worship continues to cause debate, as does the use of various aids such as the rosary.

In the New Testament religion is the translation of *threskeia* and is cultic actions which show reverence for the gods (Acts 25:19, 26:5). The application is to Jewish worship but it is also used of the Athenian cult of the unknown god in Acts 17:22. The early Christians understood religion as charity and self-control (James 1:27), which may be a reaction to religion in cultic forms. It is also insisted that one can have a form of godliness but no power. *Threskeia* is related to *eusebeia* or piety or reverence for the gods and the order in society that they uphold.[1]

An institutional definition?

Many people cannot think about religion except in the institutional sense, but the founders of religions have often protested about its bureaucracy and rituals. There is Buddha's criticism of brahmanic Hinduism, Jesus's judgements on legalistic attitudes within Judaism, and Muhammad's criticisms of pre-Islamic Meccan religion. In Hinduism there is no central institution and no control over the magic and superstition which some scholars see dominant in the villages of India. dharma is close to what religion means, which is the law, order, truth and duties of the Hindu people, but its practice is diverse, resulting in Vaishnavism, Shaivism and Shaktism, and it has different philosophical approaches. Hence it is very difficult to define religion even within Hinduism itself. Perhaps seeing the dharma as a way of life is the best we can do.[2]

A credal definition?

All religions have beliefs and in some they are more important than others. In Christianity correct belief is important (1 Tim. 3:16, 6:3; Titus i:i) and leads to a way of life (1 Tim. 2:2, 10; 5:4; 2 Pet. 1: 5–7, 3:11). A consideration of the letters of the Apostle Paul shows that they usually begin with beliefs, and proceed to argue that if God has done this in Christ then correct behaviour should follow. Doctrine became so important for the faith that men and women were burned at the stake for not assenting to the proper creed. But in other religions conduct is more important than creeds. Some say that Judaism is a religion of conduct only, but it is a half-truth since it rests on the belief in God and His acts which dominate their history.

Moses Maimonides (1135–1204), who is regarded as one of the greatest of the Jewish philosophers, produced a creed consisting of thirteen articles of faith which are considered to summarize the beliefs of the Jews. The most important are belief in the existence of God, the revelation of the Torah to Moses, the coming of the Messiah and the resurrection of the dead. How far he himself was attached to these beliefs is debatable and his reaction against any human characteristics being attributed to God meant that there was a gulf between this philosophical understanding and the devout believer at worship. He did incur the charge of heresy during and after his death.[3] Mainstream Islam has also been worried about heresy and the mystical Sufis have come under attack not only for their spiritual interpretation of the Pillars but also for the claim of some of them to have achieved union with Allah.

Beliefs are important and require a mention in any definition of religion.

A personal definition?

In a post-modern context there is an emphasis on the experience of individuals and the choices they make and often in the religions there is a conflict between what the institution is offering and the individual pursuit of religion. Whitehead, we recall, in his definition thought of the individual and while we have criticized it as limited to the experience of religion in 'solitariness' and not taking into account the operation of the institutions, he is right about personal experience. It is seen not only in the founders of the religions but also in their followers.

As might be expected William James, as a psychologist, concentrates on the personal. We recall that he said that religion cannot stand for any single principle or essence but is instead a collective name. According to him, religion cannot be limited to rituals which seek to please the deity for that would mean defining it by its external trappings which are aimed at winning the favour of the gods. In personal religion the focus is on the inner dispositions, the conscience, helplessness and incompleteness which the individual feels. Hence, in order to enter into the knowledge of God it is necessary to enter into personal relationship with Him. Nanak would have supported him since he had a personal experience of God, and such an experience in varying ways can be found in all religions. But James has to meet the criticism that this is a one-sided view with its focus on the personal which only forms part of religion.

In his last lecture he tries to meet the criticism by pointing out that institutional religion develops in a corrupt way, with meanness and lust for power, and contaminates the originally innocent thing. The prophet who had the personal experience is persecuted by the institution which he criticizes, but when his followers triumph over it eventually and form an organization, it in turn becomes the persecutor. Hence James moves to the Whitehead position with his definition:

> Religion is the feelings, acts, and experiences of individual men in their solitude, so far as they apprehend themselves to stand in relation to whatever they may consider the divine.[4]

It would seem necessary then to include the personal in any definition, but James needs to balance his account of institutions with the good as well as the bad and to include examples of those who by means of the rituals did have a personal experience of God. The founders of the religions made contact with institutional religion, not only criticizing what leaders and members believed and how they behaved but also reasoning with them about these matters. Jesus, for example, while he criticized the Judaism of his day, did not neglect attendance at worship and went as his custom was to the synagogue on the Sabbath day (Luke 4:16). And his example was followed by his early followers who met together in the Temple courts (Acts 2:46). Of course rituals must be thought out carefully and performed with purity, otherwise William James is right in saying that God is not pleased with much of their childish character, 'taking delight in toy-shop furniture, tapers and tinsel, costume and mumbling and mummery', and thinking that His glory was 'incomprehensibly enhanced thereby'.[5] But what ritual, with all its defects, points to is the deity.

A political definition?

This is implied by the definition of Aloysius Pieris which states that religion is a revolutionary urge, a psychosocial impulse to generate a new humanity. This follows the liberation theology which we have seen in Christianity and the involvement of Islam in the affairs of the state. Indeed with Islam there can be no separation. Orthodoxy in Judaism plays a role in Israelite politics and there are religious Zionists. In Britain religion is often told to keep out of politics but Anglican bishops continue to sit in the House of Lords. Buddhism has influenced emperors and political leaders, particularly Ashoka (Emperor of India 273–231 BCE), who announced in the Rock Edict IV that all cruelty would cease towards living creatures and that the sound of the war drums would be replaced by the call to the dharma of Buddhism. But there was the militancy of Nichiren (1222–82 CE) and his followers and Buddhism has been involved in the political struggles in parts of Asia and experienced persecution by the Chinese government. In general, however, Buddhism uses the non-violent methods of Gandhi, as was shown in Vietnam in the 1960s where it allied itself with Christianity. In Hinduism today there are many political groups jostling for power and threatening minorities.[6] Despite India being a secular state, religion permeates all of life.

Religion is dedicated to bringing about change in society and politics by peaceful means and can only engage in force as a last resort. Attempts, for example, to see Jesus as a political activist and revolutionary have largely failed. Religion must have its place in the political and social affairs of a nation but only as one influence among many.

A supernatural definition?

Religion has this divine dimension, as captured by Arnold Toynbee, who said that it was the presence in the world of something spiritually greater than man himself. And it conveyed a numinous or sacred quality. If this is so then it must be the primary dimension of religion. What or who points to God or Nibbana is central in the religions. In Buddhism it is the dhamma of the Buddha, in Christianity Christ, in Judaism the Torah, in Islam and Sikhism the scripture. The idea of a hierarchy in the characteristics of religion applies also to how the deity is to be contacted. Thus in Protestantism the doctrinal has been more important than the ritual as indicated by the centrality of preaching, but in other branches of Christianity, such as Greek Orthodoxy and Roman Catholicism, the sacraments claim the higher place.

When we consider other belief systems it is the belief in the sacred or supernatural which separates religions from them. The religions insist that it is the action of the divine through grace which liberates humanity from its problems. As we noted, religions believe that there is a need to be saved *from* something but also *to* something: a new lifestyle and mindset not only for the individual but also for the community. The stress on the kingdom of God or nibbana or brotherhood upon the earth is a worldly goal, but there is also the other-worldly: heaven or paradise or ultimate nibbana or where the righteous or the enlightened will dwell in a state of bliss. There are different ways of reaching these goals but, in general, apart from early Buddhism, aid is sought from God. Salvation is extended to human beings because despite their failings they have a potential for religion. It is understood in various ways, as 'the light that lighteth everyone that comes into the world' (John 1:9), the soul/principle of life in Hinduism (*atman*), or the *Tathagata-garbha*, potential for enlightenment in Buddhism. As we have argued, the world could have been given the potential to develop itself and now there appears to be a potential given to humanity for religion. It is one of the differences between mankind and the animal kingdom.

But while there is need to mention this spiritual characteristic of religions we are not too happy about the term supernatural. It gives the impression of something apart from the natural, but we learned that religions do not separate the religious and the secular and God is present everywhere. Also it is often seen as involving the existence of things which are debatable such as ghosts, spirits, the magic eye, witches, and so on. Hence in a definition we need to find some other way to express it.

Scholars tend not to use God in the definitions because of the varied meanings attached to it, but we have seen the unity of the concept behind all the various forms. In Buddhism the gods are mortal, being subject to karma, but nibbana or nirvana is stressed. What the Buddhists say about it has similarities with the theism of the other five religions. Nibbana is ultimate, absolute, unconditioned, so it is similar to those theists who stress the impersonal nature of God. And attributes of the deity are ascribed to the Bodhisattvas who possess a measureless lifespan, have supernatural power and act as saviours delivering humanity from fear, lust and folly. Hence they and the Buddha are worshipped.[7]

Dhamma also requires a closer look. It refers to the teaching of the Buddha but is also an impersonal, absolute, cosmic law without attributes or properties. It rules out a personal God but not the impersonal one that appears in Einstein's understanding. Human thought cannot grasp the concept so it is thought of as empty or *sunyata* or the void. The personal karma of the Buddhist must be brought close to dhamma, the Absolute. Once that takes place over many lives nibbana has been reached.[8]

Is there a definition that will embrace theism and the Buddhist concepts? Before settling it we glance briefly at some others which have been accepted today:

Any beliefs which involve the acceptance of a sacred, transempirical realm and any behaviours designed to affect a person's relationship with that realm.

(Peter Connolly)

The supernatural is taken into account by the phrase, 'a sacred, transempirical realm', but it is a rather narrow definition not specifying many of the aspects of religions which we have mentioned. Let us try some others:

Beliefs, actions and institutions which assume the existence of supernatural entities with powers of action or impersonal powers or processes possessed of moral purpose.

(Steve Bruce)

This is a fuller definition and is designed to include Buddhism. It could include Einstein's belief for he felt it easier to believe in an impersonal God, following Spinoza, rather than a personal. But it uses the term supernatural and does not do justice to the concept of God in the six world religions. He is the ground or source of all being and cannot be classed with supernatural entities or beings. Another one is:

A system of beliefs and practices by means of which a group of people struggle with the ultimate problems of human life.

(J. M. Yinger)[9]

This is not specific since we are not told what kind of beliefs and practices, and while it mentions community it could include other belief systems which struggle with what they would see as ultimate.

Drawing on the definitions and what we have learned from our study, let us try a definition:

Religion is a belief in God, who is the unconditioned ground of all things, and in spiritual beings, resulting in personal experience of salvation or enlightenment, communities, scriptures, rituals, and a way of life.

It is neither too broad nor too narrow, short but inclusive, and has its basis in the religions that we have examined. Such a definition allows for a belief in a spiritual dimension under various names: God, Allah, Yahweh, Brahman, Guru, unconditioned nibbana or the Absolute. It is true that some religions do not have scriptures but the definition stems from the religions we have examined. Philosophers continue to debate what the term God means, but since it is used extensively in religions we feel justified in retaining it. Those Buddhists who think positively of nibbana will equate it with the unconditioned and those who view it more negatively will still have the option of accepting it on the basis of spiritual beings in their religion.

The definition is not, of course, final, but we hope that it will lead to discussion and debate in an effort to understand religion which has been of such immense importance in the history of mankind. In our final chapter we speculate about its future.

17 The future of religion

It is difficult to forecast the future of religion as expressed in the religions which we have studied. Some have experienced decline in one part of the world but made advances in others. In a postmodern context all of them face among other things the challenge of globalization, rationalism, secularism and materialism. Travel and communication, due to the technological 'miracle', link the nations of the world in a new interaction which had not been seen in former times. Local and regional religious groups are now affected by social and political forces which may be operating very far away. What happens in India affects Hindus and Muslims in the UK and the tension in the Middle East causes problems between Jews and Arabs throughout the world. The immediate knowledge of these things is itself a spur for people to act 'in the heat of the moment' and live to regret it later. Often the motivation for action is governed not by religious values but by economics, competition, and the desire for power.

Religion is more important in some countries than others – in the USA, Latin America, Iran, Poland and Ireland. Nowadays it would be unwise to assess in local contexts and generalize the global condition of the religion. Some have done this, concentrating on the UK, but have made the point that migrants who are Hindus, Muslims or Sikhs have been greatly surprised by the lack of interest here. There are various reasons for this: mainstream churches' failure to attract the people, the loss of the sense of the supernatural, and the ability of science to explain most things naturally.

Hence religion is pushed to the periphery of society. The

media's treatment is an example of the trend, with religious broadcasts not usually at prime time and newspapers only interested in conflict between religious groups or focusing on the homosexuality of the clergy, their renunciation of celibate vows or the break-up of their marriage. Ideas about the sacred decline so that what was once considered special becomes the butt of comedians' jokes. The social and personal matters which religion used to help with are now referred to social workers and psychologists. Traditional religious institutions decline and young people turn to the new religious movements and the cults.[1]

But religion has a way of revitalizing itself and surprise those who thought that modernity would consign it to an early death. We have seen the attempts by members of the faiths to get together and discuss ways of making a social impact on the world and this ecumenicity is likely to continue. Agreements on beliefs are not likely, but a working together based on a common ethical concern for the poor and the Third World in particular would be a good goal to aim at. Modern means of communication, computers and the Internet are being used by the religions to foster revivals, evangelism, etc., throughout the world, with many faiths having their own web sites.

As we saw, sociologists differ about the effect of secularization, but one thing seems certain – that religion will not again have Durkheim's role of uniting people into a single community with a common set of beliefs. There is now a multiple choice of beliefs on offer and, according to the postmodernists, the individual not the group makes the decision. But youth in particular does not appear satisfied with the materialistic and scientific outlook which has demystified the world and in their spiritual quest they seem to want to remystify it.[2]

Religion reacts to any secular source that argues that it should disengage itself from society and politics and retire into some quiet corner of pietism. In Britain, Jewish and Christian leaders have made trenchant comments on the desire to make morality personal and not public in order to resist economic and political changes. They endorse the call for a moral renaissance, arguing that it is needed in the UK which is suffering from tolerance of crime and the victimization of the innocent. The criticism voiced by Anglican Bishops is echoed by

Jonathan Sacks, the Chief Rabbi, who calls for a more effective style of politics. He paints a devastating picture of both Britain and America who lie in a state of almost apocalyptic dreadfulness: rising crime, divorce, illegitimacy, single parenting, pulp fiction, adultery, depression, drug abuse, bad manners, shuttered shop windows, teenage abortion, and so on. But the comments did not mean that religion and the state should be united. It did not have the desire for a theocracy which can happen when secular and sacred are completely fused. Some religions over the years have wanted a theocracy: Islam, Judaism and Christianity. Today it is still seen in the Mormon faith, which was hounded from state to state by a government which believed in democracy, until eventually it found a home at Salt Lake City. The Sikhs also combined spiritual and temporal power in the Guru and later in the Akal Takht.[3]

Fundamentalism is present in all faiths. Will its resurgence continue? As we noted, it is the urge to return to fundamental values held by the people in the past and to scriptural teaching often understood in a literal way. Its goal is to make a place for an authentic expression of the faith and it reacts politically and socially against materialism and relativism and today uses modern technology to achieve its aims. The Taliban have transformed Afghanistan into an Islamic state, oppressed women, destroyed Buddhist statues, and have harboured the terrorists who caused the awful destruction of buildings in New York with the loss of thousands of lives. But reprisals against them will cause the death of many innocent people in a country which is already in a very poor condition. Mainstream Islam has condemned such extremes and pointed out that Iran was now relaxing its rules and interpreting the shari'ah in a more liberal way. In Israel the fundamentalist Neturei Karta refused to have any dealings with the state and withdrew into their own ghetto. Those in the various faiths who are more liberal and tolerant are accused by the fundamentalists of diluting the faith by their attempts to reconcile it with the secular world.[4]

Let us look at each religion in turn, starting as usual with Judaism. The religion is divided into many groups and some forecast that more splits will occur in the future. Some expect a Messiah to appear: the Hasidim think that their seventh Lubavich rabbi will return. But not all Jews practise their religion and secular Zionists believe that they must establish the nation without any divine help. Is it possible that some way might be found to reconcile the groups? It is difficult to say but it is likely that the Haredim will have strong political influence and the Reform continue to support the state. But while Israel is politically the focus of the world's attention, the faith is declining.

One factor that would help is to develop a more universal image of Judaism so that converts might be attracted to the religion and barriers removed which prevents them being Jews. A difficulty is the question about who is a Jew. It affects not only converts but whether or not there will be further divisions. The Orthodox insist that maternal ancestry and strict supervision of conversion make a Jew, while Reform has allowed converts on a more flexible basis. If the Orthodox position was accepted by the state it would mean the disenfranchisement of large numbers of American and European Jews.[5] The debate has been heated in the Knesset about the matter and shows the impact that religious parties can make. Another factor which is causing decline is 'marrying out', that is choosing a partner who is not a Jew, which in many cases means that the children are not brought up as Jews.

Currently there does not seem to be any end to the conflict between Jew and Arab in the country, with warring factions disunited even among themselves. It is likely, however, that Israel in the search for peace will be able to oppose their hard-liners and compromise with the Palestinians in their demand for land.

Christianity, with its universal message to all people, not being tied to birth or ethnicity, has expanded in Africa and Asia and is strong in the USA, Ireland, Poland and Latin America, but has declined in Europe. In the future it is likely to learn from Liberation Theology in South Africa and Latin America. Liberation cannot be restricted to the spiritual but has to be involved when there is injustice. It raised a question about mainstream religions' lack of concern for the poor and refusal to oppose the state. The situation in South Africa was aggravated by a Christian denomination, the Dutch Reformed Church, as we noted, and its support for a racist regime.

Black liberation theology dwelt on this omission, arguing that Jesus was concerned for the hungry, the naked, the oppressed and the exploited. The Church needed to oppose the oppressive state. Allan Boesak identified Jesus as a black messiah saying, 'The Jesus who represented the God of the Bible cannot be the same one whose name was carved into the bows of the Dutch slave ships in which Africans were transported to their death', and Desmond Tutu posed the question 'Why does suffering single out black people so conspicuously, suffering . . . at the hands of white fellow Christians who claim allegiance to the same Lord and Master?'[6]

In Russia the orthodox church will need to recover fully from the persecution endured under communist rule not only in leadership but also in the replacing and repairing of the churches that were damaged. Over 200,000 priests were killed and divisions also occurred, since some groups thought that the Church should have been less passive with communism. There is also the problem of how to treat other faiths in Russia and it appears that only religions registered for fifteen years or more are able to hold services and distribute literature. In 1997 a movement started to canonize Nicholas II, the last tsar. Again this raises the question of whether the Church will be an influence in any attempt to restore the monarchy.[7]

With regard to the USA we remember the resurgence of Fundamentalism which assisted the Republicans to return to power in 1980. Groups such as the Religious Roundtable in Virginia, the Christian Voice in California and the Moral Majority represent 72,000 pastors and demand Christian input with respect to social policy. The new Christian Right is involved in wanting changes in moral behaviour and in geo-political and economic issues. Making use of radio, television and the Internet to propagate their views, they exercise an influence out of proportion with a minority position. While they are divided among themselves, they are united on politics opposing homosexuals, communists, abortion, euthanasia, and so on. Some of their number have campaigned for presidential nomination and the Promise Keepers, led by a former football coach called Bill McCartney, have a budget of US$100 million, a permanent staff of 400 and, at one gathering in Washington, there were 700,000 members calling for the nation to repent.

Feminists and gays protest about the movement since it excludes women and contends that only heterosexual relationships are acceptable. It is likely that they will receive some support from George W. Bush and be more in tune with his policies than those of Bill Clinton, whose behaviour they deplored.[8]

In Northern Ireland the peace process remains fragile despite the Good Friday agreement, and the annual marching season continues the remembrance of past conflicts. It acts as a spark to ignite further troubles between Republicans and Unionists. The whole of Ireland was colonized by the British in the seventeenth century with the settlement of British landowners who took the land from the indigenous Irish population. In the parades, politics and religion are fused together. Protestants define themselves as loyalists, asserting that Ulster must remain part of the United Kingdom, whereas most Catholics see themselves as republicans. Both are more religious than people in England and exist often in segregated areas. Mixed marriages are frowned upon, education is often separate, clergy can function as members of parliament and leaders of churches, and unemployment continues to be higher among Catholics than Protestants.[9] Currently the future for religion looks much brighter but it is difficult to predict in a situation which can easily take a turn for the worse, as is seen in the bombing by the 'real IRA'.

As the twenty-first century proceeds it is likely that Christianity will still be involved in politics, become more concerned about the Third World, and endeavour to reach out towards the working class whose absence at worship is so noticeable. A more liberal attitude to the ordination of women may penetrate Eastern orthodoxy and Roman Catholicism and attitudes to gays and lesbians will take more account of the genetic debate. And much may be learned from attempts to communicate the message in context with experiments such as Father Bede Griffith's ashram in South India and Zen Buddhist techniques in Japan. One particular problem is the decline in membership of the churches in the UK and the present attenders at worship tend to be older, with a significant absence of youth and children. Mainstream Christianity is likely to learn something from the new religious movements and try to bring their forms of service more into line with modern communication in order to attract the youth.[10]

Islam is the fastest growing religion in the world. Will Islam be able to break down its hostile image as portrayed by the Western media? Or will it expand its militancy to other countries? It is the revolutionary aspect of the faith that attracts the media so that Iran is watched carefully by Western observers. It has shari'ah law at the centre of the state, but other countries such as Saudi Arabia, which has an absolute Islamic monarchy, remain stable. Why? One view is to maintain oil exports to the West, but this causes some Muslims to complain that in so doing it has compromised the faith. In Turkey secularism has been reversed, with thousands of mosques being built and a return to traditional Islamic behaviour. But the consequences of Iran's revolution are still being felt in Afghanistan where, as we noted, a purely Muslim state was established. In Iran, the Islamic Republic Party, founded by Ali Khomenei, supports the Hizbollah (Party of God) which directs terrorist attacks against Israel.[11] With the resurgence of fundamentalism in the faith it is possible that the revolutionary pattern will be repeated elsewhere.

Islam in America has been involved in race disturbances over the years and it is clear that there is pride in being both black and Muslim. Malcolm X did oppose the views of his teacher Elijah Muhammad, who was racist and had initiated a campaign against whites. He insisted on the brotherhood of all believers no matter what race or religion they adhered to, but he sought to give Muslims a pride in their religion and ethnic status. This Nation of Islam movement gained respect from orthodox Muslims and in 1985 integrated into the Islamic community. The matter is very important because it is predicted that by 2015 Islam will be the second largest religion in the USA and will be a major factor in the future of the African-American community. With respect to Russia, it is estimated that there are about 40 million Muslims and a growth in the building of Mosques. But the Muslim takeover of Afghanistan has increased the Russian worry about Islamic dissent. However, the power of Islam in Russia has been affected by the division between Sunni and Shi'ah.[12]

Islam is concerned about Western decadence with its sexual

liberation, corruption in economics, high rates of interest, and state education rather than religious. But mainstream Islam has learned to live with such modernity without engaging in revolution. One of the hindrances to the faith continues to be the divisions. The Sunni have no central hierarchy to deal with theological differences or crises that may arise because of the need for consensus. There are also disagreements as to what is the best state and how the Muslim should behave in a secular society. National and ethnic considerations do play a part, as was observed in the war between Iran and Iraq. But as in other religions there is the realism that a perfect state cannot be realized and the turning to a Messianic hope, with the Shi'ah expecting the 'hidden imam'. It is part of the larger hope of religions to believe that it requires someone or something greater than humanity to bring about peace and prosperity on earth.

In India there is the spiritual force of the new gurus, some of whom have reached international status, who do not belong to the traditional orders, nor have they been ordained by them, but are charismatic leaders. One of them, Sathya Sai Baba, born in 1926, is reported to have performed miracles and attracts thousands of followers. As well as men there have been female gurus, for example, Ananadamayi Ma (1896–1983), who, though illiterate and coming from a small village, intuitively grasped religious truths. Her work resulted in many Ananadamayi Centres in India and abroad. But some gurus have not been able to resist the temptation of Western money when they have travelled abroad and have been involved in sexual abuses and financial scandals.[13]

However, it is the force of nationalism that is attracting world attention. We mentioned earlier the Bharatiya Janata Party (BJP) which is the political wing of the Rashtriya Swayamsevak Sangh (RSS). It started at the beginning of the twentieth century and stressed Hindu culture, martial arts, religion, and anything that would support the Hindu nation. Foreigners are outsiders, especially Muslims whose Mosques, it is alleged, are built on the site of Hindu temples and must be removed. Muslims and Christians are like 'drug addicts' because of the foreign culture that they subscribe to. The BJP and the Vishva Hindu Parishad (VHP), founded in 1964, now have a major role in government and were influential in India's decision to hold nuclear tests as a symbol of its strength. Since Pakistan, which is Muslim, immediately did the same, it heightened tension dramatically and creates a major worry for the future.[14]

Nationalism stems from fear of foreign rule and influence and missionary work on the part of other religions. Hinduism as a world religion and involvement in politics began to take shape in the twentieth century as seen in the creation of the Ramakrishna Math and Mission founded by Swami Vivekananda. He believed that Hinduism was the mother of all religions and while acknowledging one truth behind all religions, spoke in Chicago of the superiority of Hinduism. The Mission has continued to believe this, but it is more notable for its attempts to relieve the poverty of the masses. Much more aggressive is the Arya Samaj, which has caused problems not only for Muslims but also for Sikhs. It led to the founding of the Hindu Mahasabha (the Hindu Great Assembly), a right-wing military Hindu political party. They believe that Hindus must govern themselves and have the right to establish a Hindu homeland based on their own culture and tradition. It is asserted that Pakistan would not exist today if their call for a Hindustan had been heeded. Reunification of the country must be attempted, though little hope can be placed in the state or its Constitution.[15]

In contrast we have tolerance and universality stemming from Gandhi and Aurobindo, even though they were involved in Indian nationalism. Gandhi saw no separation between religion and politics and insisted that Hinduism must welcome all. His friends were Muslims and Christians to the extent that he was accused of betraying Hinduism. Aurobindo had been violent in youth but gave up conflict and welcomed those of other faiths. Both were inclusive, hence the kind of nationalism advocated in India today would be deplored by them. The Dalits (untouchables) too reject nationalism because it has not mounted public campaigns to have caste abolished. The state has declared it to be illegal but they cannot believe that in practice it will cease to exist, hence they say that they will have to live with it and call for their own caste.[16]

Which way will Hinduism go: universalism or nationalism?

If the latter triumphed, and currently it is having a great impact, it would not only create more problems for the minorities but also for the relation with Muslim Pakistan. Sikhs and others may be treated as lapsed Hindus but Muslims do not fall into this category and must be treated as foreign outsiders. The outlook for good relations between Muslims, Hindus and Sikhs remains somewhat bleak.

One of the questions regarding Buddhism is whether or not the involvement in violence in various countries will continue and even develop. Historically, the faith has had good relations with states and has acted as an adviser to rulers, but tension in Tibet and conflict in Sri Lanka continues. Hindus are trying to get a separate state in the latter for the Tamil minority, but Buddhism has added its support to the opposition. When a religion becomes dominant in any country the power motive emerges and minorities suffer. The United Monk Front in Sri Lanka supports the Sri Lankan Freedom Party (SLFP) and has departed from the traditional role of advisers. The detachment from worldly affairs has been abandoned. The same kind of nationalistic spirit has inspired Buddhism as in Hinduism and when the SLFP came to power the centrality of the faith was celebrated. Hostility was also shown to other religions in the country and Buddhist institutions dominated the landscape. They opposed any compromise with the Tamil and violence was the consequence. It is estimated that more lives have been lost in the country than during the same period in Bosnia.[17] Muslims in Bosnia suffered dreadfully with over 7000 killed.

Buddhism today shows a tendency to move away from withdrawal into monasteries and become activist, which is good so long as it seeks to challenge unjust regimes and poverty and not give support to governments who oppress minorities. Many Buddhists have undertaken marches for peace, demanding social justice and protesting about the pollution of the environment. One good aspect of the Sri Lanka situation is *sarvodaya*, which is a social programme designed to work for the rural development of all members of the various religions. Over 2000 monks are building roads, irrigating canals, and working in community kitchens and marketing. Their message is that the way to overcome personal animosity, greed and egotism is by dealing with social, economic and political problems. Enlightenment becomes very practical, so that to have the right mindfulness is to see the need which exists and do something about it. This peaceful way of achieving change, modelled on Gandhi's non-violence, will also contribute much to the future of the faith. And in other parts of south-east and east Asia and Japan there has been a resurgence of peaceful Buddhism with the Japanese favouring Zen, Pure Land Buddhism and other aspects of the faith. Most of the new religious movements in Japan have their roots in Buddhism.[18]

Buddhism is a missionary religion, likely to continue to attract Western people, and books on it are read widely in most countries. The process of sitting quietly meditating or engaging in yoga is a contrast to the bustle and rush of daily life in the West and provides new resources of inner strength. The position of women in the faith is certain to improve as Buddhism experiences the egalitarian treatment of them in Europe and the US. Today there are many more nuns and full ordination has taken place in various places.

The question of how far Buddhism has been diluted by the events and conditions which it has experienced in various countries is and will continue to be the subject of debate. Some see a form of Christian Buddhism being offered while others speak about the compromising of the ideals of the sangha. In general, will Buddhism be able to avoid sacrificing its principles in order to be relevant to life in the cities dominated by materialist values?[19] Only the future will tell.

Sikhism is the fifth largest world religion, is universal, but has never sought converts. Since many of them see the way forward in the granting of a homeland of their own, a nationalistic spirit and an exclusivist identity has developed which is not consonant with the universalism of the gurus who preached to Hindus and Muslims. The Adi Granth itself includes the writings of Hindus and Muslims. But those who participated in the battle which raged at Amritsar in 1984 (see Chapter 8) had in mind Khalistan, a separate Sikh state. At the first World Sikh Sammelan in 1995 these tragic events were not far from their minds and suspicion of the intentions of both Muslims and Hindus was evident.

Militancy has shown itself in various ways since 1984 and

tension continues to exist in India. The problem is that the faith is a small minority in the country and has always been in danger of being assimilated into Hinduism. The Hindu Arya Samai, being missionary minded, used every method to try and convert the Sikhs to their faith. Over the years the Sikhs responded with various movements intended to stop such activity and keep alive their faith. Before India became independent they turned to the British who had recognized the valour of their soldiers and who realized the advantage of sustaining Sikh identity as against the Hindus and the Muslims. They helped them economically and in other ways; Sikh preachers and teachers warned them, e.g. Kahn Singh Nabha (1861–1938), against embracing Hinduism and went on to plead for an India in which all religions would equally be recognized. But the Sikhs deplored the creation of a Muslim state, namely Pakistan, for it included their cultural region, the Punjab. Consequently, thousands of Sikhs left the Punjab and settled in India, which meant loss of property and access to the sacred sites of their faith. Their home became the new state of the Punjab (1947), but it remained one of the states of India.[20]

The question with regard to the future is whether or not they will be able to maintain the Punjab, since they are so close to Pakistan and a minority within India. Discontent with their present position stems from feelings of insecurity, a belief that India is not doing enough to recognize their identity, lack of investment by the government, and a conviction that India is not grateful for their contribution to the economy of the country. Many Sikhs have migrated abroad, causing a further diminishing of their numbers, and they have become worried by the number of Hindus who have come to work in the Punjab. Hence today Sikhs are making economic, social, constitutional and religious demands. Whether or not their demands for a Khalistan will be met is uncertain, though many are engaged in a vigorous campaign to bring it about and are prepared for martyrdom, which is characteristic of Sikh history. The events of 1984 attracted world attention and in 1995 at the World Sikh Sammelan there was a consensus reached on the authority of the Guru Granth Sahib that religion and politics can function independently in their own areas and that Akal Takht is the supreme authority.[21] Those who had participated in the events of 1984 were honoured but, in general, the tone of the Assembly was moderate, which holds out more hope of peaceful negotiations with the Indian government.

It is likely that religions in the future will remain a political force and will make more use of modern technology in communicating their message. Religion will change the organizations of its institutions and rituals to attract and meet the needs of the young, and women will become prominent and gain more access to positions of authority, even though it may mean further divisions within the faiths. With the pressure of globalization, more dialogue will take place between the religions in an effort not only to get to know one another's viewpoints, but also to persuade governments to do more for the poor, especially in the Third World.

Is religion still strong enough to make an impact? It would seem so by recent statistics. The following are percentages showing the followers of the religions: Sikhs 0.36, Hindus 13.5, Buddhists 5.99, Muslims 18.25, Jews 0.24, Christians 33.6. Jews are a minority, but quantity does not always mean quality, and they are and have been most talented and influential in all 'walks of life'.[22]

If religion continues to involve itself in changing the individual and society by peaceful means, its future is assured, but the use of force is not compatible with what the founders of the religions preached and embraces the values of the conqueror. Since greed, fear, suspicion, and survival of the fittest are the values of a materialist world, it is the ideals and self-sacrifice of religions that are impressive and attract people despite their egotism. When religion loses these its future will be uncertain. The brotherhood of mankind is the ideal of the religions and peaceful activism of religion in social, economic and political affairs is acknowledged as one way of achieving it.

Notes

1 Can religion be defined?

1 Francis Clark, *Introduction to the Study of Religion*. A101 units 19/20, pp. 12ff, Open University, Milton Keynes, 1981.
2 H. J. Richards, *Philosophy of Religion*, Heinemann, London, 1998. Quoting from the *Guinness Book of Answers*, 1991, p. 62, which bases the numbers on United Nations statistics and figures supplied by religious bodies.
3 Gwilym Beckerlegge, *Religion and Science in Context*. A103, *Introduction to the Humanities*, Book 4, pp. 33ff, Open University, Milton Keynes, 1998. Smart added the material dimension later.
4 Max Weber, *Sociology of Religion* (1st edn), Methuen, London, 1920. Quoted by John Bird, *Investigating Religion*, HarperCollins, London, 1999, p. 18.
5 D. F. Pocock, *Mind, Body, Health: A Study of Belief and Practice in an Indian Village*, Blackwell, Oxford, 1973. AD208, p. 22, Open University, Milton Keynes.

2 How is religion studied?

1 Eric Sharpe, 'Seekers and Scholars'. AD208 units 1, 2, 3, p. 62, Open University, Milton Keynes, 1981.
2 Ibid.
3 Eric Sharpe, 'The Comparative Study of Religion in Historical Perspective', in W. Foy (ed.), *Man's Religious Quest: A Reader*, Croom Helm, London, 1978, pp. 7ff.
4 Connected in particular with A. J. Ayer's book, *Language, Truth and Logic*, Penguin, Harmondsworth, 1971.
5 Paul Williams, 'The Sense of the Holy'. A101 unit 20, pp. 76ff, 87f, Open University, Milton Keynes, 1980. William James, *The Varieties of Religious Experience*, Penguin Classics, Harmondsworth, 1985. See lectures 4 and 5 for the distinction between 'once-born' and 'twice born' pp. 78ff.
6 P. Williams, op. cit., p. 93. Satori means enlightenment, the goal of Zen Buddhism.

7 A. Comte, *Positive Philosophy*, Chapman, London, 2 vols, 1853. E. Sharpe, op. cit., p. 17.

8 Peter Connolly (ed.), *Approaches to the Study of Religion*, Cassell, London and New York, 1999, pp. 199ff. See Max Weber, *Protestant Ethic and the Spirit of Capitalism* (trans. T. Parsons), Allen & Unwin, London, 1930; *The Sociology of Religion* (trans. Ephraim Fischoff), Beacon Press, Boston, 1963.

9 Bryan Wilson, *Religion in Sociological Perspective*, Oxford, OUP, 1982, deals with sectarianism and secularization. Steve Bruce (ed.), *Religion and Modernisation: Sociologists and Historians Debate the Secularization Thesis*, Clarendon Press, Oxford, 1983. It has the approaches of David Martin, Bryan Wilson and Peter Berger.

10 Clive Erricker, 'Phenomenological Approaches', in P. Connolly, op. cit., Chapter 3.

3 Rituals

1 Gwilym Beckerlegge, Study Guide 1, A213 World Religions, Open University, Milton Keynes, 1998, p. 19.

2 Jean Holm and John Bowker (eds), *Sacred Place*, Pinter, London, 1998, p. 129.

3 J. G. Davies, 'Christianity: The Early Church', in R. C. Zaehner (ed.), *Concise Encyclopedia of Living Faiths*, Hutchinson, London, 1977, pp. 40ff. Study Guide 1, p. 26, Open University, Milton Keynes, 1998.

4 J. Holm and J. Bowker, op. cit., pp. 42ff.

5 Terry Thomas and J. F. Coakley, *Christianity*. A213 units 3–4, World Religions, Open University, Milton Keynes, 1997, p. 29.

6 J. Holm and J. Bowker, op. cit., pp. 93ff.

7 J. Holm and J. Bowker, op. cit., pp. 74ff.

8 Cybelle Shattuck, *Hinduism*, Routledge, London and New York, 1999, p. 80.

9 Ibid., pp. 83ff.

10 Pushpesh Pant, *Buddhism*, Tiger Books International PLC, London, 1997, p. 32. Study Guide 1, p. 41.

11 J. Holm and J. Bowker, op. cit., p. 9. Study Guide 1, p. 42.

12 J. Holm and J. Bowker, op. cit., p. 15.

13 Gurbachan Singh, *The Sikhs*, Tiger Books International, London, 1998, pp. 79ff.

14 Terry Thomas, *Sikhism*. A213 units 14–15, World Religions, Open University, Milton Keynes, 1998, p. 26.

4 Scriptures

1 R. Crawford, *The Saga of God Incarnate*, University of South Africa, Pretoria, 1998. Here 'saga' is suggested when understanding the incarnation rather than 'myth'.

2 David Goldstein, *Judaism*. A213, World Religions, units 1–2, Open University, Milton Keynes, 1990, pp. 6ff.

3 J. G. Davies, 'Christianity: The Early Church', in R. C. Zaehner (ed.), *The Concise Encyclopedia of Living Faiths*, Hutchinson, London, 1979, pp. 44ff.

4 See K. Ward, *Christianity. A Short Introduction*, One World, Oxford, 2000.
5 Kenneth Cragg, *Islam*. A213, World Religions, units 5–6, Open University, Milton Keynes, pp. 22, 57.
6 N. J. Dawson, *The Koran*, Penguin, Middlesex, 1956, pp. 33ff, 403ff.
7 S. Weightman, *Hinduism*. A213, units 7–10, Open University, Milton Keynes, 1998, pp. 12ff.
8 Bradley K. Hawkins, *Buddhism*, Prentice Hall Inc., New Jersey, USA, 1999, p. 50.
9 Helen Waterhouse, *Buddhism*. A213, units 11–13, Open University, Milton Keynes, 2000, pp. 82ff.
10 Terry Thomas, *Sikhism*. A218, units 14–15, Open University, Milton Keynes, 1988, p. 46.

5 **Behaviour**

1 J. Holm and J. Bowker (eds), *Making Moral Decisions*, Pinter, London, 1998, pp. 3ff, 149ff. R. Crawford, *Can We Ever Kill?* Darton, Longman and Todd, London, 2000, for detailed discussions of philosophy and theology on current ethical questions.
2 David Goldstein, *Judaism*. A213, World Religions, Open University, Milton Keynes, 1997, p. 39.
3 J. Holm and J. Bowker, op. cit., p. 149. But the Jew is encouraged morally to go beyond the Torah.
4 G. Beckerlegge (ed.), *The World Religions Reader*, Routledge, London and New York, 2000, pp. 57ff.
5 David C. Gross, *1,000 Questions and Answers about Judaism*, Robson Books, London, 1987, p. 16.
6 Ibid., pp. 27ff, 32, 44ff.
7 G. Beckerlegge, *Religion at the End of the Twentieth Century*. A213, World Religions, unit 16 (2nd edn), 2000, p. 59.
8 Ibid., 3.2, 37.
9 Ibid., pp. 192ff.
10 Ibid., p. 74.
11 J. Holm and J. Bowker (eds), *Women in Religion*, Pinter, London, 1994, p. 95.
12 C. Shattuck, *Hinduism*, Routledge, London, 1999, pp. 12ff, 39ff.
13 Jean Holm, *Making Moral Decisions*, Pinter, London, 1998, p. 85. See also P. Morgan and C. Lawton (eds), *Ethical Issues in Six Religious Traditions*, University Press, Edinburgh, 1996.
14 G. Beckerlegge (ed.), *The World Religions Reader*, op. cit., pp. 308ff.
15 R. C. Zaehner (ed.), *The Concise Encyclopedia of Living Faiths*, Hutchinson, London, 1979, p. 276 note.
16 H. McLeod, *Sikhism*, Penguin, Harmondsworth, 1997, pp. 239ff.
17 Owen Cole and Pa Sambho, *The Sikhs*, Sussex Academic Press, Brighton, 1995, pp. 146ff.
18 J. Holm and J. Bowker (eds), *Women in Religion*, op. cit., p. 9.

6 Women

1 J. Holm and J. Bowker (eds), *Women in Religion*, Pinter, London, 1998, p. xii.
2 David Goldstein, *Judaism*. A213, World Religions, Open University, Milton Keynes, 1997, p. 19. G. Beckerlegge (ed.), *The World Religions Reader*, Routledge, London, 2000, p. 9.
3 Ellen M. Umansky, 'Reclaiming the Covenant: A Jewish Feminist's Search for Meaning', in G. Beckerlegge, op. cit., p. 69.
4 J. Holm and J. Bowker, op. cit., p. 127.
5 Norman Solomon, *Judaism*, OUP, Oxford, 1996, p. 122.
6 Susan Mumm, Study Guide 2, A213, World Religions, Open University, Milton Keynes, 1998, p. 69.
7 J. Holm and J. Bowker, op. cit., pp. 43, 51. S. Mumm, op. cit., p. 68.
8 J. Bowker, *Is God a Virus?* SPCK, London, 1995, pp. 240ff.
9 H. P. Fry (ed.), *Christian Jewish Dialogue: A Reader*, University of Exeter, 1996, pp. 232ff, 239ff, 248ff.
10 J. Holm and J. Bowker, op. cit., p. 109. Qur'an 4.35, 33.35.
11 J. Holm and J. Bowker, op. cit., p. 109. Reader in World Religions 3.38, Study Guide 2, 71f.
12 J. Holm and J. Bowker, op. cit., pp. 92, 109.
13 J. Holm and J. Bowker, op. cit., pp. 61f, 73ff. Cybelle Shattuck, *Hinduism*, Routledge, London, 1999, p. 33.
14 B. K. Hawkins, *Buddhism*, Prentice Hall Inc., New Jersey, USA, 1999, p. 106.
15 R. C. Zaehner (ed.), *The Concise Encyclopedia of Living Faiths*, Hutchinson, London, 1979, p. 314.
16 B. K. Hawkins, op. cit., p. 60.
17 R. C. Zaehner, op. cit., pp. 415ff, Study Guide 2, pp. 80ff.
18 J. Holm and J. Bowker, op. cit., p. 156, Study Guide 2, p. 8.
19 Andrew Chapman and Alistair Self, *Mail on Sunday*, 6 August 2000.
20 S. Mumm, op. cit., p. 61.

7 Liberation

1 R. C. Zaehner, *Encyclopedia of Living Faiths*, Hutchinson, London, 1979, p. 9.
2 Ibid., p. 36.
3 K. Cragg, *Islam*. A213, World Religions, units 5–6, Open University, Milton Keynes, 1997, p. 52.
4 *The World Religions Reader*, Routledge, London and New York, 1998, pp. 200ff.
5 'Bhagavad-Gita', ch. xviii, in G. Beckerlegge (ed.), op. cit., pp. 275ff.
6 N. Smart, *Hinduism*. A213, World Religions, units 7–10, Part 2, Open University, Milton Keynes, 1998, pp. 99ff.
7 Bradley K. Hawkins, *Buddhism*, Prentice Hall Inc., New Jersey, 1999, pp. 35ff.
8 Edward Conze, *A Very Short History of Buddhism*, One World, Oxford, 2001.

9 Joseph Masson, *Buddhism*. A213, World Religions, Open University, Milton Keynes, 1998, p. 18.
10 Edward Conze, 'Buddhism: the Mahayana', in R.C. Zaehner (ed.), *The Concise Encyclopedia of Living Faiths*, Hutchinson, London, 1979, pp. 305ff, 309ff.
11 Ibid., pp. 297ff.
12 Ninian Smart, *The Religious Experience of Mankind*, Collins, Glasgow, 1979, p. 117. H. Waterhouse, *Buddhism*, A213, units 11–13, Open University, Milton Keynes, 2001, pp. 28ff.
13 G. Singh, *The Sikhs*, Tiger Books, London, 1998, p. 13.
14 R. Crawford, *The God/Man/World Triangle*, Macmillan, London, p. 130. Terry Thomas, *Sikhism*. A213, units 14–15, Open University, Milton Keynes, 1998, p. 43.
15 G. Beckerlegge (ed.), op. cit., 6.1.6, p. 421.
16 Ibid., 6.1.18, p. 425.
17 Terry Thomas, op. cit., pp. 32ff.

8 Divisions within religions

1 G. Beckerlegge, *Religion at the End of the Twentieth Century*. A213, unit 16, Open University, Milton Keynes, 2000, p. 34.
2 Ibid., p. 27.
3 Dan Cohn-Sherbok, *Modern Judaism*, Macmillan, Basingstoke, 1996, pp. 91ff, 113, 126.
4 Ibid., pp. 130, 159. See also N. Solomon, *Judaism: A Very Short Introduction*, OUP, Oxford, 1996, p. 106.
5 Ibid., p. 177.
6 Ibid., pp. 175, 229.
7 Nicolas Zernov, 'Christianity: The Eastern Schism and the Eastern Orthodox Church', in R. C. Zachner (ed.), *The Concise Encyclopedia of Living Faiths*, Hutchinson, London, 1979, pp. 79ff.
8 Ibid., pp. 138, 147ff.
9 Ibid., pp. 132ff, 164ff.
10 Ibid., pp. 132ff.
11 Ibid., p. 172.
12 J. Elias, *Islam*, Prentice Hall Inc., New Jersey, 1999, pp. 36ff.
13 G. Beckerlegge, op. cit., p. 74.
14 G. Beckerlegge, op. cit., pp. 67ff.
15 N. Smart, *The Religious Experience of Mankind*, Fontana, 1979, pp. 171ff.
16 Ibid., pp. 183ff.
17 Herbert Ellinger, *Buddhism*, SCM, London, 1995, p. 44.
18 Bradley K. Hawkins, *Buddhism*, Prentice Hall, New Jersey, 1999, pp. 50ff. Helen Waterhouse, *Buddhism*. Units 11–13, Open University, Milton Keynes, 2000, pp. 54ff.
19 A. Conze, *A Very Short Introduction to Buddhism*, One World, Oxford, 2001, p. 77.
20 Joseph Masson, *Buddhism*. Units 11–13, Open University, Milton Keynes, 1998, p. 60.
21 B. K. Hawkins, op. cit., p. 61.

22 G. Singh, *The Sikhs*, Tiger Books International, Twickenham, 1998, pp. 35ff.
23 Ibid., p. 55.
24 Singh Kalsi, *Sikhism*, Global Books, Kent, 1999, p. 112.

9 Why can religions not unite?

1 Terry Thomas, 'The Impact of Other Religions', in Gerald Parsons (ed.), *Religion in Victorian Britain*, vol. ii, Manchester University Press, 1995, pp. 281ff.
2 Ibid., pp. 291ff.
3 John R. Cobb Jr., 'Beyond Pluralism', in G. D'Costa (ed.), *Christian Uniqueness Reconsidered*, Orbis, New York, 1990, pp. 84ff. John Hick and Paul F. Nitter (eds), *The Myth of Christian Uniqueness*, SCM, London, 1987. John Hick, *The Myth of God Incarnate*, SCM, 1977. Robert Crawford, *Saga of God Incarnate*, University of South Africa, Pretoria, 1985.
4 Qur'an 2.256. N. J. Dawood, *The Koran*, Penguin, Harmondsworth, 1956, p. 47.
5 Richard L. Rubenstein, 'Muslims, Jews, and the Western World – A Jewish View', in G. Beckerlegge (ed.), *The World Religions Reader*, Routledge, London and New York, 1998, pp. 54ff.
6 M. Cook, *A Very Short Introduction to the Koran*, OUP, Oxford, 2000, p. 142.
7 H. P. Fry (ed.), *Christian Jewish Dialogue: A Reader*, University of Exeter, Exeter, 1996, pp. 18ff, 35ff.
8 Ibid., p. 12.
9 Ibid., pp. 82, 105, 131.
10 Ibid., pp. 142, 159.
11 G. Beckerlegge, *Religion at the End of the Twentieth Century*. Unit 16, Open University, Milton Keynes, 2000, p. 54.
12 W. Foy (ed.), *Man's Religious Quest: A Reader*, Croom Helm, London, 1978, p. 669.
13 Mary Pat Fisher, *Religion in the 21st Century*, Prentice Hall, New Jersey, 1999, p. 21.
14 W. Foy, op. cit., pp. 697ff, footnote 7.

10 Confessing a murder

1 G. de Beer (ed.), *Charles Darwin: Autobiography*, OUP, Oxford, 1974, pp. 49ff. J. M. Golby (ed.), *Extract in Culture and Society in Britain 1850–1890*, OUP, Oxford, 1986, p. 60f.
2 J. M. Golby (ed.), op. cit., p. 59.
3 Ian G. Barbour, *Religion and Science*, Harper, San Francisco, 1990, p. 59.
4 Ibid., pp. 60ff.
5 Frederic Harrison, 'Neo-Christianity' 1860, in J. M. Golby, op. cit., pp. 46ff. See also Arthur Stanley, in J. M. Golby, op. cit., pp. 54ff.
6 G. Parsons *et al.*, *Religion: Conformity and Controversy*, A102, units 18–19, Open University, Milton Keynes, 1991, p. 45.
7 Ian G. Barbour, op. cit., pp. 69ff.

8 G. Parsons, op. cit., pp. 36ff.
9 Jan Wentzel Van Huyssteen, *Duet or Duel*, SCM, London, 1998, p. 92.
10 Ibid., p. 127.

11 Is the world designed?

1 Russell Stannard, *The God Experiment*, Faber & Faber, London, 1999, p. 119.
2 Howard Van Till, 'No Place for a Small God', in John Marks Templeton (ed.), *How Large is God*, Templeton Foundation Press, Radnor, PA, 1997, pp. 116ff.
3 Ibid., p. 121.
4 R. Stannard, 'Appoaching God Through Paradox', in J. M. Templeton, op. cit., p. 69.
5 J. Polkinghorne, *Quarks, Chaos, and Christianity*, SPCK, London, p. 25.
6 R. Crawford, *The God/Man/World Triangle* (2nd edn), Macmillan, 2000, p. 80. The inflation theory means that there was a very rapid expansion of the cosmos when the behaviour of the particles underwent a radical change. How such inflation happens is complicated and debatable but, if correct, the expansion will continue forever and there will not be a Big Crunch. The theory of many universes cannot be proved or disproved. R. Stannard, *The God Experiment*, op. cit., pp. 190ff.
7 J. D. Barrow and F. J. Tipler, *The Anthropic Cosmological Principle*, Clarendon Press, Oxford, 1986, p. 22. Paul Davies, *God and the New Physics*, Dent, London, 1986, p. 22.
8 Ian G. Barbour, *Religion and Science*, Harper, San Francisco, 1990, p. 209.
9 See S. Hawking, *Black Holes and Baby Universes*, Bantam Press, London, 1993, and *A Short History of Time*, Bantam Books, 1995.

12 What are we?

1 John Polkinghorne, *Searching for Truth*, Bible Reading Fellowship, Oxford, 1996, p. 52.
2 Vernon Reynolds, *The Biology of Human Action* (2nd edn), Freeman & Co, Oxford, 1980, pp. 50ff.
3 Carol Albright, 'Expedition into Neuroscience and Religion', *Zygon*, vol. 31, number 4, pp. 712ff. Blackwell, Oxford, 1996.
4 Russell Stannard, *The God Experiment*, Faber & Faber, London, 1999, p. 161.
5 *Daily Mail*, 20 January 2001.
6 Justine Burley (ed.), *The Genetic Revolution and Human Rights*, OUP, 1999, pp. 14, 63, 97. Iain Torrance (ed.), *Bio-Ethics for the New Millennium*, St Andrew Press, Edinburgh, 2000, pp. 4ff.
7 J. Burley, op. cit., pp. 22, 87.
8 R. Crawford, *Can We Ever Kill?* Darton, Longman and Todd, London, 2000, Chapter 2.
9 Richard Dawkins foreword to J. Burley, op. cit., p. xvii.
10 Sheila McLean, 'The "new" Genetics', a critique in I. Torrance, op. cit., p. 69.

13 Mind and brain

1 Susan Greenfield, BBC TV programme, July 2000.
2 John Polkinghorne, *Searching for Truth*, Bible Reading Fellowship, Oxford, 1996, p. 55.
3 H. Benson and M. Stark, 'How Large is Faith?', in John Marks Templeton (ed.), *How Large is God?*, Templeton Foundation Press, Radnor, PA, 1997, p. 105.
4 Marya Schechtman, 'The Story of the Mind: Psychological and Biological Explanations of Human Behaviour', *Zygon*, vol. 31, number 4, p. 613. Blackwell, Oxford, 1996.
5 Deborah van Deusen, 'The Master Key', in *The Spire*, Communications Publications, Princeton Seminary, New Jersey, 2001.
6 R. Crawford, *The God/Man/World Triangle*, Macmillan, Basingstoke, 2000, p. 92.
7 Jean Holm and John Bowker (eds), *Making Moral Decisions*, Cassell, London, 1998, pp. 10ff.
8 John Weight, *Designer Universe*, Monarch, Crowborough, 1994, pp. 99ff.
9 David Papineau and Howard Selina, *Consciousness*, Icon, Cambridge, 1998, p. 171.

14 Other belief systems

1 John Bird, *Investigating Religion*, HarperCollins, London, pp. 57ff, 61ff, 72ff.
2 Karl Marx, 'Contribution to the Critique of Hegel's Philosophy of Right: Introduction 1844', in L. D. Easton and K. H. Guddat (ed. and trans.), *Writings of the Young Marx in Philosophy and Society*, Doubleday Anchor, New York, 1967, pp. 249ff.
3 Stuart Brown, *Secular Alternatives to Religion*, AD 208, units 22/23, Open University, Milton Keynes, 1978, p. 40.
4 K. Marx and F. Engels, *The Communist Manifesto*, Penguin, Harmondsworth, 1967, *passim*.
5 W. Foy, *Man's Religious Quest: A Reader*, Croom Helm, London, 1978, pp. 702, 705ff. The action of Camilo Torres encouraged many Marxists to collaborate with Christians and joined forces with them on electoral, parliamentary and political levels.
6 Some argue that the British Labour Party owed more to Methodism than Marx. See G. Parsons (ed.), *Religion in Victorian Britain, Traditions and Controversies*, 2 vols, Manchester University Press, Manchester, 1988.
7 S. Brown, op. cit., p. 72. See Karl Popper, *Conjectures and Refutations: The Growth of Scientific Knowledge*, Routledge & Kegan Paul, London, 1963.
8 Ibid., p. 66.
9 Paul Kurtz, 'Humanism and the Moral Revolution', in Paul Kurtz (ed.), *Humanist Alternative: Some Definitions of Humanism*, Pemberton Books, London, 1973, pp. 49ff.
10 Ibid., pp. 58ff.
11 Bernard Phillips, 'Zen and Humanism', in P. Kurtz (ed.), op. cit., p. 164.
12 Paul Kurtz, 'Is everyone a Humanist?', in P. Kurtz (ed.), op. cit., p. 185.
13 H. J. Eysenck, 'Reason with Compassion', in P. Kurtz (ed.), op. cit., p. 92.

14 Anthony Freeman, *God in Us. A Case for Christian Humanism*, SCM, London, 1993, pp. 35ff.
15 Ibid., pp. 43ff.

15   The existence of God

1 Ian Barbour, *Religion and Science*, Harper, San Francisco, 1997, p. 241.
2 Ibid., p. 311.
3 M. Ruthven, *A Very Short Introduction to Islam*, OUP, Oxford, 1997, p. 59.
4 R. Crawford, *The God/Man/World Triangle*, Macmillan, Basingstoke, 2000, Chapter 10.
5 Denis Brian, *Einstein*, John Wiley & Son, New York, 1996, p. 119.
6 Ibid., pp. 41, 632.
7 Ibid., p. 735.
8 Frank Ashall, *Remarkable Discoveries*, CUP, Cambridge, 1994, pp. 69, 75,
9 Russell Stannard, *The God Experiment*, Faber & Faber, London, 1999, p. 214.
10 John Polkinghorne, *Searching for Truth*, Bible Reading Fellowship, Oxford, 1996, pp. 79ff.
11 Ibid., p. 46.
12 Ibid., p. 119.
13 Brian Davies, *Philosophy of Religion*, OUP, Oxford, 2000, p. 24.
14 Ibid., p. 20.
15 R. Crawford, op. cit., p. 173.

16   A definition of religion

1 Bruce M. Metzger and Michael D. Coogan, *The Oxford Companion to the Bible*, OUP, Oxford, 1993, pp. 645, 655.
2 K. Knott, *Hinduism*, OUP, Oxford, 2000, p. 115.
3 R. C. Zaehner (ed.), *The Concise Encyclopedia of Living Faiths*, Hutchinson, London, 1979, p. 22.
4 William James, *The Varieties of Religious Experience*, Penguin, Harmondsworth, 1985, pp. 26, 31, 337.
5 Ibid., p. 330.
6 G. Beckerlegge (ed.), *The World Religions Reader*, Routledge, London and New York, 1998, pp. 391ff.
7 Ibid., pp. 338, 361ff. Helen Waterhouse, *Buddhism*, A213, units 11 and 13, Open University, Milton Keynes, 2000, pp. 74ff, 92.
8 Herbert Ellinger, *Buddhism*, SCM, London, 1995, p. 3.
9 J. M. Yinger, *The Scientific Study of Religion*, Collier-Macmillan, London, 1970, p. 7.

17   The future of religion

1 John Bird, *Investigating Religion*, HarperCollins, London, 1999, p. 80.
2 Ibid., p. 93.
3 Gwilym Beckerlegge, *Religion at the End of the 20th Century*, A213,

World Religions, 17 unit 16 (2nd edn) Open University, Milton Keynes, 2000, p. 130.

4 Mary Pat Fisher, *Religion in the 21st Century*, Prentice Hall, New Jersey, 1990, p. 21.

5 G. Beckerlegge, op. cit., p. 37. G. Beckerlegge (ed.), *The World Religions Reader*, Routledge, London and New York, 1998, p. 198.

6 Robert Crawford, *Journey into Apartheid*, Epworth, London, 1989. G. Beckerlegge, op. cit., p. 47.

7 G. Beckerlegge, op. cit., p. 54.

8 G. Beckerlegge, op. cit., p. 59.

9 Robert Crawford, *Loyal to King Billy*, C. Hurst and Co, London, 1987.

10 G. Beckerlegge, op. cit., p. 42.

11 G. Beckerlegge, op. cit., pp. 65, 73.

12 M. P. Fisher, op. cit., p. 71. G. Beckerlegge, op. cit., p. 66.

13 M. P. Fisher, op. cit., p. 40. Klaus K. Klostermaier, *Hindu Writings: A Short Introduction to the Major Sources*, One World, Oxford, 2000.

14 M. P. Fisher, op. cit., p. 22. K. Klostermaier, op. cit., p. 122.

15 K. Klostermaier, op. cit., pp. 143ff. R. C. Zaehner (ed.), *Encyclopedia of Living Faiths*, Hutchinson, London, 1977, pp. 250ff.

16 K. Klostermaier, op. cit., p. 147. Reader 4.13.

17 G. Beckerlegge, op. cit., pp. 105ff. M. P. Fisher, op. cit., p. 47.

18 M. P. Fisher, op. cit., p. 48.

19 G. Beckerlegge, op. cit., pp. 114ff.

20 G. Beckerlegge (ed.), op. cit., *The World Religions Reader*, op. cit., p. 456.

21 G. Beckerlegge, op. cit., pp. 126ff.

22 M. P. Fisher, op. cit., p. 49.

23 *Daily Mail*, 16th Sept. 2001

Index

Abelard, Peter 76
Abhidhamma Pitaka 44
abortion 50ff.
Abraham 27ff., 37
action of God 154
Adi Granth 34, 41, 45
Adler, Alfred 16
Afghanistan 209
aggadah 38
Aga Khan 100
Aisha 69
Akal Takht 34, 205, 214
Al-Tashahud 27
Albright, Carol 222
Alende, Salvador 166
Ali 100
Allah 27, 176
altruism 146, 156
Amida Buddha 177
Amitabha 32, 84
amrit 34
Amritsar 213
Ananadamayi Centres 210
ancestor worship 4
Angad 45
Anglo-Catholics 97
animals 143
annica 81–2
Anselm, Saint 76, 178, 186
anthropic principle 138ff.
Antinori, Severino 148
Apostolic succession 96
Aquinas, Thomas 16, 153, 179
Arafat, Yasser 55
ardas 34

Arhats 83, 105
Arianism 92
Aristotle 153, 184
Arjan 45
Arjuna 79, 82
Arnold, Matthew 2, 4
artificial insemination 50
Arya Samaj 71, 211
Ashall, Frank 224
Ashkenazim 89
Ashoka 198
Augustine 53, 66, 135
Aurobindo, Sri 104, 211
Ayer, A. J. 157, 216

Babri 58
Baghdad 28
Baptists 95
Barbour, Ian 175, 221–4
Barrow, John 133, 138, 222
Beckerlegge, G. 216–25
Beer, G. 221
behaviourism 157
belief 196
Benaras 30
Benson, H. 223
Berger, Peter 18, 187
Bhagavad gita 31, 42, 78ff., 119
bhakti 31, 71, 79
Bhindranwale, Sant Jarnail Singh 61
bhopa 29
Big Bang 134, 140
Big Crunch 135
bimah 22
Bird, John 223–4

Blackham, J. 170
Bodhisattva 36, 44, 59, 105, 200
Boesak, Allan 207
Bohm, David 186
Bohr, Niels 181
Bonhoeffer, Dietrich 98
Bosnia 212
Bowker, J. 217–19
Bradley, K. 218–19
Brahman xii, 42
Brahmanas 42, 70
Brahmin 29, 57
Brahmo Samaj 71, 104, 118
brain 128, 151–2
Brian, Denis 224
Brown, John 168
Brown, Stuart 224
Bruce, Steve 201, 217
Buber, Martin 1, 118
Buddha 31, 43, 59, 71, 80
Buddhism 31, 153–6, 198, 212
Burley, J. 222
Bush, George W. 208

calligraphy 27
Calvin, John 95
Campaign for Nuclear
    Disarmament 169
Canada 152
capital punishment 51–2
Castro, Fidel 167
Catholicism 131
Chapman, A. 219
chimpanzees 143
Chomsky, Noam 157
Christian Humanism 170–2
Christian Right 207
Christianity 25
Christology 107–8, 115–16
Church of South India 97
Clark, Francis 216
Clifford, W. K. 130
cloning 147–8
Coakley, J. F. 217
Cobb, J. R. 221
Cohn-Sherbok, Dan 92
Cole, Owen 218
Coleridge, Samuel Taylor 187
Communism 165
community 207

computers 151
Comte, Auguste 9, 217
Connolly, Peter 2, 201, 218
Constantine 53, 92
convergent evolution 125
Conze, Edward 219–20
Cook, Michael 116
cosmological argument 179
Cragg, Kenneth 218–19
Cranmer, Thomas 95
Crawford, R. 218–19, 220, 225
creation 135ff.
creator 126, 174
criticism of evolution 129–30
culture 47

Dabar 184
Dalai Lama 32, 60, 81, 107
Dalits 78, 211
Darwin, Charles 96, 123ff., 132ff.,
    142, 179; *Descent of Man* 126;
    Essays and Reviews 126; *Origin
    of Species, The* 125, 129
Davies, Brian 224
Davies, J. G. 217
Davies, Paul 140
Dawkins, Richard 2ff., 144ff., 149,
    154ff., 222
Dawson, N. J. 218
definitions of religion 1–9, 63, 192ff.
Descartes, René 151
designer 126ff., 132, 179
dhamma 31, 41, 63, 193
dharma 79, 81, 84, 87, 193
Diana, Princess 160
din 63, 193
diwan 33
DNA 132, 145
Dolly 148
Dutch Reformed Church 53

earthquakes 189
Easton, L. D. 224
eightfold path 59
Einstein, Albert 141, 180ff., 200ff.
Eldredge, Niles 133
Elias, J. 221
Elizabeth I 95
Ellinger, H. 220–4
empiricism 14

Engels, Friedrich 164, 224
episkopos 26
Erricker, Clive 217
euthanasia 50ff.
evolutionary approach 9ff.
existence of God 174ff.
Eysenck, H. J. 223

father 175
feminists 21, 64ff., 73–4, 208
festivals 24, 28, 30, 35
Feuerbach, Ludwig 161
Fisher, Mary Pat 119, 222, 224–5
fittest 125ff.
five Ks 34
five pillars of Islam 54
Fourth Gospel 40
Foy, W. 219–21, 223
Freeman, A. 171–3
Freud, Sigmund 2, 6, 16
Fry, H. P. 220–2
functional x, 4–5
fundamentalism 5, 101, 205,
    216–17
future of Religion 203–15

Galileo 123
Gandhi, Indira 61, 110
Gandhi, Mahatma 6, 56–7, 78–9,
    119, 211
garbhagriha 30
genes 132, 145ff.
genetic engineering 146
genetic research 147
Ghazali, Al 102
God and philosophy 190
Gödel, Kurt 137
Golby, J. M. 221
Golden Temple 33ff., 61
Goldstein, David 218–19
Gould, Stephen 133
Grand Canyon 125
granthi 33
Gray, Asa 129
Greek Orthodoxy 93
Greenfield, S. 224
Griffiths, Bede 208
Gross, David C. 218
Guddat, K. H. 223
gurmukh 86

gurdwara 19, 33
Guru Granth 33
Gush Emunim 90

Hadith 42, 100
halakhah 38, 48ff.
Hamas 55, 101
haram 28
Hardy, Alister 186
Haredim 89, 206
Harper, E. B. 77
Harrison, F. 221
Hasan 99
Hasidic 50
Hasidim 89, 205
haumai 86
Hawking, Stephen 136ff., 189, 222
Hegel, G. F. 157, 161–2
Height, John 224
Heisenberg, Werner Karl 181–2
Herzl, Theodore 91
Hick, John 114, 221
High Priest 117–18
Hillel, Rabbi 50
Hindu philosophical divisions 103
Hinduism 43, 56ff., 176
Hindustan 211
Hizbollah 101
homosexuality 204
Hoyle, Fred 138
Hubbard, L. Ron 159
human genome 145–6
Humanist Association 168
Humanist Manifesto, A 170
Hume, David 180
Husain 99
Huxley, T. H. 127–8

iconostasis 26
icons 26
Ignatius, Bishop of Antioch 26
image of God 66, 75, 158
imaginary time 136
iman 63
Indian religions 22
industrialization 163
information processing 152
intention 47, 55, 62
Internet 204
Iran 55, 100, 209

Isaiah 15, 182
Ishmael 28
Islamic Republican Party 209

James, William 8, 15, 197, 216, 224
Janata Vimukti Perumana 60
janeu 30
Japan 106
Jats 62
Jeans, James 137
Jesuits 96
Jesus 40, 68, 80, 112–13, 117, 181
Jewish Prayer Book 66
Jewish Temple 22
Jews: and Christians 116; and
    Muslims 115
Job 188
Jonah 184
Judaism 176
Julian of Norwich 66
Jung, Carl Gustav 16
Just War 53

Ka'bah 27
kabbalism 89, 176
Kabir 45, 79
Kali 177
kalpas 131
Kalsi, Singh 221
Kama Sutra 70
Kant, Immanuel 130, 178
Kaplan, M. 91
kadah prasad 33
karma 43, 79, 83, 188
Katami Muhammed 101
Khalistan 61, 213–14
Khalsa 19, 34, 45
Khrushchev, Nikita 167
King, Martin Luther 6, 162
Kingsley, Charles 129
kirtan 33
Klostermaier, K 225
Knesset 206
Knott, K. 224
Krishna 30, 71
Kuhn, Hans 119
Kuhn, T. S. 191
Kurtz, Paul 224

Lang, Andrew 9

langar 33
language of religion 14
law 51, 94
law giver 136
Lawton, C. 219
Lenin, Vladimir Ilich 167
Liberation Theology 53, 162, 166ff.,
    206ff.
liturgy 66
logical positivism 13
logos 39, 113ff., 184
Lotus Sutra 44
love 51
Lubatvitch 90
Luther, Martin 66, 94
Lutheran Church 98
Lux mundi 130

Madhi 99
Madhva 103
Mahabharata 42
Mahayana Buddhism 32, 44, 59, 72,
    81, 194–5, 177
Maimonides, Moses 196
Maitreya 85
Malcolm X 209
Malinowski, Bronislaw 2
Malthus, Thomas 124
manjidars 72
manmukh 86
mantras 32, 176
Manu 42, 57, 78
many universes 138
Mao Tse-tung 166
Marriot, McKim 78
Martin, David 20
Marx, Karl x, 2, 6, 18, 224
Marxism 161ff.
Mass 25, 93
Masson, Joseph 219–20
materialist 151
maya 82
McLean, Sheila 222
McLeod, H. 218
Mecca 29, 41
Medina 28
meditation 84, 86
Mendel, Gregor 132
Messiah 40, 76, 89, 90, 117
Metzger, B. M. 224

mihrab 27
Mill, J. S. 157
minaret 27
mind 137, 151–2
Mishnah 38, 68
missionaries 113, 124
Mitnaggedim 90
mitzvah 38, 47, 193
monasticism 52
monks 84
Moon, Sun 159
Moral Majority 54, 207
morality 47
Morgan, P. 218
Mormons 205
Mother Ganges 30, 70
Muhammad 28, 41ff., 54, 68ff., 77, 115, 183
Mujhadin 101
Mumm, Susan 219
Muslims 24
mutations 132, 190
Mu'tazila 42

Nabha, Kahn Singh 214
Namdhari 109
Nanak, Guru 10, 33–4, 44–5, 61, 85–6, 98, 110–11, 197
Nation of Islam 209
nationalism 210–11
natural selection 124–6
necessity 143
neo-Darwinism 142, 144
Neturei Kara 89, 205
neurons 156
New Age religion 5ff., 160–1
new religious movements 159
Newman, John Henry 95
Newton, Isaac 123–4, 181
nibbana 199, 200
Nichiren 44, 198
Nicholas I 1, 207
niddah 65
Nirankari 110
nirvana 44, 82ff., 177
Northern Ireland 208
numinous 187
nuns 71–2

Open University xii

Oral Law 38
orang-utan 126
ordination of women 67
original sin 49, 76, 126
Orthodox Jews 89, 206
oscillating universe 135
Otto, R. 3, 7, 15, 187

pacifism 52–3
Pakistan 211–12
palaeontology 132–3
Palestinians 90
Paley, William 179
Pant, Pushapesh 217
Papineau, David 223
Paranas 43
Parliament of World Religions 118–19
Parsons, G. 221–3
Pascal, Blaise 187
Pavlov, Ivan 157
Penrose, Roger 156
Pentateuch 39
Personalists 82
Pesach 24
Pharisees 23
phenomenological approach 20
philosophical approach 12ff.
Pieris, Aloysius 3, 198
pilgrimage 60
Plato 78, 138
Plotinus 176
Pocock, D. F. 8, 216
Polanyi, Michael 155, 186
Polkinghorne, John 137, 222–4
polygamy 51
Pope 93
Popper, Karl 167ff., 186, 223
pornography 51
postmodernism 158, 204
prasad 29
prayer beads 36
presbuteros 26
priesthood of all believers 68
Progressives 91
Promise Keepers 207
Protagoras 168
psychological approach 15–16
Puja 29
punctuated equilibrium 142

Punjab 215
Pusey, Edward 96

qiblah 27
quantum fluctuations 136
Qur'an 27, 39, 41ff., 69, 101, 116, 183, 221

rabbis 23
Radha 30
Radhasomi movement 110
Rahner, Karl 115
Ram Mohan Roy 104
Ramadan 28
Ramakrishna, Sri 104, 118
Ramakrishna Math and Mission 211
Ramanuja 80, 103
Ramayana 43
rebbes 89
reconstructionist Judaism 66, 91
reincarnation 50
relativity 47
religious experience 130, 186–7
Renaissance 168
resurrection 153
revelation 182
Richards, H. J. 217
Rig Veda 42
ritual 22–36, 194ff.
Roman Catholic 93
rosary 36
Rosh Hashanah 24
Rubenstein, R. L. 221
Ruether, Rosemary 68
Rushdie, Salman 101
Ruskin, John 187
Russell, Bertrand 132, 157
Russia 207
Ruthven, M. 224
Ryle, G. 157

Sacks, Jonathan 205
sacraments 93
Sadat, Anwar 55
Sadducees 23
sadhus 30
Sahajdhari 109
saltus 142
Sambho, Pa 218

samsara 79
samskaras 30
sangha 32, 43, 213
Sanghera, Rajinda 73
Sartre, J.P. 169
sarvodaya 212
Satan 188
Saul 182
Savitri 70
Schach, Rabbi 90
Schechtman, Marya 223
Schleiermacher, Friedrich 130
Schneerson, M. M. 90
science x, 5, 39
secularization 204
seder 24
self 156
selfish gene 156
Selina, Howard 223
Semitic 11, 22
Sephardim 89
Shabbat 22ff.
Shakti 29
Shankara 80, 103, 155
Shari'ah 54
Sharpe, Eric 10, 216
shastras 44
Shattuck, Cybelle 217–19
Shi'ah 28, 54ff., 98ff., 210
Shiva 29, 43, 102–3, 176
shofar 24
shraddha 30
Sikh Gurus 108ff.
Sikh Sammelan 213–14
Sikhism 33, 45, 60, 72–3, 213–14
Singh, Beant 61
Singh, Guru Gobind 62, 73, 109
Sita 70
skandhas 82
Skinner, B. F. 157
sleeping foetus 56
Smart, Ninian 3, 7, 15, 219–20
sociobiology 156–7
Solomon, Norman 219–20
Son of God 40–1
soul 153–4
species 124, 142
Spencer, Herbert 2–3, 130
Spinoza, Baruch 201
spirit 175

Sri Lanka 212
Sri Lanka Freedom Party 212
Stalin, Joseph 167
Stannard, Russell 137, 222–4
Stark, Marg 223
stem cells 148
stupas 32
subordination of women 67
Sufism 101–2
suicide 49–50
sukkoth 24
Sunni 28, 54, 99, 210
supernatural 199–200
sutras 43–4
Sutta Pitaka 44
synagogue 22

Taliban 55, 205
tallith 23
Talmud 38, 64, 117
Tamil Tigers 60, 212
Tantras 43, 106
Tantrism 57, 70
tanzil 41
Templeton, John Marks 222
thematic xi
theological approach 11
Theravada 31ff., 44, 58, 72, 80ff.,
    104, 177
Thomas, Terry 218, 220–1
three-body doctrine 105, 112
Tibet 60, 107
Tibetan Buddhism 63
Till, Howard Van 222
time 136
Tipler, Frank 138, 223
Torah 22, 38ff., 48ff., 64, 90ff.,
    194
Torrance, Iain 223
Torres, Camilo 167
Toynbee, Arnold 2, 4, 199
Trade Union Movement 167
traditionalists 90
Trinity 11
Trotsky, Leon 167
Turkey 69, 209
Tutu, Desmond 207
Twelver Shi'ah 69, 99
Tylor, E. B. 1
Tyndall, J. 130

Umansky, Ellen M. 219
Unitarianism 95, 120
United Monk Front 212
United Reformed Church 97
Upanishads 42ff., 70, 79
Ussher, James 128

van Deusen, Deborah 223
van Huyssteen, J. W. 222
Vajrayana 32, 59, 72, 81, 106
Vatican Council, First 96
Vatican Council, Second 97, 166
Vedanta 80
Vedas 42, 70
veil 69, 73
verbal inspiration 183
Vesak 31
Vietnam 152, 198
Vinaya Pitaka 43
virgin birth 113
Vishnu 29, 30, 31, 57, 79, 102–3,
    176, 182
Vivekananda, Swami 104, 118,
    211

Wallace, A. R. 127ff.
war 51
Ward, Keith 218
Waterhouse, H. 220–4
Weber, Max 6ff., 18, 217
Wesley, John 5
Whitehead, A. N. 2, 5, 197
Whitsun 25
Wilberforce, Samuel 129
Williams, Paul 216
Wilmut, Ian 149
Wilson, Bryan 20, 217
Wilson, John 14
Wittgenstein, Ludwig 13ff., 190
women 27, 213
word 183
Wordsworth, William 16
World Conference on Religion 119
World Council of Churches 97ff.,
    116–17

X-Files, The 161

Yahweh 176
Yama 30

Yinger, J. M. 20, 201, 224
yoga 84
Yogi, M. M. 160
Yom Kippur 24

zaddikim 89

Zaehner, R. C. 219–20, 224–5
Zen Buddhism 16, 84, 169ff., 213
Zernov, N. 220
Zionism 51, 91
Zoroastrianism 188
Zwingli, Ulrich 95